AF789117

Data Protection Compliance

A Guide to GDPR and Irish Data Protection Law

DATA PROTECTION COMPLIANCE

A Guide to GDPR and Irish Data Protection Law

By

LAURA L KEOGH

CLARUS
PRESS

Published by
Clarus Press Ltd,
Griffith Campus,
South Circular Road,
Dublin 8.
www.claruspress.ie

Typeset by
Gough Typesetting Services,
Dublin

Printed by
SprintPrint
Dublin

ISBN
978-1-911611-24-0

A catalogue record for this book is available from the British Library

All rights reserved.
No part of this publication may be reproduced, or transmitted in any form or by any means, including recording and photocopying, without the written permission of the copyright holder, application for which should be addressed to the publisher. Written permission should also be obtained before any part of the publication is stored in a retrieval system of any nature.

Disclaimer
Whilst every effort has been made to ensure that the contents of this book are accurate, neither the publisher and/or author can accept responsibility for any errors or omissions or loss occasioned to any person acting or refraining from acting as result of any material in this publication.

Copyright © Laura L Keogh 2019

Preface

It is wonderful, data protection has become a household phrase since the GDPR aroused attention, gained via the threat of high fines. So much of our society depends on the collection and transfer of personal data so it is heartening that organisations now take serious notice of it. The GDPR is the EU law for data protection and certain elements of it are also within Irish national law via the Data Protection Act 2018. Organisations are often confused about what they have to do with data protection and find it daunting that the GDPR encourages the need for everyone in an organisation to somewhat understand the data protection obligations of where they work. Thus, the list for data protection compliance can seem endless. I wrote this book because many people had the same questions. I wanted to provide a concise handbook to guide people through what they need to do to ensure their organisation is compliant with data protection law. With data protection, it is so important to know the whole picture. It is no use just having a data protection agreement or a privacy policy in place – that is just a piece of the jigsaw, there is a whole series of building blocks. I tried to compartmentalise these blocks to show how achievable it actually is to be data protection complaint and how easy it is to understand what obligations are contained within the GDPR.

First, of course, there is the introduction, this is for anyone that is interested in the scene setting of the GDPR and it is not required reading. Thereafter, the book is divided into four parts. At the beginning of each part is a helpful guide to the chapters in that part of the book. These guides are your path to compliance – if you can understand each step, that is the majority of the work over. Part 1 provides the elementary blocks explaining in what circumstances you are required to comply with data protection law; Part 2 explains the obligations on organisations; Part 3 describes the circumstances around transferring personal data between countries and between entities; and Part 4 deals with the miscellaneous topics, such as liability issues, which I am sure many people will be eager to read.

I tried to keep the writing and references as simple as possible, mostly simply referring to the actual law and related working party documents and guidelines. There is a further discussion section at the end of most chapters, which lists the most relevant guidelines only. If you are interested in a more academic discussion there are a host of other wonderful resources available, the primary focus of this book is practicality; for everyone, from the in-house legal counsel to the IT developers and administrators, to have in their back pocket.

I have to say a huge thank you to David McCartney at Clarus Press and everyone that helped with the proofs of the book. I am so grateful.

I do hope that you find this book useful.

Best of luck on your data protection compliance journey,
LLK
6 May 2019

Table of Contents

PART 2
CONDITIONS UNDER WHICH A CONTROLLER CAN PROCESS PERSONAL DATA

PART 4
MISCELLANEOUS

Abbreviations

2018 Act: Data Protection Act 2018 [No 7 of 2018]

ASHS: Archiving in the public interest, scientific research, historical research and statistical purposes

EDPB: European Data Protection Board as established by Article 68 GDPR

EEA: European Economic Area

European Charter: Charter of Fundamental Rights of the European Union

GDPR: General Data Protection Regulation (EU) 2016/679 of the European Parliament and of the Council of 27 April 2016

ICO: The Information Commissioner's Office

LSA: Lead Supervisory Authority

OIS: Online Intermediation Services

PNR: Passenger Name Record

SCC(P)s: Commission Decision of 5 February 2010 on standard contractual clauses for the transfer of personal data to processors established in third countries under Directive 95/46/EC of the European Parliament and of the Council (notified under document C(2010) 593) *OJ L 39, 12.2.2010*

Set I SCCs: Commission Decision of 15 June 2001 on standard contractual clauses for the transfer of personal data to third countries, under Directive 95/46/EC (Text with EEA relevance) (notified under document number C(2001) 1539) *OJ L 181, 4.7.2001*

Set II SCCs: Commission Decision of 27 December 2004 amending Decision 2001/497/EC as regards the introduction of an alternative set of standard contractual clauses for the transfer of personal data to third countries (notified under document number C(2004) 5271) *OJ L 385, 29.12.2004*

TEU: Treaty on the European Union, Official Journal of the European Union C 326, 26 October 2012

TFEU: Treaty on the functioning of the European Union, Official Journal of the European Union, C 83, 30 March 2010

WP29: the Article 29 Working Party as established by Article 29 Directive 95/46/EC

Key Terms

- Agent: Processor that receives data via the Privacy Shield mechanism
- Article 29 Working Party (WP29): Issued independent non-binding advice on the data protection law in place pre GDPR (Directive 95/46/EC)
- ASHS: Acronym for "Archiving in the public interest, scientific research, historical research and statistical purposes"
- Controller: The entity who has primary control of the personal data
- Data exporter: Entity that receives data from the EU under the SCCs
- Data importer: Entity that transfers data outside the EU under the SCCs
- Data Protection Commission (Irish Commission): Supervisory authority for Ireland
- Data Protection Act 2018 (DPA 2018): The Irish data protection Act
- Data Protection Agreement (DPA): It is the agreement between a controller and a processor or between a processor and a further sub-processor
- Data Protection Impact Assessment (DPIA): Assessment required where there is a high risk from processing activity
- Data Protection Officer (DPO): Employed by entities to assist with internal compliance with data protection law
- Data Protection Representative: EU representative for a non-EU controller or processor caught by the GDPR
- Data Subject Access Request (DSAR): Where data subject requests access to their data
- Data Subject: The identifiable individual related to the personal data
- Establishment: The location where an entity is situated via a stable relationship with that location, such as where a company is legally registered; however, the understanding of the term is wide enough to reflect the true reality of where an entity is situated regardless of where there may be a legal registration
- European Data Protection Board (EDPB): Issues independent non-binding advice on the GDPR
- European Data Protection Supervisory Authority (EDPS): The EU's independent data protection authority

- General Data Protection Regulation (GDPR): The current EU law on data protection
- Lead supervisory authority (LSA): The main supervisory authority where there is a cross border issue
- Personal data: Any data that relates to an identifiable individual
- Processor: The entity that processes personal data on the basis of instructions from the controller
- Recipient: Controller that receives data via the Privacy Shield mechanism
- Standard Contractual Clauses (SCCs): Standard clauses used to transfer data outside the EU – there are different types of SCCs used for transfer to a controller (Set I or Set II SCCs) and to a processor (SCC(P)s).
- Supervisory authority: The authority within each member state that facilitates compliance with data protection law

Introduction

This book is intended as a practical compliance guidebook, to aid any entity toward compliance with data protection law contained within the General Data Protection Regulation (EU) 2016/679 (the GDPR)[1] and requisite Irish law. The layout of the book is to facilitate quick access to certain questions. This introductory section is intended to explain the broader elements relating to the GDPR, thereafter each chapter deals with a different element of the GDPR, setting out the steps towards compliance.

While the GDPR provides the means to facilitate the flow of personal data within the EU, it requires a high level of security and transparency on the use of individual's personal data. The GDPR's effectiveness is attributed to high fines and the clear enforceability mechanisms via the supervisory authority.[2]

The GDPR became effective on 25 May 2018. Note that the GDPR

---

1 Regulation (EU) 2016/679 of the European Parliament and of the Council of 27 April 2016 on the protection of natural persons with regard to the processing of personal data and on the free movement of such data, and repealing Directive 95/46/EC (General Data Protection Regulation) Official Journal of the European Union, Vol L119 (4 May 2016), pp 1-88; Hereinafter referred to as the GDPR.

2 See Ch 18 re supervisory authority.

is a text with European Economic Area (EEA) relevance,[3] thus it is also applicable in Iceland, Lichtenstein and Norway.[4] The GDPR replaced the previous Directive 95/46/EC.[5]

Within Ireland, the Data Protection Act 2018 [No 7 of 2018] (DPA 2018)[6] implements the derogations provided for within the GDPR.

Note that any collection or processing of personal data that took place prior to the implementation of the GDPR on 25 May 2018, must comply with the GDPR as of 25 May 2018.

Digital Single Market

In May 2015 the European Commission published a Digital Single Market Strategy.[7] This emphasised the need for the free flow of data within the EU for the functioning of the internal market and to grow the EU digital economy. The free movement of data has become known as the "fifth freedom" within the EU, adding to the original four freedoms of free movement of goods, services, capital and people. It was emphasised that the GDPR was necessary for the success of the digital economy; to increase trust in digital services, as well as to provide a common set of rules on data protection law across the EU.[8] In order to regulate the free movement of personal data, the GDPR was formulated to balance the free flow of personal data with the rights of individuals.[9]

Regarding non-personal data (which does not fall within the scope

---

3 Hereinafter referred to as the EEA; See European Economic Area, Decision of the EEA Joint Committee, No 154/2018 of 6 July 2018 amending Annex XI (Electronic communication, audio-visual services and information society) and Protocol 37 (containing the list provided for in Art 101) to the EEA Agreement [2018/1022]; See also Art 7(a), Agreement on the European Economic Area (OJ No L 1, 3.1.1994, p 3), as amended

4 Hereinafter any reference to EU Member States will also be a reference to EEA Member States.

5 Directive 95/46/EC of the European Parliament and of the Council of 24 October 1995 on the protection of individuals with regard to the processing of personal data and on the free movement of such data (OJ L 281, 23.11.1995, p 31); Hereinafter referred to as Directive 95/46/EC.

6 Data Protection Act 2018 [No 7 of 2018]; Hereinafter referred to as DPA 2018.

7 Communication from the Commission to the European Parliament, the Council, the European Economic and Social Committee and the Committee of the Regions, A Digital Single Market Strategy for Europe /* COM/2015/0192 final */ {SWD(2015) 100 final}.

8 Sec 3.4, Digital Single Market Strategy for Europe /* COM/2015/0192 final */ {SWD(2015) 100 final}.

9 See Art 1 GDPR.

of this book), a regulation on the free flow of non-personal data has come into force and will be directly applicable from May 2019.[10]

Objectives of the GDPR

The GDPR has four primary objectives.[11] The objectives must be followed throughout the personal data lifecycle; from collection of the personal data to final deletion or anonymisation of the personal data. The objectives should be used to gain an initial overview to check for data protection compliance. Any use of personal data, within the scope of the GDPR, must be (1) limited, (2) secure, (3) transparent and (4) challengeable.

(1) Limited

The collection and use of personal data must be limited to what is necessary. Necessity is determined via what the needs are *at the time of collection of the data*. Only personal data that is needed should be collected and only personal data that is needed should be retained. This concept shall arise and be developed throughout the book. All stages of the personal data lifecycle (collection, use and retention) must be limited to what can be justifiably necessary.

(2) Secure

Personal data should always be protected by appropriate security measures that are proportionate to the risks associated with the data processing activity. Adherence to the limited objective is imperative as the less data that is collected and or retained, the less data that is exposed to risks.

(3) Transparent

The individual must be informed of all information collected about them, what is being done with their information and who is collecting it. This is applicable to all forms of personal data collection. For example, where CCTV monitoring occurs there must be a clearly visible sign indicating the CCTV and who operates the CCTV.

10 Regulation (EU) 2018/1807 of the European Parliament and of the Council of 14 November 2018 on a framework for the free flow of non-personal data in the European Union (Text with EEA relevance.) PE/53/2018/REV/1OJ L 303, 28.11.2018, p 59–68

11 Derived mainly from Art 5(1) GDPR.

(4) Challengeable

The individual, whose information is being collected, must be able to query and challenge what is being done with their data. The fact that the individual knows who is collecting their data and what is being done with their data via the transparency objective enables the challengeable objective.

Sources of Data Protection Law: Directive versus Regulation versus National Law

The Treaty on the Functioning of the EU (TFEU)[12] and the Treaty on the EU (TEU)[13] specify the competencies of the EU, i.e. what the EU may legislate on. The EU may legislate for data protection law via Article 16(1) TFEU. This states:

> Everyone has the right to the protection of personal data concerning them.

Article 16(2) TFEU states that the EU shall lay down such data protection rules to protect this right. The EU first legislated in this area via Directive 95/46/EC and revised data protection law under the GDPR, repealing Directive 95/46/EC. Thus, there was a shift from the provision of EU data protection law via a directive to a regulation:

- Directive: A directive is binding as to the results to be achieved, but the choice of form and method is left for the Member State national authorities to decide.[14] As such, while Directive 95/46/EC provided the overarching law, national law was required to essentially fill in the details. The Irish Data Protection (Amendment) Act 2003 gave effect to Directive 95/46/EC.
- Regulation: A regulation is binding in its entirety and directly applicable on all Member States of the EU.[15] As such, the GDPR is directly applicable in Ireland and further national law is not required.

While the GDPR is directly applicable in Ireland, national law may legislate further where such derogations are specified within

12 The consolidated version of the Treaty on the functioning of the European Union, Official Journal of the European Union, C 83, 30 March 2010 (TFEU).
13 The consolidated version of the Treaty on the European Union, Official Journal of the European Union C 326, 26 October 2012 (TEU).
14 Art 288 TFEU.
15 Art 288 TFEU.

the GDPR. The GDPR states that derogation from the GDPR is permissible via national law in certain situations, in particular:

- Provision for a lower age of consent to the processing of personal data below the default age of 16 years, provided that such age is not below 13 years;[16]
- Processing special categories of personal data, for example for social protection, legal claims, health, security;[17]
- Processing for journalistic, artistic or literary purposes;[18]
- Processing national identification numbers;[19]
- Processing and access to official public documents;[20]
- Processing for archiving purposes in the public interest, scientific research, historical research or statistical purposes;[21]
- Processing in the context of employment;[22]
- Establishment of the respective national data protection supervisory authority.[23]

Furthermore, it is noted within Recital 10 GDPR that the GDPR does not exclude Member State law that sets out the circumstances for specific processing situations, including the precise determination of the conditions under which the processing of personal data is lawful.

The DPA 2018 makes provisions for these derogations within Ireland, which shall be flagged throughout this book. Furthermore, the DPA 2018 also implements the 2016 Directive regarding criminal data,[24] which shall not be dealt with in this book.

The following is a list of the EU Member States who have adopted, or are in the process of adopting, national legislation regarding the derogations allowed within the GDPR. The use of the word

---

16 Art 8(1) GDPR.
17 Recital 52–53 GDPR.
18 Art 85 GDPR.
19 Art 87 GDPR.
20 Art 86 GDPR.
21 Art 89 GDPR.
22 Art 88 GDPR.
23 Art 54 GDPR.
24 Directive (EU) 2016/680 of the European Parliament and of the Council of 27 April 2016 on the protection of natural persons with regard to the processing of personal data by competent authorities for the purposes of the prevention, investigation, detection or prosecution of criminal offences or the execution of criminal penalties, and on the free movement of such data, and repealing Council Framework Decision 2008/977/JHA (2016 Directive).

"Draft" indicates that the law has not been officially adopted in that country. Note that in some countries, different parts are adopted into law at different stages and by different laws. The age of consent is provided here for ease of reference.

Country	Status of national implementation of GDPR derogations[25]	Age of consent to data processing
Austria	Passed (Federal Data Protection Act)	14
Belgium	Passed (the Act of 3 December 2017 establishing the data protection authority; other derogations entered into force on the 5 September 2018 Belgian Privacy Act)	13
Bulgaria	Passed (Personal Data Protection Act)	14
Croatia	Passed (No. NN 42/2018)	16
Cyprus	Passed (Protection of Natural Persons as to the Processing of their Personal Data and the Free Movement of such Data Law 125(I) of 2018)	14
Czech Republic	Passed (Data Processing Act)	15
Denmark	Passed (Danish Data Protection Act)	13
Estonia	Passed (Personal Data Protection Act)	13
Finland	Passed (Act on Data Protection (1050/2018))	13
France	Passed (French law no 2018-493)	15
Germany	Passed (Data Protection Act)	No reference (default 16)
Greece	Draft	16 by default (draft law states 15)
Hungary	Passed (amendment of Act No. CXII of 2011 on the Right of Informational Self-Determination and on Freedom of Information (the Amendment))	16
Ireland	Passed (Data Protection Act 2018)	16
Italy	Passed (Legislative decree no. 101 of 10 August 2018)	14
Latvia	Passed (Personal Data Processing law)	13

[25] Valid as of March 2019.

Lithuania	Passed (GDPR Implementation law)	14
Luxembourg	Passed (Act implementing the GDPR)	No reference (default 16)
Malta	Passed (Maltese Data Protection Act 2018 (Chapter 586 of the Laws of Malta))	13 (however, valid consent can only be provided via a 18 year old or older)
Netherlands	Passed (Dutch GDPR Implementation Act)	16
Poland	Passed (Personal Data Protection Act of 10 May 2018, Journal of laws 2018, item 1000); but further data protection items in Draft law	16
Portugal	Draft	16
Romania	Passed (Romanian Law 190)	No reference (default 16)
Slovakia	Passed (Slovakian Data Protection Law (no. 18/2018 Coll.))	16
Slovenia	Draft	16 by default (draft law states 15)
Spain	Passed (Data Protection and Digital Rights Act)	14
Sweden	Passed (Swedish Data Protection Act (2018:218) and the Swedish Data Protection Regulation (2018:219))	13
United Kingdom	Passed (Data Protection Act 2018)	13
Iceland (EEA)	Passed (Act No. 90/2018 on Data Protection and the Processing of Personal Data)	13
Liechtenstein (EEA)	Passed (Liechtenstein Data Protection Act)	No reference (default 16)
Norway (EEA)	Passed (Norwegian Personal Data Act of 15 June 2018)	13

Right to Privacy versus Data Protection

The detailed nuances between data protection and privacy are beyond the scope of this book; however, a brief discussion is warranted. The right to privacy is a fundamental right.[26] The right to privacy is considered an unenumerated right within the Irish constitution and has been developed via common law.[27] However, the statutory right to data protection is provided via DPA 2018 and the GDPR.

The protection of personal information, i.e. data protection, was generally considered part of the right to privacy. The Information Commissioner's Office (ICO), the UK's independent authority to uphold information rights for the public, provided an explanation of the privacy/data protection distinction.[28] The ICO stated that the right to privacy can take two main forms:[29]

(1) Physical privacy – the ability to have physical solitude; and
(2) Informational privacy – the ability to control, edit, manage and delete information about oneself and to decide how and to what extent such information is communicated to others.

Thus, it may be stated that data protection law, via the GDPR,

---

[26] Art 8(1), Convention for the Protection of Human Rights and Fundamental Freedoms, 4 November 1950, 213 *United Nations Treaty Series* 221, at 230 (entered into force 3 September 1953); Art 12, Universal Declaration of Human Rights, GA Res 217 (III) A, UN GAOR, 3rd Sess, at 71, UN Doc A/810 (1948); Art 17, International Covenant on Civil and Political Rights, *entered into force* 23 March 1976; Art 11, Inter-American Convention on Human Rights, *entered into force* 22 November 1969; Art 8, European Convention for the Protection of Human Rights and Fundamental Freedoms (ECHR), as amended by Protocols Nos. 11 and 14 4 November 1950 (Art 8 ECHR became part of Irish domestic law via s 2(1) European Convention on Human Rights Act 2003) – note that The concept of what the right to privacy means differs throughout the world, see for further discussion Whitman 'The Two Western Cultures of Privacy: Dignity Versus Liberty' 113 [2004] Yale Law Journal 1151.

[27] Recognised as one of the unenumerated rights in of Art 40.3 Irish constitution in *Kennedy and Arnold v Attorney General* [1987] IR 587; also recognised as part Art 41, right to protection of family life, in *McGee v Attorney General* [1974] IR 284.

[28] The ICO is, among other things, the supervisory authority as required by Art 28 Directive 95/46/EC, see Art 6 Data Protection Act 1998 (as amended); The Data Protection Act 2018 repealed Data Protection Act 1998 and provided that the ICO will be the supervisory authority for the purposes of the GDPR. ICO website, available at https://ico.org.uk/.

[29] Information Commissioner's Office, Conducting privacy impact assessments code of practice, Version 1.0, 2014, at 6, available at https://ico.org.uk/media/for-organisations/documents/1595/pia-code-of-practice.pdf; Venice Commission, Opinion on video surveillance in public places by public authorities and the protection of human rights, 70th Plenary Session (Venice, 16-17 March 2007), available at http://www.statewatch.org/news/2007/aug/venice-commission-video-surveillance.pdf.

addresses "informational privacy". Within Europe, in the Charter of Fundamental Rights of the European Union (European Charter),[30] the right to privacy and the right to data protection are viewed as two distinct rights:

- Right to respect for private life is provided in Article 7 European Charter;
- Right to personal data protection is provided in Article 8 European Charter.

These rights were officially recognised and brought into EU law via Article 6(1) TEU, and as such were brought into Irish law.[31] As stated above, Article 16 TFEU also specifically provides for the right to data protection within the EU. Therefore, the right to "physical privacy" and "informational privacy" can be considered as two components of the right to privacy, or, they can be considered as two distinct rights.

In either regard, the purpose of the GDPR is to protect personal data or "informational privacy".[32]

Article 29 Working Party versus the European Data Protection Board

Reference shall be made throughout this book to the Article 29 Working Party (hereinafter referred to as WP29) and the European Data Protection Board (hereinafter referred to as EDPB). Their opinions and recommendations can be used to further understand and interpret the GDPR.

In order to aid in the correct and coherent interpretation of data protection law, WP29 was set up via Article 29, Directive 95/46/EC. WP29 provided independent non-binding advice on the meaning of Directive 95/46/EC. Recital 139 GDPR states that the work of WP29 shall be taken over by the EDPB. WP29 ceased to exist on 25 May 2018 and the EDPB came into existence. Article 68 GDPR specifically establishes the EDPB and Article 70 GDPR lays out the EDPB's duties, which includes the continuing practice of issuing advice on the interpretation of data protection law.

Article 94 GDPR states that any previous references to WP29 or the

---

30 Charter of Fundamental Rights of the European Union, 2000 OJ (C 364)

31 Twenty eighth Amendment of the Irish Constitution (Treaty of Lisbon) Act 2009.

32 Recital 1, GDPR, specifies Art 8 European Charter and Art 16 (1) TFEU.

Directive 95/46/EC shall be construed as references to the EDPB and the GDPR. Thus, the work of WP29 can be used in the interpretation and understanding of the GDPR, where the EDPB has not issued any replacing advice. As such, any references to WP29 opinions in this book are used to aid in the explanation of the GDPR. All of the WP29 and EDPB guidelines and opinions may be found online.[33]

The EDPB published their programme for 2019/2020, please refer to this to see upcoming guidelines that were unfinished at the time of the publication of this book, as it may be beneficial.[34]

European Data Protection Supervisor and the EU Institutions

The European Data Protection Supervisor (hereinafter referred to as EDPS) was set up as the EU's independent data protection authority under Regulation (EC) No 45/2001.[35] The purpose of the EDPS is to ensure the EU institutions act in compliance with EU data protection law. Regulation 2018/1725 came into force on 11 December 2018 and repealed Regulation (EC) No 45/2001 and brought the data protection practices of EU institutions up to date, in line with the GDPR.[36] Regulation 2018/1725 sets out the obligations of the EU institutions when processing personal data and restated that it is the role of the EDPS to monitor the compliance of the EU institutions with said obligations.[37]

The EDPS advises the EU institutions on all matters relating to the GDPR and Regulation 2018/1725, in particular regarding new EU legislation and policies. The EDPS is to also monitor new technology, with regard to its compliance with the GDPR, and cooperate with national supervisory authorities in this light. In this

---

33 Currently WP29 Documents 1997—2016 can be found at: http://ec.europa.eu/justice/article-29/documentation/index_en.htm. Guidelines from the EDPB and WP29 Guidelines endorsed by the EDPB can be found at: https://edpb.europa.eu/our-work-tools/general-guidance/gdpr-guidelines-recommendations-best-practices_en.

34 European Data Protection Work Programme 2019/2020, published at 12.02.2019.

35 Art 1(2) Regulation (EC) No 45/2001 of the European Parliament and the Council of 18 December 2000 on the protection of individuals with regard to the processing of personal data by the Community institutions and bodies and on the free movement of such data (OJ L 8, 12.1.2001, p 1).

36 Regulation (EU) 2018/1725 of the European Parliament and of the Council of 23 October 2018 on the protection of natural persons with regard to the processing of personal data by the Union institutions, bodies, offices and agencies and on the free movement of such data, and repealing Regulation (EC) No 45/2001 and Decision No 1247/2002/EC (OJ L 295, 21.11.2018, p 39–98)

37 Art 1(3) Regulation (EU) 2018/1725

regard, for the purposes of the book, the EDPS is most relevant in Chapter 22.

Irish Data Protection Commission

The Irish Data Protection Commission is the supervisory authority for Ireland, for the purposes of the GDPR,[38] whose function is to ensure and facilitate compliance with the GDPR among entities in Ireland. Furthermore, any functions that were previously vested in the Data Protection Commissioner are transferred to the Irish Data Protection Commission.[39] The Irish Data Protection Commission also issues guidance notes to aid entities in compliance, which are available online and shall be referenced, where applicable, in this book.[40]

---

38 s 10-11 DPA 2018.

39 s 14 DPA 2018; in addition, any prior reference to the Data Protection Commissioner or to the Office of the Data Protection Commissioner is now considered a reference to the Irish Data Protection Commission.

40 See www.dataprotection.ie.

PART 1:

WHETHER COMPLIANCE WITH THE GDPR IS REQUIRED

Guide: Is Compliance with the GDPR Required?

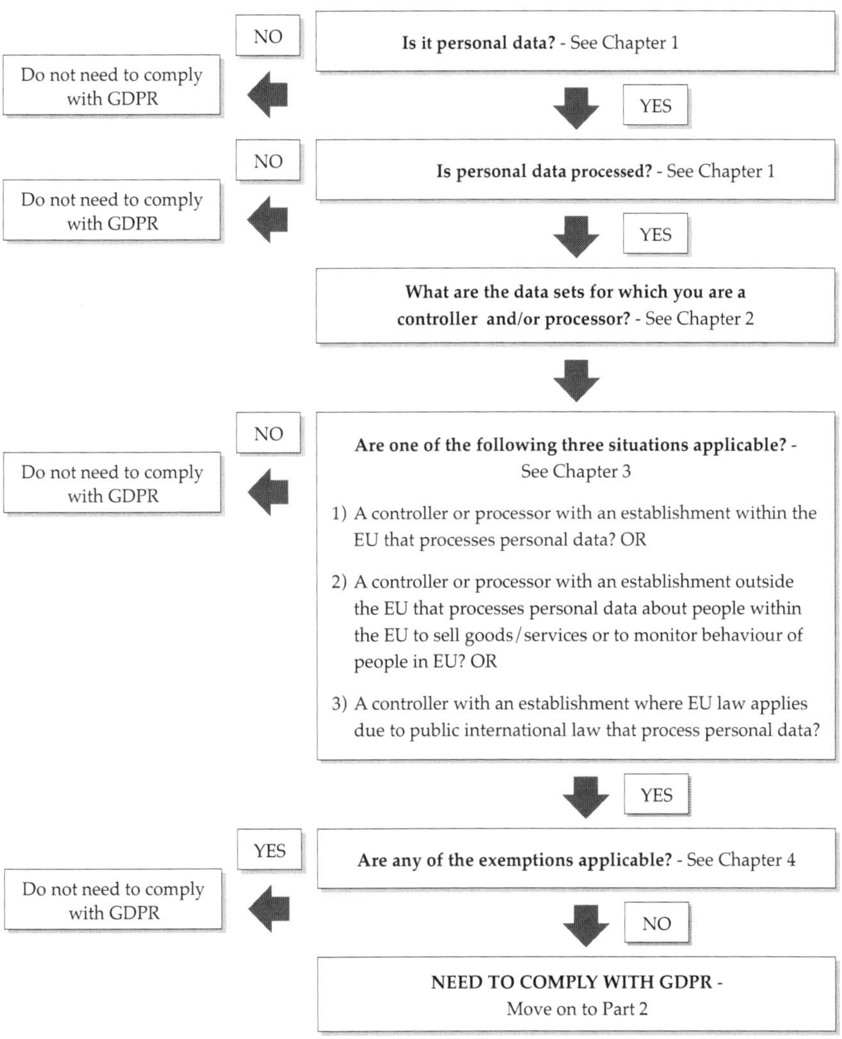

Chapter 1

Identify Whether Personal Data is Being Processed

Relevant Law: Recital 26 GDPR, Recital 30 GDPR, Article 4(1) GDPR, Article 4(2) GDPR, Article 4(5) GDPR

There are three elements that need to be satisfied in order for the GDPR to be applicable:[1]

1. The data is personal data;
2. The personal data is processed;
3. The personal data is processed within the scope of the GDPR.

This Chapter shall deal with the first two elements and the third element shall be dealt with in Chapter 3.

Identify Personal Data

The GDPR provides a very broad definition of personal data. Article 4(1) GDPR defines personal data as:

> any information *relating* to an identified or identifiable natural person ('data subject').

Thus, in order for data to be considered personal data, it needs

[1] Art 3 GDPR.

to be established if a person is (1) identifiable and (2) if a piece of information *relates* to the identifiable person.

Identifiable person

Article 4(1) GDPR specifies that an identifiable natural person is a person that can be identified directly or indirectly, in particular by reference to an *identifier* such as:

- Name;
- Identification number;
- Location data;
- Online identifier e.g. forum user name, social media tag;
- Factors (a single factor or multiple factors) specific to the physical, physiological, genetic,[2] mental, economic, cultural or social identity of that natural person e.g. salary, religion, blood type, whether receiving social services, DNA code, disability.

Recital 30 GDPR lists possible online identifiers, including internet protocol addresses,[3] cookie identifiers and radio frequency identification tags. Every smart device has at least one unique identifier. Thus, it is important to thoroughly check the processes in place to see what personal data may be collected in less obvious areas. For example, many companies that offer analytic software (i.e. to track interaction with a website or advertisement) often collect IP addresses.

Furthermore, there are the other well-known identifiers, such as email addresses, dates of birth, home addresses and images of individuals. Ensuring whether imagery collects personal data is very important with the increased use of optical technologies, particularly CCTV cameras and drones.

Indirectly identifiable

A piece of information by itself may not be personal data but when combined with other information, may become personal data. Essentially, if there is a piece of information A, and when it is joined with piece of information B, and a single individual may be identified, both pieces of information would be then classified as personal data. For example, when an entity tracks the location

2 Recital 34 GDPR.
3 The CJEU determined in case C-582/14 that IP addresses are personal data.

of a truck, the purpose of the location data is for tracking the truck; however, it also indirectly gives the location data of the employees within the truck. Thus, the location data can become personal data if it is possible to combine the location data with the employee data.

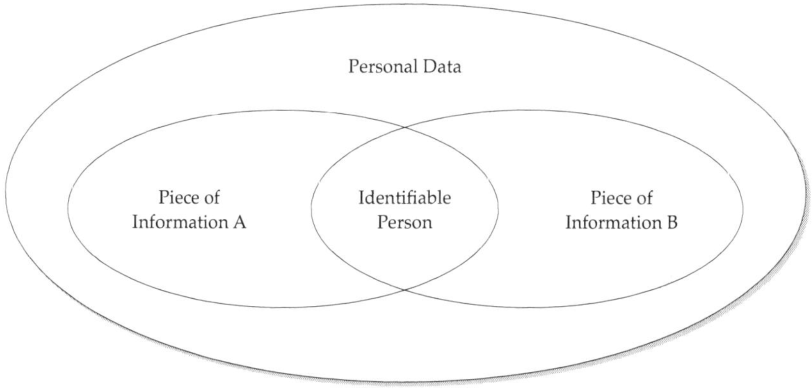

Furthermore, a combination of factors, particularly, online identifiers may be used to create a profile of an individual that relates to a single identifiable individual.[4] Thought needs to be given to the fact that information may be combined with publicly available information, such as on public social media, thereby making the information personal data.

Note that when the topic of transfers between controllers and processors is considered in Part 3 it is important to note that if processor's normal operations do not include personal data, a request from a certain controller may result in the data collected for that controller being personal data. For example if a processor is a tracking company, and they simply track what their clients (the controller's) request; the GDPR may need to be considered when tracking something that may indirectly reveal personal data. However, this would be clarified in any related agreements between a controller and processor; but it is important for processors to be aware that even if they may not have direct access to the identifiable piece of information, data still may be considered personal data.

Test for whether data "relates" to an identifiable person

Recital 26 GDPR outlines a general test that can be used to determine whether a piece of information relates to an identifiable person, thereby making it personal data. Account should be taken of all

[4] Recital 26 GDPR.

methods that could *reasonably* be used to identify an individual.[5] The general test is whether it would be *reasonably likely* for an individual to be identified considering the objective factors of:

(1) Time;
(2) Cost; and
(3) Available technology.

The use of the word reasonably within Recital 26 GDPR is important because any data could be identifiable using sufficient time and finance. However, the GDPR focuses on what is reasonably likely to be identifiable. Thus, a balancing test would need to occur that takes into account the nature of the data. For example, more time would be used to discover the identity relating to credit card information. However, less time would be used to discover the identity of a person who claimed a free coffee using their loyalty card. Therefore, if after reasonable effort (considering the type of data and based on the three factors) it is determined that it is not possible to "relate" a piece of information to an identifiable individual, it is not considered personal data and may be deemed anonymous (see below). Note that this may change as new technologies become available and may make it easier and less costly or time consuming to identify an individual. Thus, where a decision is made that certain data is not considered personal, it is important that it is documented and under constant review.

Furthermore, as the definition for personal data states "any information relating…" this extends to information arising out of an individual's personal data. For example, it was held that any comments made by an examiner on a data subject's exam sheet are the personal data of that data subject.[6]

Pseudonymisation

Article 4(5) GDPR defines pseudonymisation:

> 'pseudonymisation' means the processing of personal data in such a manner that the personal data can no longer be attributed to a specific data subject without the use of additional information, provided that such additional

5 Recital 26 GDPR.

6 See *Nowak v DPC* (20 December 2017) (C-434/16); however, there is a limit as personal data was not extended to the contents of certain work carried out by the data subject as an employee and documentation arising out of a complaint made by a data subject, see *Nowak v DPC and Price Waterhouse Coopers* [2018] IEHC 117 (26 February 2018).

information is kept separately and is subject to technical and organisational measures to ensure that the personal data are not attributed to an identified or identifiable natural person;

Thus, pseudonymisation is where an individual cannot be identified without the use of additional information. An example of this is the use of customer identification numbers or reservation numbers rather than using a data subject's name. Personal data that has undergone "pseudonymisation" is still considered personal data because such data still *relates* to the data subject.[7] The purpose of utilising pseudonymisation is for required security measures, detailed in Chapter 9. Pseudonymisation reduces the risk that personal data may be exposed if there is a data breach.[8]

Anonymisation

Anonymised personal data is *not* governed by the GDPR because it is not capable of being related to an identifiable individual.[9] Data is rendered anonymous when it is not possible to relate an identifiable person to that piece of information. There is discussion to the effect that no data can be rendered completely anonymous;[10] therefore, if reliance is placed on anonymisation, ensure that an external security company is used to check whether an individual may be linked to the anonymised information retained to guarantee that a person is not identifiable in accordance with the test outlined above on whether data "relates" to a data subject.

Identify whether Personal Data is Processed

Personal data is processed when any activity is carried out on the personal data. In accordance with Article 4(2) GDPR, the concept of processing includes any activity, from the collection of data to the storage of data.[11] Therefore, even at the point of collecting personal data, processing is considered to have already occurred.

---

7 Recital 26 GDPR.

8 Data breach procedures are detailed in Chapter 10.

9 Sentence 5, Recital 26 GDPR.

10 See the works of Yves-Alexandre de Montjoye, a full list can be found at https://scholar.google.com/citations?user=LVJtdoEAAAAJ&hl=en.

11 Art 4(2) GDPR defines the concept of processing: "processing" "means any operation or set of operations which is performed on personal data or on sets of personal data, whether or not by automated means, such as collection, recording, organisation, structuring, storage, adaptation or alteration, retrieval, consultation, use, disclosure by transmission, dissemination or otherwise making available, alignment or combination, restriction, erasure or destruction".

Further Discussion

Article 29 Working Party, Opinion 4/2007 on the concept of personal data.

Article 29 Working Party, Opinion 05/2014 on Anonymisation Techniques.

Article 29 Working Party, Opinion 8/2014 on the on Recent Developments on the Internet of Things.

Article 29 Working Party, Opinion 03/2017 on processing personal data in the context of Cooperative Intelligent Transport Systems (C-ITS).

Chapter 2

Identify Data Sets: Controller versus Processor

Relevant Law: Article 4 GDPR, Article 26 GDPR

Once it is established that an entity is processing personal data, the different "data sets" for which an entity is a controller or processor should be identified. It is important to identify each "data set" to establish whether an entity is a controller or a processor for that data set.

Definitions

The controller is the entity who has primary control of the personal data. Article 4(7) GDPR defines controller:

> Controller means "the natural or legal person, public authority, agency or other body which, alone or jointly with others, determines the *purposes and means* of the processing of personal data; where the purposes and means of such processing are determined by Union or Member State law, the controller or the specific criteria for its nomination may be provided for by Union or Member State law" [emphasis added].

Thus, the controller is the entity that:[1]

1. Decides on *why* processing of the personal data occurs (i.e. decides on the purpose) and

1 Art 29 Working Party, Opinion 1/2010 on the concepts of "controller" and "processor", at 13

2. Decides on *how* the personal data is processed (i.e. decides on the means).

The controller can be any entity from an individual, to a charity, to a multinational corporation, as long as it has the competence to "control".

Article 4(8) GDPR defines processor:

> Processor means "a natural or legal person, public authority, agency or other body which processes personal data on behalf of the controller".

The processor is the entity that carries out processing on personal data on behalf of the controller. The controller determines what the processor can and cannot do with the personal data. The processor can be any entity from an individual to a company.

Examples

Consider a gym. A gym collects data on its members, employees, and anyone that may have signed onto their mailing list. Thus, the gym decides what to do with three different data sets; (1) gym member's data, (2) employee data and (3) marketing data. The gym decides why the data is collected and how. Thus, the gym is the controller for all three data sets.

Next, consider a company that builds smart fitness machines. The company develops machines that scan real time information on the health of a person to indicate progress in fitness and offer suggestions on what exercises to do next. The gym approaches this company and contracts them to supply this information on members who choose to opt into this additional service. The gym uses this company to provide this additional service to members at an extra cost. This fitness machine company has access to three different data sets; (1) the personal data of the gym's members, (2) its own employees and (3) marketing data that is gathered via subscriptions to their own mailing list or other. The fitness machine company has no decision-making power on what to do with the first data set and must do what the gym asks - the fitness machine company is therefore a processor of the first data set. However, the fitness machine company is the controller of the second and third data set.

Remember an entity will always be the controller for their employee/ human resource data.

Joint Controller versus Separate Controllers

There may be some instances in which it is determined that more than one entity is the controller of a certain data set, meaning such entities might be "joint controllers". Article 4(7) GDPR states that the controller can be an entity that controls the personal data "either jointly or alone". Article 26(1) GDPR makes it clear that an entity is only a joint controller where all joint controllers "jointly determine the purposes and means of processing". Where there is no joint determination, the entities are separate controllers. The difference between being separate controllers and joint controllers is important in terms of satisfying data protection law. Separate controllers fulfil and satisfy all the data protection requirements separately. However, joint controllers would fulfil these obligations together. Article 26(1) GDPR states that joint controllers must determine their respective responsibilities for compliance with the GDPR. This shall be further considered in Part 3.

WP29 gave an example of separate controllers;[2] an employer must collect information from employees to pay salaries, etc.; however, the employer must also send some of this data to the tax authority. The tax authority collects this data to determine tax liabilities. The employer and the tax authority have a different purpose and means (why and how). Therefore, both are controllers in their own right and not joint controllers.

A recent case provided an example of joint controllers:[3] An entity X used a social media site to collect user cookies in order to gain statistical information on users and to push behavioural advertisements; however, the user cookies were collected from X's page on the social media site. The social media site also used X's cookie data for their own statistical usage and to push advertisements, meaning the social media site is a data controller. Thus, X argued that they could not also be data controller as the cookies were collected and used by the social media site. However, the social media site only collected that cookie information and generated those statistics because X created that social media page on their platform. The CJEU determined that X and the social media site were joint controllers for that particular data set. This is because

---

2 Art 29 Working Party, Opinion 1/2010 on the concepts of "controller" and "processor", at 20

3 5 June 2018, C-210/16

both entities determined why cookie collection occurred (to gain further insight into users) and how (via the social media platform).

Why is it Important to Determine if an Entity is a Controller or a Processor

Whether the entity is a controller or processor, the entity must adhere to the principles of data protection law. While the controller is generally responsible for informing and carrying out the rights of the data subject, the processor must ensure that it cooperates with the controller to carry out those rights and must not collect or further process personal data than what is permitted. The obligations of the controller are outlined in Part 2; however, obligations on the processor shall be outlined in an agreement between the controller and processer, which is further detailed in Part 3.

Further Discussion
Article 29 Working Party, Opinion 1/2010 on the concepts of "controller" and "processor".

Chapter 3

Identify Whether Personal Data is Processed within the Scope of the GDPR

Relevant Law: Recital 14, Recital 22 GDPR, Recital 23 GDPR, Recital 24 GDPR, Recital 25 GDPR, Article 3 GDPR, Article 4(2) GDPR

The GDPR is applicable if *personal data* is *processed* within the *scope* of the GDPR.[1] Chapter 1 outlined how to determine whether the data is personal data and whether it is processed. Where it is established that personal data is processed, the next step is to make an assessment on whether a "data set" falls within the scope of the GDPR.

Note that the EDPB adopted the draft guidelines on the territorial scope of the GDPR and are referred to herein;[2] however, these guidelines are subject to a public consultation and may alter.

Article 3 GDPR lays out three categories where the processing of personal data falls within the scope of the GDPR:

1. Controller or processor established in the EU;
2. Controller or processor established outside the EU but processing personal data of data subject's within the EU;

---

1 Art 3 GDPR.
2 EDPB Guidelines 3/2018 on the territorial scope of the GDPR (Article 3) - Version for public consultation, Adopted on 16 November 2018.

3. Controller or processor established outside the EU but applicable due to public international law.

In order to determine the applicability of one of the three categories, it is first essential to identify the establishment of the controller or processor.

Identify Establishment

While there is no strict definition of an establishment within the GDPR, Recital 22 GDPR details the term "establishment":

> "Establishment implies the effective and real exercise of activity through stable arrangements. The legal form of such arrangements, whether through a branch or a subsidiary with a legal personality, is not the determining factor in that respect."

Thus, an establishment is the location with which there is a stable arrangement for the processing of personal data or the coordination of such processing. The term "establishment" is given a broad understanding within the GDPR to reflect the true reality of where an entity is located, regardless of where there may be a legal registration. Recital 22 GDPR indicates that the legal form of the establishment is not important, rather the determining factor is whether a stable arrangement is in place.

The EDPB provided clarity on the following situations:

- A non-EU controller is not considered to have an EU establishment by virtue of utilising an EU based processor and vice versa. [3] Thus, non-EU controllers may utilise processors within the EU without fear of being caught by the GDPR automatically;
- An entity that only has an Article 27 GDPR representative within the EU,[4] is not considered to have an establishment within the EU. [5]

The EDPB recommended that an assessment of whether there is an EU located establishment should take place on a case by case

[3] EDPB Guidelines 3/2018 on the territorial scope of the GDPR (Article 3) - Version for public consultation, Adopted on 16 November 2018, at 9.

[4] See Chapter 16 on EU representatives.

[5] EDPB Guidelines 3/2018 on the territorial scope of the GDPR (Article 3) - Version for public consultation, Adopted on 16 November 2018, at 20.

basis and the individual characteristics need to be considered.[6] Legal counsel should be consulted where there is uncertainty on this point.

1. Controller or Processor Established Within the EU

Article 3(1) GDPR provides:

> This Regulation applies to the processing of personal data *in the context of the activities* of an establishment of a controller or a processor in the Union, *regardless of whether the processing takes place in the Union or not* [emphasis added].

The most important facet is identifying whether an establishment is located in the EU (see above). Article 3(1) GDPR covers a wide ambit of situations:

Situation	Details
EU establishment processing personal data of individuals located in the EU.	Once the establishment is within the EU, all personal data processing activities in and related to that establishment fall within the scope of the GDPR. For example, employee data, client data, mailing lists, etc.
EU establishment processing personal data of individuals not located in the EU.	For example, where a company is established in the EU and provides services in the United States, all personal data collection outside the EU must also comply with the GDPR. The EDPB emphasised that any personal data processing *in the context of the activities* of an EU establishment falls within the scope of Article 3(1) GDPR, regardless of the location or nationality of data subjects.[7]

6 EDPB Guidelines 3/2018 on the territorial scope of the GDPR (Article 3) - Version for public consultation, Adopted on 16 November 2018, at 5.
7 EDPB Guidelines 3/2018 on the territorial scope of the GDPR (Article 3) - Version for public consultation, Adopted on 16 November 2018, at 9.

Establishment outside the EU processing personal data *in the context of the activities* of an establishment in the EU.	The EDPB noted that a situation may arise where entities are "inextricably linked" to the extent that a non-EU entity may be considered to have an establishment in the EU.[8] A common example of this is where a non-EU establishment is an inextricable part of the processing operations on personal data for an EU establishment. In this context only the personal data that arises from the EU establishment shall be governed by the GDPR. The EDPB recommends a thorough analysis on a case by case basis to determine the applicability of Article 3(1) GDPR.

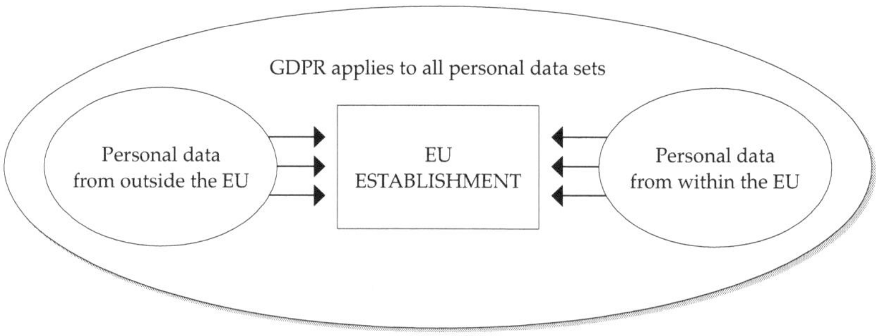

2. Controller or Processor Established Outside of the EU

Article 3(2) GDPR states:

> This Regulation applies to the processing of personal data of data subjects who are in the Union by a controller or processor not established in the Union, where the processing activities are *related* to:
> a. The offering of goods or services, irrespective of whether a payment of the data subject is required, to such data subjects in the Union; or
> b. The monitoring of their behaviour as far as their behaviour takes place within the Union [emphasis added].

Thus, in order for the GDPR to be applicable to non-EU entities, the processing must be in relation to "targeting" data subjects located within the EU.[9] Where data subjects located in the EU are "targeted" by a non- EU entity, the GDPR shall govern the EU

[8] EDPB Guidelines 3/2018 on the territorial scope of the GDPR (Article 3) - Version for public consultation, Adopted on 16 November 2018, at 6-7.

[9] EDPB Guidelines 3/2018 on the territorial scope of the GDPR (Article 3) - Version for public consultation, Adopted on 16 November 2018, at 13-14.

data set only where the processing takes place in relation (a) to the offering of goods or services to people within the EU or (b) to monitor the behaviour of people within the EU. For example, if there is a company from Canada who provides a gaming app to people within the EU - any personal data about those users located in the EU must comply with the GDPR. However, if an EU individual utilises a service while travelling outside the EU, this is not covered by the GDPR. The monitoring must take place within the EU and the offering of goods and services must be to individuals physically within the EU. Note that where this situation applies an EU representative must be appointed (see Chapter 16).

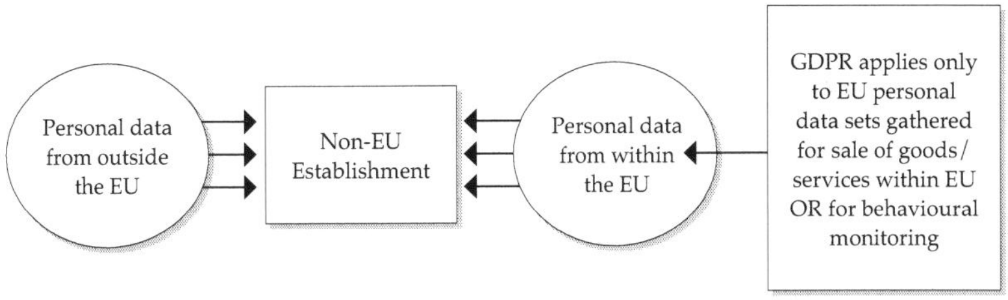

(a) Offering goods or services

The determining factor in establishing whether an entity is offering goods or services within the EU is that of *intention*. Just because a data subject can access a non-EU entity's website from the EU, does not mean that the entity is offering services within the EU.[10] Recital 23 GDPR clarifies that if there is a clear indicator that an entity actually intends to offer a good or service within the EU, then the GDPR is applicable. It states that such an indicator would, for example, be a particular currency option, or language option.[11] Thus, if there is an option to pay in Euro, this is an indicator showing that there is an intention to offer goods and services within the EU. The EDPB clarified several items regarding the criteria for offering goods or services within the context of the GDPR:[12]

- The offering of goods and services also includes the offering of online goods and services.
- If the goods or services are offered for free, this is not a mitigating factor.

---

10 Recital 23 GDPR.

11 For a longer list of examples see EDPB Guidelines 3/2018 on the territorial scope of the GDPR (Article 3) - Version for public consultation, Adopted on 16 November 2018, 15-16.

12 EDPB Guidelines 3/2018 on the territorial scope of the GDPR (Article 3) - Version for public consultation, Adopted on 16 November 2018, at 14-15.

- There needs to be a direct or indirect connection between the personal data processing activity and the offering of the good or service, i.e. the collection of an address (personal data) to deliver the goods.

(b) Monitoring

The term monitoring is not defined within the GDPR. Recital 24 GDPR indicates that it is most likely monitoring if it is gathered in order to make decisions or predictions about data subjects. The most obvious situation is monitoring for the purposes of behavioural advertisements. However, there are many forms of monitoring such as monitoring of employees and having CCTVs in operation in a public area. The EDPB stated that the fact that there is a purpose or reason for such monitoring is an important factor to consider and that monitoring with no purpose would not automatically bring the activity within the scope of the GDPR. [13]

Recital 24 GDPR refers to online monitoring as one form of monitoring. It states that in order to assess whether online monitoring occurs, it needs to be determined whether data subjects are tracked on the internet, and/or their preferences are calculated i.e. for targeted advertisements. Thus, non-EU businesses that unintentionally track EU individuals online will not be captured by the GDPR if not used for a purpose.

3. Controller Established Outside EU but where EU Law Applies via Public International Law

Article 3(3) GDPR provides:

> This Regulation applies to the processing of personal data by a controller not established in the Union, but in a place where Member State law applies by virtue of public international law.

Thus, the GDPR applies where a controller, not a processor, has an establishment in which EU law applies via public international law. Recital 25 GDPR states Member State's diplomatic missions or consular posts are examples of such situations. The EDPB provided the example that a Dutch consulate located in Jamaica

[13] For a list of usual purposes see EDPB Guidelines 3/2018 on the territorial scope of the GDPR (Article 3) - Version for public consultation, Adopted on 16 November 2018, at 18.

that is recruiting local staff would need to act in compliance with the GDPR.[14]

Further Discussion

EDPB Guidelines 3/2018 on the territorial scope of the GDPR (Article 3) – Version for public consultation, Adopted on 16 November 2018

14 EDPB Guidelines 3/2018 on the territorial scope of the GDPR (Article 3) - Version for public consultation, Adopted on 16 November 2018, at 19.

Chapter 4

Identify if an Exception is Applicable

Relevant Law: Recital 27, 56, 153, 159 GDPR, Article 2 GDPR

The GDPR does not apply to:

- Anonymised data;[1]
- Processing that falls outside EU law[2] (for example tax and criminal law);
- Processing within the scope of Chapter 2 of Title V of the TEU[3] (common foreign and security policy);
- Processing for a purely personal or household activity[4] (discussed below);
- Processing for criminal prevention and prosecution;[5]
- Data of a deceased person.[6]

There are also partial exemptions to the GDPR provided for within Irish law (further discussed below):

- Journalism and art;
- Archiving in the public interest, scientific research, historical research and statistics (ASHS);
- Public documents;

---

1 See Ch 1.
2 Art 2(2)(a) GDPR.
3 Art 2(2)(b) GDPR.
4 Art 2(2)(c) GDPR.
5 Art 2(2)(d) GDPR.
6 Recital 27 GDPR.

- An objective of general public interest;
- Processing for election purposes.

Thus, ensure that national law is checked prior to assuming that there is an exemption.

Where such exemptions differ from one Member State to another, the law of the Member State to which the controller is subject shall apply.[7] This is determined by the controller's place of establishment.[8]

Household Exemption

The household exemption excludes personal data processing from the scope of the GDPR where it is conducted for purely personal purposes. For example, collecting the dietary requirements of friends in preparation for a birthday party. Once the general public is monitored the household exemption does not apply. This must be remembered specifically for when an individual utilises a CCTV camera for security purposes; it must not look onto a public space or else the GDPR shall apply.[9] The Irish Data Protection Commission stated that this is an issue for cars that use "Dash Cams".[10] Where a person uses a dash cam they are a controller for the purposes of the GDPR; therefore, individuals using one should remember to delete such footage regularly and be wary against publishing footage on social media, or other, so as not to breach the GDPR.[11] This is likewise the case for the use of drones with camera capabilities,[12] and for the use of certain "internet of things" devices, such as smart glasses,[13] as they may monitor the public.[14] Just because a non-commercial entity is the owner of the device, does not stop the GDPR from being applicable. Even an individual or group with no commercial purpose can be classified as a controller.

---

7 Recital 153 GDPR.

8 See Ch 3 re how to identify establishment.

9 *FrantišekRyneš v* Úřad ECJ Case C-212/13, 11 December 2014.

10 Irish Data Protection Commission, Guidance for Drivers on use of "Dash Cams", see https://www.dataprotection.ie/en/guidance-landing/guidance-drivers-use-dash-cams.

11 For example see Case C–345/17 where publishing a video to YouTube did not qualify for the household exemption.

12 Part 3.1 art 29 Working Party, Opinion 01/2015 on Privacy and Data Protection Issues relating to the Utilisation of Drones.

13 Part 3.4 art 29 Working Party, Opinion 8/2014 on the on Recent Developments on the Internet of Things

14 European Data Protection Supervisor, Technology report No 1, Smart glasses and data protection, Brussels January 2019.

Journalistic and Artistic Purposes

Journalistic and artistic purposes is a category that the GDPR specifically allows for derogation by Member States.[15] Section 43 DPA 2018 specifically exempts journalistic and artistic purposes from compliance with the GDPR only where the right to freedom of expression could not otherwise be achieved. Therefore, a balancing act must take place on the part of the journalistic or artistic entity that wishes to make use of this exemption: can freedom of expression be achieved without disregarding the right to personal data protection? If freedom of expression can reasonable be achieved even though the GDPR is applicable, then the GDPR is still applicable. If freedom of expression cannot be achieved while being constrained by the GDPR, then the GDPR is not applicable. For example, where possible under this rule, a journalist should inform a person if an article is being published about them.

If freedom of expression can be achieved > GDPR applicable
If freedom of expression cannot be achieved > GDPR not applicable

Note that the journalism category can apply to non-traditional media, such as amateur journalists, blogs, video publishing platforms etc., as long as the object of the publication is the disclosure of information, opinions or ideas to the public.[16]

Archiving in the Public Interest, Scientific Research, Historical Research and Statistical Purposes (ASHS)

Archiving personal data in the public interest or processing personal data for scientific research, historical research or statistical purposes shall be referred to as ASHS activities. These terms are very broad and may be interpreted as such;[17] however, WP29 noted that these terms may not be stretched beyond their common meaning.[18] Processing for ASHS purposes is a category that the GDPR specifically allows for derogation by Member States.[19] Section 42 DPA 2018 states that controllers do not need to ensure the provision of data subject rights (detailed in Chapter 8 of this book) if it would impair or render impossible the intended ASHS

---

15 Recital 153 GDPR, art 85 GDPR.
16 See Case C–345/17
17 Recital 159 GDPR.
18 See Art 29 Working Party, Guidelines on consent under Regulation 2016/679, as last Revised and Adopted on 10 April 2018, at 27.
19 Recital 156, 157, 158 GDPR; Recital 159, 161 GDPR (scientific); Recital 160 GDPR (historical); Recital 162, 163 GDPR (statistical); Art 89 GDPR Recital 154 GDPR; Art 86 GDPR.

purposes. Thus, where it is not reasonably possible to provide data subject rights while processing personal data for ASHS purposes, the data subject's rights do not need to be provided for. However, where it is possible to provide data subject rights without impeding the ASHS purposes, then such rights must be provided for.

Possible to provide data subject rights without hindering the ASHS activity > proactively ensure data subject rights are fulfilled
Impossible or a hindrance to the ASHS activity to provide data subject rights > data subject rights are limited

As such, the obligations under the GDPR are significantly lessened. For example, if historical records with personal data need to be analysed and it would be impossible to contact the individuals that are detailed within the records, the data subject rights do not need to be provided for. There are four factors to keep in mind for this limited exemption:

Information should still be available	There should be publicly available information on the fact that an entity is relying on this exemption, either via the entity's website or other.[20]
Data subject's right to object still remains	Where personal data is processed for ASHS purposes, the right of the data subject to object to the processing activity shall remain (detailed in Chapter 8), unless the processing is necessary for the performance of a task carried out for reasons of public interest.[21]
Further processing automatically permissible	Where data is collected on an established legal basis (outlined in Chapter 5) further processing for ASHS purposes shall be considered to be compatible with the initial purpose for which that data was gathered.[22] Thus, a new legal basis need not be established. Therefore, where personal data was gathered in accordance with the GDPR on a legal basis and the entity that gathered the data wishes to, in addition, carry out processing for ASHS purposes, this is permissible under the original legal basis.

20 Art 29 Working Party Guidelines on transparency under Regulation 2016/679, at 31.

21 Art 21(6) GDPR. See Ch 8.

22 Art 5(1)(b) GDPR.

Anonymised data always exempt from the GDPR	Anonymised data is exempt from the GDPR, thus where the ASHS data is aggregated and may be rendered anonymous, the GDPR automatically does not apply.

Public Access to Official Documentation

Public access to official documentation is a category that the GDPR specifically allows for derogation by Member States.[23] Regarding public access to official documentation, s 44 DPA 2018 states personal data contained in such a record may be disclosed where a request for access is granted in accordance with the Freedom of Information Act 2014.

Objectives of General Public Interest

Processing for tasks carried out in the public interest is a category for which derogation by Member States is permissible, in accordance with Recital 10 GDPR. Section 60 DPA 2018 states that where the personal data processing is for an objective of general public interest, provision may be made via further legislation to limit the obligations of controllers (obligations detailed in Chapter 7 and Chapter 8). Section 60(7) DPA 2018 provides a substantial list of objectives of general public interest, several of which are: provisions for safeguarding national security, national financial interests, national public services and national social services. Another objective is protecting members of the public against any one of the following:

- Financial loss due to malpractice;[24]
- Risks arising from the employment relationship;[25]
- Discrimination or unfair treatment in the provision of goods or services to them.[26]

Further objectives of general public interest may be provided for via regulation.[27] Specific regulations may also be introduced and/or amended in accordance with s 60.[28] There should be publicly available information on the fact that an entity is relying on a

---

23 Recital 154 GDPR; Art 86 GDPR.
24 s 60(7)(k) DPA 2018.
25 s 60(7)(l)(i)DPA 2018.
26 s 60(7)(l)(ii) DPA 2018.
27 s 60(8) DPA 2018.
28 Data Protection Act 2018 (Section 60(6)) (Private Security Services Act 2004, Property Services (Regulation) Act 2011 and Personal Insolvency Act 2012) Regulations 2018; Data Protection Act 2018 (Section 60(6)) (Central Bank of Ireland) Regulations 2018.

national law exemption, either via the entity's website or other, except where such information would prejudice the purpose of the legislation.[29] Furthermore, s 94 DPA 2018 re law enforcement provides for several instances in which a data subject may not exercise their rights, of which many of the instances resemble s 60, including instances of national security and ensuring fairness of criminal proceedings, among others.

Processing for Election Purposes

Recital 56 GDPR provides that the processing of personal data for election purposes may be permitted by Member States for reasons of public interest. Section 59 DPA 2018 provides that the right of the data subject to object[30] does not apply to processing carried out by political parties or a candidate for election in the course of Irish electoral activities. Furthermore, the right does not need to be satisfied by the Referendum Commission in the performance of its duties. There should be publicly available information on the fact that an entity is relying on this exemption, either via the entity's website or other.[31] Remember that political opinions constitute a special category of personal data and must be respected in the context of political campaigns.[32]

Further Discussion

Article 29 Working Party, Opinion 8/2014 on the on Recent Developments on the Internet of Things.

Article 29 Working Party, Opinion 01/2015 on Privacy and Data Protection Issues relating to the Utilisation of Drones.

---

29 Art 29 Working Party Guidelines on transparency under Regulation 2016/679, at 31, 33-34.

30 Art 21 GDPR, see Ch 8.

31 Art 29 Working Party Guidelines on transparency under Regulation 2016/679, at 31.

32 European Data Protection Board, Statement 2/2019 on the use of personal data in the course of political campaigns, Adopted on 13 March 2019.

PART 2

CONDITIONS UNDER WHICH A CONTROLLER CAN PROCESS PERSONAL DATA

Guide: Under what Circumstances can a Controller Process Personal Data?

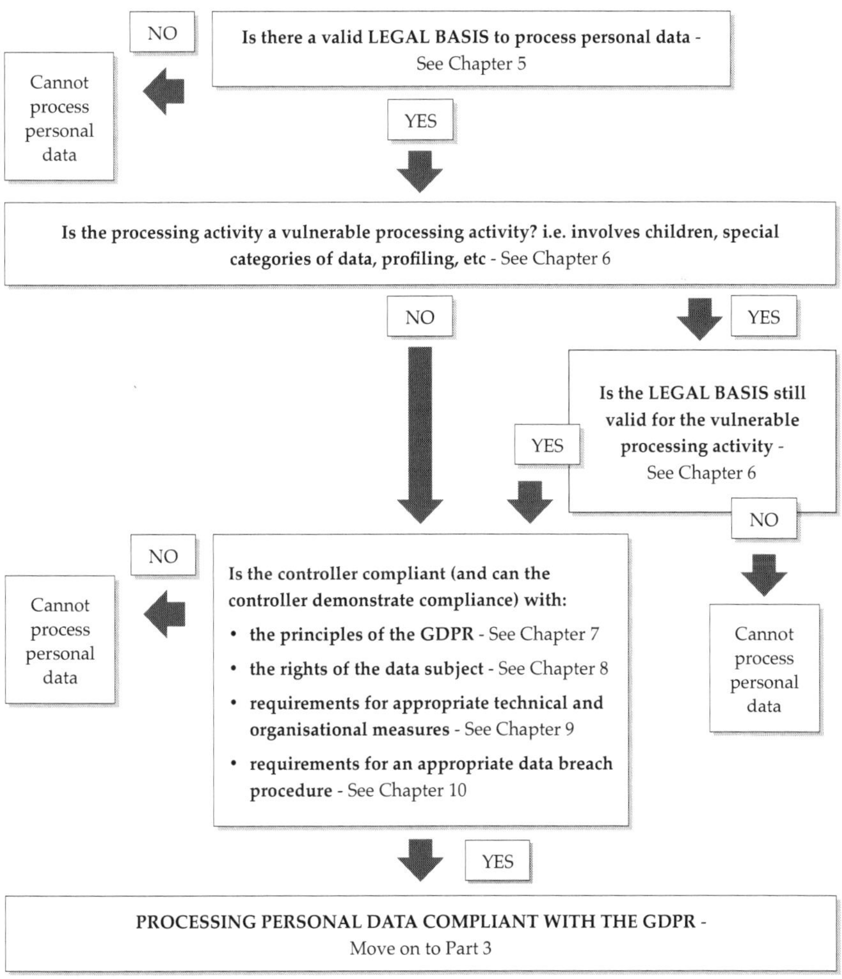

Chapter 5

Identify Legal Basis to Process Personal Data

Relevant Law: Recital 40–50 GDPR, Article 5–7 GDPR

In order to process personal data there needs to be at least one legal basis upon which the personal data may be processed. The legal basis must be established by the controller.[1] Article 6 GDPR sets out the six possible legal bases:[2]

(1) Consent;[3]
(2) Contractual necessity;[4]
(3) Compliance with a legal obligation to which the controller is subject to;[5]
(4) Vital interests of a natural person;[6]
(5) Necessary for the performance of task carried out in the public interest or in the exercise of official authority vested in the controller;[7]
(6) Necessary for pursuance of the legitimate interests of the

1 See Ch 2 for definition on personal data.
2 Note that in Ch 6 variances occur within the traditional legal bases to process certain categories of personal data or for certain types of processing.
3 Art 6(1)(a) GDPR.
4 Art 6(1)(b) GDPR.
5 Art 6(1)(c) GDPR.
6 Art 6(1)(d) GDPR.
7 Art 6(1)(e) GDPR.

> controller (or third party) except where such interests are overridden by the rights of the data subject.[8]

The *purpose* for the processing should be established in order to determine the most appropriate legal basis. The purpose is why the personal data is being collected and processed. For example, if the purpose is to complete a contract, then the contractual basis may be most appropriate; if it is to aid a customer, then the legitimate interest may be appropriate; if it is to stop the spread of disease, then vital interest may be appropriate.

Therefore, the purpose should be determined first and then the legal basis:

1.	Why is the personal data being gathered / processed? Answer = Purpose
2.	What is the legal basis for this purpose?

Each legal basis shall be detailed below.

1. Consent

Consent is where the data subject agrees to their personal data being processed for a specified purpose. Where consent is used as the basis to process personal data, the controller must specifically state the purpose of the personal data processing – why is the personal data being collected and what will the controller do with the personal data? Consent simply to the gathering of personal data does not entitle the controller to do whatever the controller wants with the data. Consent is only provided for the purpose that was specified to the data subject.

Article 4(11) GDPR defines consent:

> "consent" of the data subject means any freely given, specific, informed and unambiguous indication of the data subject's wishes by which he or she, by a statement or by a clear affirmative action, signifies agreement to the processing of personal data relating to him or her

Thus, consent shall only be deemed to be valid consent if (a) data subject is informed, in particular of the purpose for the data

8 Art 6(1)(f) GDPR.

processing (b) controller can show unambiguous consent for that purpose and (c) data subject provided freely given consent.

(a) Informed

Consent is informed if the data subject is made aware of the following six items in clear plain language:[9]

(1) The identity of the controller;
(2) Purpose of the processing activity;
(3) What data will be collected;
(4) Existence of the right to withdraw consent;[10]
(5) Whether data is used for automated decision making;[11]
(6) Whether data is transferred outside the EU and the appropriate safeguards in place.[12]

Three items to be aware of regarding the need for the data subject to be informed:

Multiple controllers	Where consent is sought to cover joint controllers or other controllers, all those entities must be named for consent to be informed.[13]
Consent for data processing must be distinguishable from other	Where consent is gathered via a document that also concerns other (non-data protection) matters, the request for consent to process personal data must be clearly distinguishable.[14] This is why privacy statements are usually kept separate.
Right to be informed	This information is usually provided alongside the required information per the right to be informed, as detailed in Chapter 8, and in line with the transparency principle detailed in Chapter 7.

(b) Unambiguous

Consent is unambiguous if the controller can demonstrate consent for the specified purpose i.e. provide proof.[15] The controller must be

9 Recital 42 GDPR.
10 Art 7(3) GDPR.
11 See Ch 6.
12 Art 46 GDPR and see Part 3 herein.
13 Art 29 Working Party, Guidelines on Consent under Regulation 2016/679 , at 13.
14 Art 7(2) GDPR.
15 Recital 42 GDPR ; Art 7(1) GDPR.

able to demonstrate that the data subject unambiguously consented and provided consent for the specified purpose:

i. Unambiguously consented

Consent cannot be implied or assumed. For consent to be unambiguous there needs to be a proactive step to consent. The language used must be very clear, with no jargon. Thus, a tick box seeking consent cannot be pre-ticked.

ii. Provided consent to the specified purpose

Consent must be provided for a specific purpose, and where consent is needed for multiple purposes it must be set out separately. For example, where consent is required to send marketing emails and to sell the emails to a third party, it must be clear both items were separately and specifically consented to. Therefore, at the end of a document the several processing purposes that require consent must be laid out and it must be possible to consent or not consent to each purpose separately.

> i. An example of how to gain unambiguous consent:
>
> The controller wishes to collect your name and email address to send you marketing materials about the controller's activities. The controller also wishes to use this information to sell on to third parties to use for their marketing mailing lists.
>
> ☐ Tick box to consent to receiving marketing emails from the controller
>
> ☐ Tick box to consent to your name and email address being provided to third parties for such parties marketing activities.

(c) Freely Given

Consent is freely given where it is free from pressure and where there is no unreasonable adverse effect for not providing consent.[16] For example, imagine there is a company that will only sell Sally a car if she provides consent to allowing the company to track the car location. Making the sale of the car conditional on consent places undue pressure on Sally to provide consent. Therefore, consent to the tracker would not be freely given. The essence of consent is choice. If Sally was given a choice to provide consent, where if she provided consent she got additional tracking capabilities and if not, then she would not be able to benefit from those capabilities — there would be a real choice. Another example of this is where

[16] Art 7(4) GDPR.

an employer tells an employee that the employee must consent to internet surveillance. As the employer is exerting undue pressure, and there is a clear imbalance in power between the employee and employer, the employee would not be able to provide freely given consent.[17]

2. Contractual Necessity

The contractual basis revolves around the word *necessity* - processing personal data is lawful where it is necessary to carry out a contract or to enter into a contract.[18] A very common situation in which the contractual basis is used is that of the employment relationship — the gathering of an employee's name, address, bank details, details of annual leave, etc., is required because it is necessary to carry out or enter into the employment contract i.e. for the employee to be paid. The controller must be very aware of the point where necessity ends. For example, gathering an employee's photo is generally not necessary to enter into the employment contract, thus another legal basis would need to be established to collect the photo — usually consent.

3. Legal Obligation

The legal obligation basis only concerns a legal obligation to which the controller is subject to. Recital 45 GDPR states that the legal obligation must have an actual basis in the law. Where this legal basis is relied upon, it should be very clear that such a legal obligation is applicable. The law should provide sufficient clarity and precision to the extent that it is foreseeable that the controller would need to abide by such legal obligation.[19] For example, there may be a legal requirement for personal details to be collected when an individual is admitted to hospital.

4. Vital Interest

A vital interest is one that is necessary to protect the life of a data subject or other individual.[20] This legal basis may only be utilised where no other legal basis may be used.[21] Recital 46 GDPR provides

---

17 Recital 43 GDPR.

18 Recital 44 GDPR. EDPB Guidelines 2/2019 on the processing of personal data under Art 6(1)(b) GDPR in the context of the provision of online services to data subjects, Adopted on 9 April 2019, Version for public consultation.

19 Recital 41 GDPR.

20 Recital 46 GDPR.

21 Recital 46 GDPR.

examples of when such basis may be used, including processing of personal data to monitor epidemics or disaster situations.

5. Public Interest or Exercising Official Authority

Similar to the legal obligation basis, anything carried out in the public interest or in exercising official authority should have a basis in the law that is sufficiently clear and precise.[22] Section 38 DPA 2018 further states that a controller may only process personal data on this basis where it is conferred by an enactment or the constitution.

6. Legitimate Interest

The legitimate interest basis includes the interest of a controller or third party. "Third party" is defined in Article 4(10) GDPR as a:

> "natural or legal person, public authority, agency or body other than the data subject, controller, processor and persons who, under the direct control of the controller or processor, are authorised to process personal data."

A legitimate interest may only be relied upon after a balancing assessment has taken place between the legitimate interest and the rights of the data subject. The legitimate interest can be established via the reasonable expectations of the data subject arising out of the relationship between the data subject and controller.[23] For example, when a data subject considers a CCTV that is in operation in a shop – the data subject has no contractual connection with the shop and would not have provided consent, etc. However, the controller has the legitimate interest of security and the data subject has a reasonable expectation that the CCTV is used for security purposes. Thus, there is a legitimate interest for any personal data that is collected via the CCTV to be used for security purposes. This means that such data may not be used for other purposes of which the data subject has no reasonable expectation, for example monitoring data subjects' shopping habits. The GDPR provides for certain instances where a legitimate interest may be assumed:

- Activities for the prevention of fraud;[24]

---

[22] Recital 41 and 45 GDPR.
[23] Recital 47 GDPR.
[24] Recital 47 GDPR.

- Transferring personal data within the controller group of entities i.e. for internal administration.[25]

Furthermore, Recital 47 GDPR states that direct marketing may be regarded as carried out for a legitimate interest where a reasonable expectation exists that a data subject would expect that information, for example in business to business communications.[26]

Establish Legal Basis for Each Purpose

A legal basis needs to be established for each purpose of data processing. The purpose is why the personal data is being collected and processed. The concept of a legal basis is intrinsically linked to the purpose for which the personal data is to be gathered and processed. For example, where someone consents to the collection of their email address to receive marketing emails from the controller. The purpose is to send marketing emails. Consent is only provided for that purpose. If the controller than sells the email addresses onto a third party - consent was not provided for this purpose. Therefore, another legal basis would need to be established to support this new purpose of selling emails to third parties. Personal data may be used for a wide variety of purposes, and the controller must ensure that there is a legal basis for each purpose.

Further Processing Beyond Purpose

Relevant Law: Article 6(4) GDPR

Where the controller wishes to perform further processing on personal data beyond the purpose for which the legal basis was established - is that further processing permissible without establishing a new legal basis? It is permissible where the processing is *compatible* with the initial purpose. Article 6(4) GDPR states that the following elements need to be taken into account to determine whether it is compatible:

1. The link between the initial purpose and the further processing;
2. The context in which the personal data was initially

[25] Recital 48 GDPR (but remember additional obligations for transfers outside the EU, see Chapter 13-14).

[26] For further see Ch 20.

collected i.e. the relationship between the data subject and the controller;
3. The nature of the personal data i.e. whether it is a special category or not;[27]
4. The consequences of the further processing;
5. The security measures in place.[28]

Therefore, an assessment needs to be made considering the above five factors as to whether this further process is compatible with the initial purpose for which the personal data was collected. For example, a gym collects data on gym members to ensure the members have paid their membership and to enable them to have access to the gym facilities. This does not mean that the gym is allowed to automatically add them to the gym mailing list. However, a compatible purpose would be to inform them when their gym membership needs to be renewed. This is compatible with the initial purpose of collecting their data, which was to enable them to become a gym member.

The DPA 2018 provides that certain further processes are automatically deemed compatible with the initial purpose in Ireland, which are:[29]

- Preventing a threat to national security, defence or public security;
- Preventing, detecting, investigating or prosecuting criminal offences;
- For providing or obtaining legal advice or otherwise necessary for defending legal rights.

Furthermore, further processing is automatically considered compatible for ASHS purposes.[30]

In any situation where it is found that the further processing is incompatible with the initial purpose, the controller may only further process if it is permissible in accordance with a law or with the data subject's consent. The controller could also initiate the processing activity again and establish an appropriate legal basis.

---

27 See Ch 6 on special categories.
28 See Ch 9.
29 s 41 DPA 2018.
30 Art 5(1)(b) GDPR; See Ch 4; Art 89(1) GDPR.

Further Discussion

Article 29 Working Party, Opinion 15/2011 on the definition of consent.

Article 29 Working Party, Opinion 03/2013 on purpose limitation.

Article 29 Working Party, Opinion 06/2014 on the notion of legitimate interests of the data controller under Article 7 of Directive 95/46/EC.

Article 29 Working Party, Guidelines on Consent under Regulation 2016/679.

EDPB Guidelines 2/2019 on the processing of personal data under Article 6(1)(b) GDPR in the context of the provision of online services to data subjects, Adopted on 9 April 2019, Version for public consultation.

Chapter 6

Identify whether Legal Basis Appropriate for a Vulnerable Processing Activity

There are vulnerable processing activities for which there are variances in the six legal bases outlined in Chapter 5, including:

1. Special categories of personal data;
2. Children;
3. Processing on the basis of automated decision making, including profiling;
4. Processing the content of communications;
5. Cookies.

These shall be discussed in detail below.

1. Special Categories of Personal Data

Relevant Law: Article 9 GDPR

Article 9(1) GDPR prohibits the processing of special categories of personal data except under certain conditions. Special categories of personal data are:

- Data that reveals racial or ethnic origin;
- Data that reveals political opinions;
- Data that reveals religious or philosophical beliefs;
- Data that reveals trade union membership;
- The processing of genetic data and or biometric data for the purpose of uniquely identifying a natural person, i.e. facial images or finger prints;
- The processing of data concerning health and or data concerning a natural person's sex life and or sexual orientation.

Exemptions to prohibition

Article 9(2) GDPR provides for exemptions to the general prohibition on processing special categories of personal data. Furthermore, Recital 52-53 GDPR allows for derogation by Member States to authorise other exemptions. In accordance with the GDPR and the DPA 2018, an entity may process special categories of personal data where one of the following ten situations are satisfied:

1. Explicit consent (except where Member State law states consent will not lift prohibition);[1]
2. Necessary for employment, social security, social protection law or for a collective agreement with the necessary safeguards;[2]
3. Necessary to protect the vital interests of the data subject, where the data subject is incapable of providing consent;[3]
4. Forms part of legitimate activities of a non-for-profit body with a political, philosophical, religious or trade union aim;[4]
5. The data was already made "manifestly" public by the data subject;[5]
6. For legal proceedings and administration of justice;[6]
7. For public interest;[7]
8. For medical reasons;[8]
9. For public interest in the area of public health;[9]

---

1 Art 9(2)(a) GDPR.
2 Art 9(2)(b) GDPR; s 46 DPA 2018.
3 Art 9(2)(c) GDPR.
4 Art 9(2)(d) GDPR.
5 Art 9(2)(e) GDPR.
6 Art 9(2)(f) GDPR; s 47 DPA 2018, s 49 DPA 2018.
7 Art 9(2)(g) GDPR; s 51 DPA 2018.
8 Art 9(2)(h) GDPR, Art 9(3) GDPR; s 52 DPA 2018.
9 Art 9(2)(i) GDPR; s 53 DPA 2018.

10. For ASHS purposes.[10]

In addition to those ten situations, the DPA 2018 (and not the GDPR) has legislated for further situations in which the special categories of personal data may be processed:

1. For preventing a threat to national security, defence or public security;[11]
2. For preventing, investigating or prosecuting criminal offences;[12]
3. For compiling data on political opinions;[13]
4. For the performance of a function conferred on a person by or under an enactment of the Constitution.[14]

Section 41 DPA 2018 provides instances in which further processing of special categories of personal data may occur for purposes other than the purpose for which it was collected:

- Preventing a threat to national security;
- Preventing, detecting, investigating or prosecuting criminal offences;
- Establishing, exercising or defending legal rights and or providing legal advice in connection with same.

Explicit consent

The most commonly used exemption is *explicit consent*. The term consent was detailed within Chapter 5. This concept of consent already lays down a high standard for consent; the extra requirement for *explicit* consent arises from the manner in which the data subject expresses their consent.[15] It must be insured that the data subject provides a very express and clear statement of consent, for example in a signed written statement.

Profiling

Profiling is detailed in item 3 of this chapter; however, note that profiling can generate special categories of personal data, i.e. via the combination of different data. WP29 gave the example that it

---

10 Art 9(2)(j) GDPR; s 54 DPA 2018; See Ch 4 on ASHS.

11 s 41 DPA 2018; s 45 DPA 2018.

12 s 55 DPA 2018.

13 s 48 DPA 2018.

14 s 49(b) DPA 2018.

15 Art 29 Working Party, Guidelines on consent under Regulation 2016/679, as last Revised and Adopted on 10 April 2018, at 18.

is possible to infer someone's health information from their food shopping list.[16] If special categories of personal data may be inferred from profiling, the controller must be adamant to ensure that there is a legal basis for this processing and that the data subject is informed, in accordance with their rights.[17]

Genetic, biometric or health data

The GDPR details these items:

- Genetic data: "personal data relating to the inherited or acquired genetic characteristics of a natural person which result from the analysis of a biological sample from the natural person in question, in particular chromosomal, deoxyribonucleic acid (DNA) or ribonucleic acid (RNA) analysis, or from the analysis of another element enabling equivalent information to be obtained.";[18]
- Biometric Data: "personal data resulting from specific technical processing relating to the physical, physiological or behavioural characteristics of a natural person, which allow or confirm the unique identification of that natural person, such as facial images or dactyloscopic data."[19]
- Data concerning health: "all data pertaining to the health status of a data subject which reveal information relating to the past, current or future physical or mental health status of the data subject...".[20]

---

16 Art 29 WP, Guidelines on Automated individual decision-making and Profiling for the purposes of Regulation 2016/679, as last revised and adopted on 6 February 2018, at 15.

17 See Ch 8.

18 Recital 34 GDPR, art 4(13) GDPR.

19 Art 4(14) GDPR

20 Recital 35 GDPR, art 4(15) GDPR; Recital 35 GDPR continued "...This includes information about the natural person collected in the course of the registration for, or the provision of, health care services as referred to in Directive 2011/24/EU of the European Parliament and of the Council (9) to that natural person; a number, symbol or particular assigned to a natural person to uniquely identify the natural person for health purposes; information derived from the testing or examination of a body part or bodily substance, including from genetic data and biological samples; and any information on, for example, a disease, disability, disease risk, medical history, clinical treatment or the physiological or biomedical state of the data subject independent of its source, for example from a physician or other health professional, a hospital, a medical device or an in vitro diagnostic test."

Article 9(4) GDPR provides that Member States may further legislate re processing for genetic, biometric or health data.

In accordance with s 50 of the DPA 2018, the processing of data concerning health shall be lawful where "necessary and proportionate" for any of the following purposes:

- A policy of insurance, including health insurance
- A policy of life assurance
- Pension purposes, including retirement annuity
- Mortgaging of a property

The Disability Act 2005, as amended,[21] still applies to the processing of genetic data of persons (with or without disabilities[22]). In order for genetic data to be processed, consent is required.[23] In any regard genetic processing may not take place vis a vis employment, life assurance, health and or other insurance, pension arrangements, or mortgages for property.[24] Note that where genetic processing takes place further information is required to be provided to the data subject.[25] Note that information on a data subject's family history may be used for insurance purposes.[26]

Health research

The Data Protection Act 2018, s 36(2) (Health Research) Regulations 2018 (Health Research Regulations) came into effect on 8 August 2018.[27] For any health research that started prior to such date, a transition period is provided for until 30 April 2019. The Health Research Regulations apply to the processing of personal data for the purposes of "health research", which is defined as "scientific research for the purpose of human health". The regulation sets out an exhaustive list of examples of such research.[28] The Health

21 See s 202 DPA 2018.

22 For informational purposes s 2, Disability Act 2005 provides: "disability", in relation to a person, means a substantial restriction in the capacity of the person to carry on a profession, business or occupation in the State or to participate in social or cultural life in the State by reason of an enduring physical, sensory, mental health or intellectual impairment.

23 Disability Act 2005, s 42.

24 Disability Act 2005, s 42(2).

25 Disability Act 2005, s 42(3) provides that the data subject must be informed of purpose and possible outcomes of the proposed processing, as well as any potential implications for the health of the data subject which may become known as a result of the processing.

26 See Disability Act 2005, s 43.

27 SI No 314 of 2018.

28 Reg 3(2).

Research Regulations provide that the processing of personal data for health research purposes requires "explicit consent".[29] Explicit consent is defined as consent meeting the requirements of Article 4 GDPR,[30] outlined in Chapter 5. Such consent is not required where a committee, as provided for within the Health Research Regulations, makes a declaration that such consent is not required.[31] Entities may apply to the committees for such declaration.

Such a declaration is compliant with the GDPR in that Recital 54 GDPR provides that the processing of special categories of personal data may be necessary for reasons of public interest in the areas of public health without consent of the data subject. It should be noted that such processing of health data without consent should not result in personal data being processed by employers, insurance companies or banking companies as this would unjustly impact on the rights of the data subject.[32]

The Clinical Trials Regulation harmonises the process for clinical trials in the EU.[33] The EDPB issued an opinion on the GDPR vis a vis the new regulation.[34] The EDPB discussed the need for a legal basis. Under the Clinical Trials Regulation, consent is required. However, the EDPB questions the validity of such consent for the purposes of the GDPR and recommends that another legal basis may need to be established for the purposes of fulfilling the GDPR. WP29 stated that the consent needed under the Clinical Trials Regulation may be considered as an additional safeguard, rather than as the legal basis under the GDPR.[35] It remains to be seen whether this is an issue vis a vis the Health Research Regulations, as consent is permissible as the legal basis for GDPR purposes.[36]

2. Children

Relevant Law: Recital 38 GDPR, Article 4(25) GDPR, Article 8 GDPR

Note that in December 2018 the Irish Data Protection Commission

---

29 Reg 6(1).
30 Reg 6(2).
31 Reg 6(4)-(5).
32 Recital 54 GDPR.
33 Clinical Trial Regulation EU No. 536/2014, which will replace EU Clinical Trial Directive (EC) No. 2001/20/EC.
34 EDPB Opinion 3/2019 concerning the Questions and Answers on the interplay between the Clinical Trials Regulation (CTR) and the GDPR.
35 See Art 29 Working Party, Guidelines on consent under Regulation 2016/679, as last Revised and Adopted on 10 April 2018, at 28.
36 See further Part 4.

launched a public consultation on the "Processing of Children's Personal Data and the Rights of Children as Data Subjects under the GDPR" and thereby the below may alter as a result of this consultation.[37]

Parental consent and or authorisation is required where the following four factors are met:[38]

	Criteria	Details
1	Data subject under 16 years of age	0-15 years old
2	Legal basis needed is consent	If a different legal basis as provided in Chapter 5 is applicable then parental consent is not required
3	The processing activity relates to offering "information society services"	Article 4(25) GDPR defines the concept of an "information society service" in relation to Article 1(1) of Directive 2015/1535 on information society services. This defines the service as having four components: (i) A service that is *normally* (could be a "freemium" service) provided for remuneration, (ii) The service is provided at a distance, (i.e. not a face to face service) (iii) The service is provided by electronic means (i.e. online games, mobile applications) (iv) The service is provided at the request of the individual If these four components are satisfied, the service is an "information society service".
4	The "information society services" are offered directly to a data subject under 16 years of age	If there is no intention to offer the service to a child, it need not comply with Article 8 GDPR. For example, often mobile applications will specify the age to whom they are offering their service to.

37 Data Protection Commission "Public Consultation on the Processing of Children's Personal Data and the Rights of Children as Data Subjects under the GDPR", see https://www.dataprotection.ie/en/news-media/public-consultation-childrens-data-protection-rights. See also Data Protection (Amendment) Bill 2018.

38 Art 8 GDPR.

Where all four factors are met parental consent is required. The controller has the obligation to verify that consent is provided or authorised by the appropriate person with parental responsibility.[39] Article 8(2) GDPR specifically refers to available technology, in that current technology should be used to comply with this provision. For example, when a child signs up to a service where consent would be required, often they will be prompted to enter in a parent's email address and the child only receives access where the parent has verified their permission via email.

Variances within the Member States

Article 8 GDPR provides that Member States may provide for an age lower than 16 years, provided it is not below 13 years. Please refer to the chart in the Introduction "Sources of Data Protection Law: Directive versus Regulation versus National Law" for a list of the ages of consent of the different Member States. Section 31(1) of the DPA 2018 provides that in Ireland the age a child can consent to data processing under Article 8 GDPR is 16 years of age. Note that this age of consent will be reviewed in three years.[40] Irish law provides further provisions regarding children. Section 30 of the DPA 2018, states that it is illegal to profile,[41] direct market or micro target a child under Irish law.[42] This prohibition is absolute, regardless of consent or other legal bases. In accordance with s 31(2) of the DPA 2018, "information society services" does not include a reference to preventative or counselling services.

Note that other countries outside the EU also have restrictions on personal data processing of children's data. Furthermore, as many Irish companies have branches within the US and offer services within the US, it is important to be aware of the US Children's Online Privacy Protection Act of 1998 (COPPA), as amended. This applies to the collection of personal data of persons under the age of 13.[43]

Communicating with children and parents

Note that children are entitled to all the rights as detailed in

---

39 Art 8(2) GDPR.
40 DPA 2018, s 31(3).
41 See below on "Processing on the basis of automated decision making, including profiling".
42 DPA 2018, s 29.
43 The Federal Trade Commission has a compliance guide to aid businesses, see https://www.ftc.gov/tips-advice/business-center/guidance/childrens-online-privacy-protection-rule-six-step-compliance.

Chapter 8 of this book, including the right to be informed. Thus, when communicating with children it must be done in a method that is appropriate for children,[44] i.e. use of cartoons and simple language. Attention is required when communicating with children because they would be less aware of the risks and consequences of personal data processing.[45] The rights in Chapter 8, including the right to be informed, do not need to be provided to the holder of parental responsibility. However, WP29 recognised that the information required to be provided to a child to fulfil their rights, in accordance with Chapter 8, may also need to be provided to the holder of parental responsibility too, particularly where the target audiences are pre-literate children.[46]

3. Processing on the Basis of Automated Decision Making, including Profiling

Relevant Law: Recital 70–72 GDPR, Article 4(4), Article 22 GDPR

Automated decision making and profiling are viewed as two separate but related concepts within the GDPR:

- Automated decision making is where a decision is made using technological means, without human interaction;[47]
- Profiling is defined within Article 4(4) GDPR as "any form of automated processing of personal data", where there is an objective to evaluate or analyse certain aspects of the data subject. Recital 71 GDPR provides specific examples of profiling, including analysing or predicting the data subject's "performance at work, economic situation, health, personal preferences, interests, reliability, behaviour, location or movements".

For example, where a data subject is the 100th customer in a café and the cash register calculates that the data subject gets a free coffee for being the café's 100th customer - that is an automated decision. However, this would become a decision based on profiling

[44] Art 12(1) GDPR. For an example on child friendly writing see the "UN Convention on the Rights of the Child in Child Friendly Language " and Art 29 Working Party Guidelines on transparency under Regulation 2016/679, at 10.

[45] Recital 38 GDPR.

[46] Art 29 Working Party Guidelines on transparency under Regulation 2016/679, at 11.

[47] Art 29 Working Party, Guidelines on Automated individual decision-making and Profiling for the purposes of Regulation 2016/679, at 8.

if the only type of free coffee a data subject can receive is based on the data subject's preferences provided by an analysis of their café loyalty card.

Article 22 GDPR states that there is a general prohibition against a data subject being subject to a decision based solely on automated decision making, including profiling, where the decision will have a legal or similarly significant effect. Thus, personal data processing is prohibited where:

(a) There is no human involvement in the decision outcome, AND
(b) The decision would have a legal or similar significant effect

No human involvement	WP29 warned against fabricating human involvement to by-pass Article 22 GDPR. WP29 stated that any human involvement must be meaningful and be carried out by "someone who has the authority and competence to change the decision."[48] The human should be capable of considering all the relevant data.
Legal effect	A decision that has a legal effect is one that impacts a data subject's legal rights. WP29 provided the following examples of decisions that would have a legal effect: • Cancellation of a contract • Denial of a social benefit • Denial of citizenship
Similar significant effect to a legal effect	A decision that has a similar significant effect to a legal effect is one that may impact a data subject's choices, behaviour or circumstance.[49] Recital 71 GDPR provides examples of items that would have a significant similar legal effect: • Refusal of an online credit application • E-recruiting practices WP29 provided further examples of items that would have a "similar significant effect":[50] • Decisions that impact on financial circumstances • Decisions that impact on health services • Decisions that impact on employment opportunities

48 Art 29 Working Party, Guidelines on Automated individual decision-making and Profiling for the purposes of Regulation 2016/679, at 21.
49 Art 29 Working Party, Guidelines on Automated individual decision-making and Profiling for the purposes of Regulation 2016/679, at 21.
50 Art 29 Working Party, Guidelines on Automated individual decision-making

	• Decisions that impact on admission into education services WP29 noted that targeted advertising often uses profiling, but that this will often not reach the barrier of a "similar significant effect".[51] An example of targeted advertising that may have a similar significant effect is where a person is profiled as being in debt and they are targeted with many advertisements for high interest loans. Furthermore, WP29 stated that profiling causing a "similar significant effect" may occur based on data gathered about other individuals, where such data on other individuals is assumed to also be true for the data subject.[52] For example, a credit company that provides credit rates to a data subject based on an analysis of customers living within the area of the data subject, i.e. bad credit rates if "bad area".[53]

Thus, the café loyalty card example provided above would not be prohibited as it would not have a legal or similar significant effect.

Exemptions to the prohibition

Article 22(2) GDPR states that decisions based solely on automated decision making, including profiling, are not prohibited where there is a legal basis of:

i. Contractual necessity,[54] (show that the automated decision is necessary as opposed to an alternative method);
ii. Consent;[55] OR
iii. Authorisation via Member State law.[56]

Where contractual necessity or consent is used for this purpose, the controller has the obligation to implement further safeguards, including at a minimum, the ability for the data subject:[57]

- To obtain human intervention;

---

and Profiling for the purposes of Regulation 2016/679, at 22.

51 Art 29 Working Party, Guidelines on Automated individual decision-making and Profiling for the purposes of Regulation 2016/679, at 22.

52 Art 29 Working Party, Guidelines on Automated individual decision-making and Profiling for the purposes of Regulation 2016/679, at 22.

53 Art 29 Working Party, Guidelines on Automated individual decision-making and Profiling for the purposes of Regulation 2016/679, at 22.

54 See Ch 5.

55 See Ch 5.

56 See DPA 2018, s 57.

57 Art 22(3) GDPR.

- To express their viewpoint; and
- To contest any decision made via automated decisions, including profiling.

Variances to the prohibition

There are three situations in which there is a variance to the general prohibition:

Variances within national law	Irish law provides a further safeguard to data subjects. Section 89 DPA 2018 re law enforcement states that a decision that has an adverse result on the relevant data subject may not be based solely on automated decisions, including profiling.[58] Thus, any negative decision on a data subject resulting from any automated decision is prohibited. However, s 89(2) DPA 2018 re law enforcement provides an exemption to this prohibition, stating that such decisions may still occur where it is authorised by the law or where the controller has taken adequate safeguards to protect the interests of the data subject. In addition, note that s 57 DPA 2018 provides that the prohibition against automated decision making as provided for in Article 22 GDPR, may be lifted where provided for via law.
Special categories of personal data	Regarding special categories of personal data, automated decisions, including profiling, can only take place with the legal basis of consent or public interest (not contractual necessity).[59] Furthermore, s 89(3) DPA 2018 re law enforcement states that profiling is prohibited where it is based on a special category of personal data that results in discrimination toward the data subject. Thus, where discrimination occurs due to profiling from a special category of personal data, that profiling is prohibited regardless of the legal basis.
Children	According to s 30 DPA 2018, it is illegal to profile a data subject under the age of 16. Note that Article 30 DPA 2018 refers only to "direct marketing, profiling and micro-targeting" and no reference is specifically made to automated decisions.

4. Content of communications

There is a general prohibition against the processing of the content of communications, for example letters, telephone calls, text messages, etc. The only basis upon which processing the content

58 DPA 2018, s 89(1).

59 Art 22(4) GDPR.

of communications is permissible is on the basis of consent. See Chapter 21 for further details.

5. Cookies

Cookies can only be collected on the legal basis of consent. See Chapter 21 for further details.

Further Discussion

Article 29 Working Party, Opinion 1/2008 on the protection of Children's Personal Data (General Guidelines and the special case of schools).

Article 29 Working Party, Opinion 2/2009 on the protection of children's personal data (General Guidelines and the special case of schools).

Article 29 Working Party, Guidelines on Automated individual decision-making and Profiling for the purposes of Regulation 2016/679.

Chapter 7

Demonstrate Compliance with the GDPR Principles ("Accountability")

Relevant Law: Recital 39–40 GDPR, Article 5, 12 GDPR

There are six principles for which the controller must comply with and demonstrate compliance with:[1]

1. Lawfulness, fairness and transparency;
2. Accuracy;
3. Integrity and confidentiality (security);
4. Purpose limitation;
5. Data minimisation;
6. Storage limitation (retention).

These principles are also reiterated within s 71 DPA 2018. The controller is ultimately responsible for compliance with these principles.[2] This means even if personal data is transferred to another entity (like a processor) the controller still has ultimate responsibility. The requirement for the controller to be responsible for compliance with the principles necessitates that the controller must be able to demonstrate compliance with such principles. This requirement to demonstrate compliance with the principles is known as the *requirement of accountability*.

1. Lawfulness, Fairness and Transparency

Personal data must be processed lawfully, fairly and in a

1 Art 5 GDPR.
2 Art 5(2) GDPR.

transparent manner vis-a-vis the data subject. These three elements are intertwined, and the way they feed into each can be viewed in a specific order:

Lawful	It is self-evident that nothing can happen unless it is lawful. Thus, this should be the starting point for an assessment of this principle. For processing to be lawful, it must be processed on an established legal basis (as laid out in Chapter 5 and 6) and in a manner compliant with the GDPR.[3] It feeds into the other principles because in order to process personal data lawfully, it must be done fairly and transparently.
Fair	Fairness adds flexibility to the principle as fairness can adapt to the situation. Something that may be technically legal may still be considered unfair. For example, how a controller should provide information to an elderly person is perhaps different to how information should be provided to a teenager. The entire process of obtaining, using and retaining personal data must be fair. A large part of fairness is that it is clear what is being done with the data, and that nothing is done with the data that a data subject would not expect; this can be guaranteed via transparency.
Transparent	To process personal data transparently information about the data processing operation must be provided in an accessible manner; this includes all information about how the data is processed lawfully and fairly. The requirements for transparency are outlined below.

Transparency

Transparency within the GDPR is "user-centric",[4] it enables the user to be in control of their personal data by becoming aware of the situation surrounding the processing operations, as well as their rights. Furthermore, it enables the data subject to challenge processing operations that may not be GDPR compliant. The GDPR contains specific requirements for transparency in terms of:

- (a) Content, i.e. information that must be provided to the data subject;
- (b) Form, i.e. how the information must be provided to the data subject;
- (c) Time, i.e. when the information must be provided.

---

3 Recital 40 GDPR.

4 Art 29 Working Party Guidelines on transparency under Regulation 2016/679, at 5.

Transparency is an obligation throughout the data processing operation, from when the data is being collected, until it is deleted.

(a) Content (information that must be provided to the data subject)

Regarding content, there are five major situations in which the data subject must be informed of certain information (these will be further elaborated on in the respective parts of this book):

Consent legal basis	Where consent is being sought as the legal basis, the data subject must be informed about the details of what they are consenting to and of any detriment for not providing consent;[5]
Right to be informed	Data subject must be informed about the data processing operations and about their rights, including how to implement their rights;[6]
Exercising rights	When a data subject seeks to exercise their rights, the controller must respond within a reasonable time and must confirm when the action required was carried out;[7]
Security	Transparency needs to be integrated into the controller's technical and security measures, including that the design of the processing operation enables transparency from the outset;[8]
Personal data breach	Data subject must be informed when a high-risk breach occurs.[9]

(b) Form (how the information is to be provided to the data subject)

Regarding form, all information that is required to be provided to the data subject must be accessible. The information must be accessible, in terms of being physically accessible and accessible in terms of understandability.

Physically accessible: The information must be physically accessible.[10] It should be easy for the data subject to access the information and it should be obvious how the information may be accessed.[11]

5 See Ch 5 – 6.
6 See Ch 8 on the right to be informed.
7 See Ch 8.
8 See Ch 9.
9 See Ch 10.
10 Recital 39 GDPR; Art 12 GDPR.
11 Art 29 Working Party Guidelines on transparency under Regulation 2016/679, at 8.

Thus, generally, information should be provided in writing. Information may also be provided by "other means", such as via cartoons, infographics or flowcharts;[12] however, to fully comply with the principle of transparency, it is recommended that all the requisite information is always provided in one single place or in a complete document in written form.[13] Where requested by the data subject, the information may be provided orally.[14] Furthermore the information should be freely accessibly, in that the information must generally be provided free of charge.[15] WP29 noted that this aspect of "freeness" means that any information provided cannot be made conditional upon payment, such as the payment for services or goods.[16] Thus, any information that needs to be provided to the data subject must be provided prior to payment. For example, when buying groceries online, the privacy policy must be displayed prior to any payment occurring.

Accessible in terms of capable of being understood: In order to ensure information is understood, the information must be provided in clear plain language and in a concise and intelligible way.[17] It is recognised that certain techniques such as standardised icons may be used alongside text to increase clarity.[18] The information must be definitive and specific to the situation and may not be vague, general or uncertain.[19] Furthermore, it is not sufficient for the information to be understood generally, the information must be able to be understood by the intended audience. The way the information is provided must mirror the needs of the data subject. For example, the way information is provided to a child, must reflect the fact that the data subject is a child, using perhaps more pictures and simple language, etc. Thus, the controller has the obligation to assess how to comply with transparency obligations where the controller is aware of the audience, including people with disabilities.[20] Furthermore, if the controller is aware that the

---

12 Art 29 Working Party Guidelines on transparency under Regulation 2016/679, at 12.

13 Art 29 Working Party Guidelines on transparency under Regulation 2016/679, at 11-12.

14 Art 12(1) GDPR, further details within Ch 8.

15 Art 12(5) GDPR, further details within Ch 8.

16 Art 29 Working Party Guidelines on transparency under Regulation 2016/679, at 13.

17 Recital 39 GDPR; Art 12(1) GDPR; Art 34(2) GDPR.

18 Recital 49 – 53 GDPR; Art 12(7) GDPR states that the Commission may take steps to create standardised icons

19 Art 29 Working Party Guidelines on transparency under Regulation 2016/679, at 8.

20 Art 29 Working Party Guidelines on transparency under Regulation 2016/679, at 11.

data subject only understands one language, then the information should be available in that language. This is also linked with fairness.

(c) Time (when the information is to be provided to the data subject)

Regarding time, all information that is required to be provided, must be provided within a reasonable time. Where there are specific time requirements, these will be detailed within the relevant section of this book.

2. Accuracy

All personal data held must be accurate and, where possible, kept up to date. Every reasonable step must be taken to ensure that personal data that is inaccurate is erased or rectified without delay.[21] The right to rectification and right to erasure, as outlined in Chapter 8, enforce this principle. Furthermore, accuracy is ensured via appropriate security measures, as provided in Chapter 9.

3. Integrity and Confidentiality (Security)

Personal data must be processed in a manner that ensures appropriate security of the personal data, including protection against unauthorised or unlawful processing and against accidental loss, destruction or damage.[22] The requirement to use appropriate technical or organisational measures to ensure such security is outlined in Chapter 9. This principle is linked to the accuracy principle, in that the appropriate measures must be in place to ensure accuracy, in that there has been no tampering with personal data or loss of personal data.

4. Purpose Limitation

Purpose limitation means that the purpose for processing of personal data must be specified, and no personal data processing can occur beyond that purpose. The purpose of data processing must be documented from the outset. Thus, the concept of purpose limitation has two elements: purpose specification and compatible use.[23]

---

21 Art 5(1)(d) GDPR.
22 Art 5(1)(f) GDPR.
23 Art 5(1)(b) GDPR.

Purpose specification: Purpose specification means that personal data may only be collected for "specified, explicit and legitimate" purposes. This requires that at the outset the purpose is specified, and per the transparency principle, the data subject is informed of the specific purpose for the data processing activity.[24] In addition, such purpose must have a legal basis, as provided for within Chapter 5 and 6.

Compatible use: Compatible use means that personal data must not be "further processed in a way incompatible" with the purpose that was specified. This enforces the fact that further processing can only occur in the instances outlined within Chapter 5. For example, further processing for ASHS purposes is always considered a compatible purpose.[25]

5. Data Minimisation

Personal data may only be processed if it is necessary for the specified purpose established via the purpose limitation principle. Thus, any personal data that is processed must satisfy three elements:[26] The personal data processed must be *adequate, relevant* AND *limited to what is necessary* for the purpose for which personal data is processed.

Thus, only personal data that is appropriate and necessary for the purpose specified may be processed. Data minimisation requires a continuous assessment of what personal data is collected, processed and retained and why; any personal data that is not required for the purpose, should not be collected and or continue to be processed. This principle may be fulfilled by the implementation of appropriate security measures as detailed in Chapter 9, for instance via data protection by design and data protection by default.

6. Storage Limitation (Retention)

Storage limitation requires that data is deleted or anonymised when no longer needed for the specified purpose in accordance with the purpose limitation principle and data minimisation principle. Personal data may only be kept in a form that permits identification of data subjects where it is necessary for the specified purpose.[27]

---

24 See Ch 8, the right to be informed.
25 See Ch 4 and Art 89(1) GDPR.
26 Art 5(1)(c) GDPR.
27 Art 5(1)(e) GDPR.

This requires an assessment of the retention of the personal data i.e. why personal data is retained throughout the processing activity. This must be continuously assessed throughout a processing activity. Thus, this principle requires that retention periods are formulated and justified. Technical and organisational measures, as required in Chapter 9, may be used to automatically review and delete or anonymise un-needed personal data. Note personal data may be stored for longer periods where it is an ASHS activity as it qualifies as being compatible for further processing.[28]

Further Discussion

Article 29 Working Party, Opinion 03/2013 on purpose limitation.

Article 29 Working Party Guidelines on transparency under Regulation 2016/679.

[28] See Ch 4 and Art 89(1) GDPR.

Chapter 8

Ensure Data Subject Rights Are Provided

Relevant law: Recital 58–71 GDPR, Article 12–22 GDPR

Every data subject has the fundamental right to the protection of their personal data.[1] Therefore, appropriate levels of security are paramount. Security shall be dealt with substantively within Chapter 9.

Chapter III GDPR deals with the specific rights of the data subject under the GDPR. These are the rights that the data subject may exercise as against the controller. There is also the right to withdraw consent under Article 7(3) GDPR, where data subject's personal data is being processed on the legal basis of consent. The controller must have in place mechanisms that will enable the data subject to exercise all rights. The rights include the right to:

1. Be informed;
2. Access;
3. Data portability;
4. Rectification;
5. Erasure (right to be forgotten);
6. Restriction of processing;
7. Object to processing;
8. Not be subject to automated decision making;
9. Withdraw consent.

Note that a processor will be required to aid the controller in satisfying these rights, where needed.[2] Further note, that certain rights need not be provided in accordance with an exemption as specified within Chapter 4. There are also further rights of the data subject contained in Chapter VIII GDPR, which include:

- The right to lodge a complaint with the supervisory authority;
- The right to an effective judicial remedy.

These are general rights and not particular to the controller and shall be dealt with in more detail within Chapter 18 -19.

1 See Ch 1 on the explanation of the right to personal data.
2 See Ch 12.

1. Right to be Informed

Relevant law: Recital 60–62 GDPR; Article 13–14 GDPR

The controller must provide the data subject with information on:[3]

1. Who is doing the processing, what is being processed and why;
2. How the personal data will be handled;
3. The rights of the data subject.

The contents of the three categories of information are as follows:

1	Information as to who, what and why	i) The name, address and contact details of the controller and, where applicable, the controller's representatives ii) The contact details of the data protection officer, where applicable[8] iii) What personal data is collected[9] and what processing takes place iv) Why the processing takes place (the purpose) v) The legal basis of the processing vi) The legitimate interest pursued by the controller or third party (where legitimate interested is used as a legal basis for the processing)

3 Recital 39 GDPR; Arts 13-14 GDPR.

4 See Ch 15.

5 Art 14(1)(d) specifically states that the categories of personal data must be provided where the controller did not collect the personal directly from the data subject; however it would likewise need to be informed to the data subject, where the data is obtained directly from the data subject, as the data subject would need to know what personal data is being obtained.

6 This is evidently not applicable where the controller did not collect the personal directly from the data subject, as the controller would already have the information.

7 This is evidently not applicable where the controller did not collect the personal directly from the data subject as the controller would already have the information.

8 See Ch 15.

9 Art 14(1)(d) specifically states that the categories of personal data must be provided where the controller did not collect the personal directly from the data subject; however it would likewise need to be informed to the data subject, where the data is obtained directly from the data subject, as the data subject would need to know what personal data is being obtained.

		vii) Whether the data subject is obliged to provide the personal data (via statute or under contract)[10] viii) Whether there is any detriment for the data subject in not providing personal data[11] ix) The origin of the personal data, i.e. where the controller gathered the personal data from, including whether it came from a publicly accessible source or other (relevant where the controller did *not* collect the personal data directly from the data subject) [12]
2	Information on how personal data is handled	i) The recipients or categories of recipients of the personal data, if any, including: • all other controllers or joint controllers – (including the general details of the agreement between the joint controllers)[13]; • the category of processors should be provided, rather than a list of all processors; however, the category should be as specific as possible i.e. by reference to the activities it carries out, • the industry, sector and sub-sector and the general location of the recipients ii) The fact that the personal data may or will be transferred to a third country outside of the EU, if applicable, and the legal permissibility for the transfer iii) Whether automated decision making takes place, including profiling, and if so, the extent of it and possible consequences for the data subject (this applies to profiling generally, and not just profiling captured by Article 22 GDPR, as detailed in Chapter 6)[14]

[10] This is evidently not applicable where the controller did not collect the personal directly from the data subject, as the controller would already have the information.

[11] This is evidently not applicable where the controller did not collect the personal directly from the data subject as the controller would already have the information.

[12] Art 14(2) (f) GDPR; Recital 61 GDPR states "where the origin of the personal data cannot be provided to the data subject because various sources have been used, general information should be provided".

[13] Art 26(2) GDPR; Art 29 Working Party Guidelines on transparency under Regulation 2016/679, at 23.

[14] Art 29 Working Party Guidelines on transparency under Regulation 2016/679, at 22.

		iv) The period for which the personal data will be stored, or the criteria used to determine that period (retention period) v) Any risks and consequences for the data subject in relation to the processing of personal data; such risks should become apparent during the required risk assessment as detailed in Chapter 9 (if a data protection impact assessment took place a controller may choose to publish such assessment;[15] however, this is not mandatory) vi) Rules and safeguards in place re the processing of personal data;[16] there does not need to be detailed information on this; such information could include items specified in Chapter 9, including; • the adherence to a certain code of conduct or privacy standard, • how the controller adheres to data protection by design or default
3	Information on data subject rights	i) The existence of the right to access, rectify and erase the data subject's data, the right to data portability and the right to restrict processing — WP29 recommended that controllers should clearly explain the difference between the types of data that a data subject can receive via the right to access and the right to data portability.[17] ii) The existence of the right to object to data processing – this must be presented separately and distinctly from all the other rights. For example, within a privacy policy it should be presented in a separate section. The data subject must be specifically informed of: [18] • The right to object where the legal basis is 'Public interest or exercising official authority'; • The right to object to direct marketing.

[15] See Guidelines on Data Protection Impact Assessment (DPIA) and determining whether processing is "likely to result in a high risk" for the purposes of Regulation 2016/679, WP 248 rev.1.

[16] For detail of what safeguards would be required see Ch 9.

[17] Art 29 Working Party Guidelines on the right to data portability, adopted on 13 December 2016, at 13.

[18] Art 21(4) GDPR.

		iii) The existence of the right to withdraw consent (where consent as detailed in Chapter 5 is the legal basis used for the processing) iv) The right to lodge a complaint with a supervisory authority[19] v) How a data subject can exercise those rights. For example, the rights can often be exercised by contacting the controller's data protection officer

The requirement to provide these three categories of information is in line with the transparency principle. In consideration of the principle of fairness and transparency, the controller may provide further information beyond what is outlined above.[20] Note that there may be many types of personal data processing operations being conducted on the data subject's personal data, and all such processing operations must be informed to the data subject. Furthermore, the above information must be provided in a specific manner and at a specific time, which is detailed below.

How must the information be provided?

In line with the transparency principle regarding form,[21] the above stated content must be provided in a transparent manner, i.e. in an accessible and understandable way. As such the below eight criteria should be followed in the provision of the information under the right to be informed:

1	No discretion	All the above information should be provided to the data subject, there is no discretion as to what information may be withheld – all information is of equal importance.[22] Where a piece of information does not exist for a certain data processing operation i.e. there are no transfers outside the EU, then the data subject should still be informed that no such transfers occur.
2	Proactive	The controller must actively provide the information – the data subject should *not* need to request the information.[23]

[19] See Ch 18.
[20] Recital 39 GDPR.
[21] See Ch 7 on form of transparency.
[22] Art 29 Working Party Guidelines on transparency under Regulation 2016/679, at 14.
[23] Art 29 Working Party Guidelines on transparency under Regulation 2016/679, at 16, 18.

3	Findable	It should be obvious to the data subject how to access the information.[24] For example, often the information is provided via a privacy statement on a website; therefore, it should be noticeable upon reaching the website where the privacy statement is, i.e. the controller should use appropriate font and colouring so that it is easily discoverable.
4	Distinct	The information must be presented distinctly from other information; the data subject should not have to search for it within general terms or other information.[25] Particularly in the context of online activities, it is appropriate to provide this information via a privacy statement that is distinct from other terms.
5	Definitive	The information may not be provided in vague or general terms, it must be clear, explicit and specific given the true nature of the processing operation.[26] In particular, the legal basis must be absolutely clear.[27] Definitive language in the active form must be used, such as "we will" rather than "we may."[28]
6	Written	The information must be provided in written form. The information should be provided in writing, including by electronic means.[29] In addition, the data subject may request for such information to be provided orally.[30] WP29 gave examples of methods in which information could be provided:[31] • Online access, i.e. via a website or mobile phone application • Hard copies, i.e. via leaflets or alongside an instruction manual • Oral explanation, i.e. over the phone or person to person, but there should be the ability to re-listen or have access to the information again[32] • Public signage i.e. for CCTVs

[24] Art 29 Working Party Guidelines on transparency under Regulation 2016/679, at 8, 18.

[25] Art 29 Working Party Guidelines on transparency under Regulation 2016/679, at 7, 16-18.

[26] Recital 42 GDPR; Art 12(1) GDPR.

[27] Art 29 Working Party Guidelines on transparency under Regulation 2016/679, at 9.

[28] WP29 also stated that language involving "may", "might", "some", "often" and "possible" should be avoided; Art 29 Working Party Guidelines on transparency under Regulation 2016/679, at 8-9.

[29] Art 12(1) GDPR.

[30] Art 12(1) GDPR.

[31] Art 29 Working Party Guidelines on transparency under Regulation 2016/679, at 18-19.

[32] Art 29 Working Party Guidelines on transparency under Regulation 2016/679, at 13.

		• Newspaper/media notices i.e. to give notice that drones will be flying overhead, capturing images • QR codes i.e. where a smart device has no screen via which a privacy statement could be provided, there could be a QR code that a data subject could scan to view the privacy statement. WP29 emphasised that the method chosen to provide the information must be appropriate to the circumstances.[33] Furthermore, multiple methods may be used to ensure the data subject's right to be informed is fulfilled. For example, if a controller is selling a smart watch, it may be more appropriate to provide the privacy statement on a leaflet within the packaging for the smart watch, in addition to a privacy statement online. The controller is encouraged to test different mechanisms that are the most appropriate, given the circumstances, to ensure transparency.[34]
7	Reflect audience	The way information is provided should reflect the audience, i.e. children, teenagers. In accordance with transparency, information must be provided in an intelligible and understandable way, meaning it should be able to be understood by the "average member of the intended audience".[35] Thus, the method used to provide the information must also be appropriate for the data subject; for example: • Oral explanation may be used for data subjects that are visually impaired, in such instances a visually impaired person must have access to the information and be able to re-listen to the information • Oral explanation via video footage or via pictures or cartoons may be used for data subjects that may not be fully literate or have a low attention span[36]

33 Art 29 Working Party Guidelines on transparency under Regulation 2016/679, at 12.

34 Art 29 Working Party Guidelines on transparency under Regulation 2016/679, at 14.

35 Art 29 Working Party Guidelines on transparency under Regulation 2016/679, at 7.

36 Art 12(1) GDPR ; For an example on child friendly writing see the "UN Convention on the Rights of the Child in Child Friendly Language " and Art 29 Working Party Guidelines on transparency under Regulation 2016/679, at 10.

		• Where the controller is aware that their audience only speaks a certain language, the information should be available in the requisite language. Note that the controller must ensure that any translation of information is accurate.[37] The way the information is provided should reflect the known audience. The controller should have reasonable knowledge of who their audience is. The controller is encouraged to test different mechanisms in which the information may be provided where there is uncertainty as to its intelligibility.[38]
8	Engaging	The information should be presented in such a way to avoid "information fatigue."[39] There are many methods and tools used to present information in such a way that it may be more accessible for data subjects. A considerable amount of information needs to be conveyed to the data subject, thus, controllers must think of innovative ways to avoid information fatigue to ensure the data subject is aware of the information. WP29 recommended utilising a combination of the following methods: • A layered format for the privacy statement should be used. This gives an overview of the terms first, but then allows the data subject to learn more about each term.[40] In an online environment there could be a headline and the data subject can click on it to find more information. This overview approach is suggested so that there is no information overload – it should not be provided as a block text chunk that is inaccessible. • The controller could prioritise information that has the largest impact on the data subject, or information that may not be expected by the data subject. Thus, the data subject could immediately understand the consequences of the processing and then can read further details as needed.[41] This would be most appropriate

37 Art 29 Working Party Guidelines on transparency under Regulation 2016/679, at 10.

38 Art 29 Working Party Guidelines on transparency under Regulation 2016/679, at 7.

39 Art 29 Working Party Guidelines on transparency under Regulation 2016/679, at 7.

40 Art 29 Working Party Guidelines on transparency under Regulation 2016/679, at 17.

41 Art 29 Working Party Guidelines on transparency under Regulation 2016/679, at 19.

		for offline environments. For example, where information is provided orally, the data subject may be informed of this priority information and can be directed to a privacy statement elsewhere for further details.[42] Another example is that of public signage, i.e. a sign may say that a CCTV is in operation in the area and provide details of the website to go to for further information. • Online platforms could have a "privacy dashboard" where a data subject can view data protection information easily and exercise their rights and alter their settings.[43] The platform could draw the user in, for example, via "learn more" video tutorials.[44] • "Just in time" notices could be utilised where appropriate. These are push notifications that appear when it is most relevant for the data subject to be aware of the use of their data.[45] WP29 noted that this approach is optimal as it spreads the provision of information so that it does not cause information overload. • Standardised icons,[46] videos, cartoons, infographics, flowcharts or voice alerts should be used in combination with text.[47] WP29 noted that at least one of the above methods (or other innovative methods) should be used to ensure engagement and guarantee the principle of transparency is satisfied.

Considering the methods or tools used to provide the information, the entirety of the information should still be available to the data subject in one single place or in a complete document in written form.[48] Likewise, where oral information was provided, the information should equally be available to re-listen or be accessible

42 Art 29 Working Party Guidelines on transparency under Regulation 2016/679, at 20.

43 This compliments the requirement for privacy by design, see Ch 9.

44 Art 29 Working Party Guidelines on transparency under Regulation 2016/679, at 21.

45 Art 29 Working Party Guidelines on transparency under Regulation 2016/679, at 18.

46 Art 12(7) GDPR states that the Commission may take steps to create standardised icons.

47 Recital 60 GDPR; Art 29 Working Party Guidelines on transparency under Regulation 2016/679, at 11.

48 Art 29 Working Party Guidelines on transparency under Regulation 2016/679, at 11-12.

in another format of which the data subject was informed of.[49] It is imperative that all eight criteria are followed to ensure the principle of transparency is guaranteed and to ensure the right to be informed is satisfied.

When must the information be provided?

Where the information is collected from the data subject, the controller must provide such information at "the time the personal data is obtained".[50] Due to the requirement that the information must be provided free of charge in accordance with the principle of transparency,[51] this means that the information must be provided prior to any payment taking place,[52] i.e. where goods or services are being bought, the right to be informed must be satisfied prior to payment. WP29 noted that even where the controller is providing a free service, the information must be provided prior to rather than after any signing up process.[53] Where the controller is observing the data subject, i.e. by CCTV or WiFi tracking, it must be clear to the data subject that they are entering an area where they are being observed.[54] Thus, it is best practice, where practical, to fulfil the right to be informed prior to any data processing occurring.

Where the controller did not obtain the personal data from the data subject: Where the controller did not obtain the personal data from the data subject, the controller still has the obligation to provide the information listed above.[55] This may happen where the data was initially collected via third parties, publicly available sources, data brokers or other data subjects.[56] In such instances the information must be provided to the data subject either:

- Within one month after obtaining the personal data;
- When the data subject is first contacted by the controller;
- At the time when the personal data is first disclosed to someone other than the controller.

---

[49] Art 29 Working Party Guidelines on transparency under Regulation 2016/679, 13.
[50] Art 13(1) GDPR.
[51] Art 12(5) GDPR.
[52] Art 29 Working Party Guidelines on transparency under Regulation 2016/679, at 13.
[53] Art 29 Working Party Guidelines on transparency under Regulation 2016/679, at 13.
[54] Art 29 Working Party Guidelines on transparency under Regulation 2016/679, at 15.
[55] Art 14 GDPR.
[56] Art 29 Working Party Guidelines on transparency under Regulation 2016/679, at 15.

The time period which occurs first must be complied with. Thus, the maximum time limit possible is one month. In light of the principles of fairness and transparency, the controller should take into account the expectations of the data subject when determining at what point the information should be provided,[57] i.e. it may be optimal to inform the data subject earlier than the required time limit. The principle of fairness requires that controllers are able to justify the rationale for when the personal data is provided.[58]

What if the information changes?

The right to be informed continues throughout the processing operations, from collection to deletion. Thus, where there is a change to the information initially provided, the data subject must be informed. The GDPR does not state a time for when a data subject needs to be informed of the information changing (other than further processing). Thus, it is for the controller to assess the situation. If it is a minimal change, then simply informing that data subject there was a change and letting them know where to find the updated information would be sufficient. Stylistic changes would not need to be informed.[59] If it is a substantial change, that may impact upon the data subject, WP29 stated that the controller should notify the data subject in advance to enable the data subject to have enough time to exercise their rights i.e. object to data processing or withdraw consent.[60] A substantial change may be a change in controller, a change concerning the legal basis on which they are processing the data, or a change regarding a transfer outside the EU. Where the changes are significant, the controller should also explain what the likely impact of those changes will be on the data subject.[61] The principle of fairness and transparency must be recognised in this context.

As with when the information is initially provided, the updated information must be provided in a transparent manner (see above). Thus, the data subject must be able to notice that a change occurred i.e. via an email, letter sent or a pop-up on a website.[62]

---

57 Recital 60 GDPR.

58 Art 29 Working Party Guidelines on transparency under Regulation 2016/679, at 16.

59 Art 29 Working Party Guidelines on transparency under Regulation 2016/679, at 17.

60 Art 29 Working Party Guidelines on transparency under Regulation 2016/679, at 15-16.

61 Art 29 Working Party Guidelines on transparency under Regulation 2016/679, at 18.

62 Art 29 Working Party Guidelines on transparency under Regulation 2016/679, at 17.

Any attempt to avoid the requirement to inform the data subject of changes, either via a clause in the privacy statement or other,[63] will be deemed unfair in line with the principle of transparency and fairness. For example, where there is a clause in the privacy statement which reads that the data subject should regularly check the privacy statement for changes, this not sufficient to satisfy the right to be informed. Also note that any changes to the information, in terms of what those changes mean, must still comply with all GDPR requirements.

Should the data subject be reminded of the information?

Even where there have been no changes to the information, WP29 stated that the controller should remind the data subject of the information where the processing continues on an ongoing basis. For example, a reminder of the privacy statement may be provided yearly. WP29 further recommended that controllers should facilitate for data subjects to have continuing easy access to the information provided in accordance with the right to be informed.[64]

What if further processing occurs?

Recall from Chapter 5 that further processing may only occur for compatible purposes, including ASHS activities.[65] Further processing for a non-compatible purpose is not permissible even if it is informed. For the purposes of the right to be informed, the following must be satisfied, where further processing occurs:

1) *Data subject must be notified:* Where the controller intends to further process the personal data of the data subject for a purpose other than what the data subject was informed of, the controller must provide the data subject with information on such further processing before the further processing begins. For example, if health data was collected via a smart watch as a service for the data subject, and then the controller wanted to use the data for scientific research, the data subject would need to be informed of the further processing before the research commenced (if it did not fall within an exception, see Chapter 4) . The reason it must be provided *before* is to

[63] Art 29 Working Party Guidelines on transparency under Regulation 2016/679, at 17.

[64] Art 29 Working Party Guidelines on transparency under Regulation 2016/679, at 18.

[65] See Ch 5 on "Further processing beyond purpose".

allow the data subject to have time to consider whether the further processing is reasonable and whether they should exercise one of their rights. The controller must be able to justify any decision regarding the timing of the provision of the information, namely whether it was in line with the principle of fairness and transparency.[66] Thus, if further processing may not be expected by the data subject, more notice should generally be provided before commencing the further processing.[67]

2) *Further information to be provided re compatibility*: The data subject must also be provided with an explanation justifying why the further processing is compatible with the initial purpose.[68] If the controller chooses to not provide such an explanation within a privacy statement, WP29 stated that the controller should make it clear that such information is available on request.[69]
3) *Changes must be informed*: Information should be provided on any changes to the information initially provided.[70]

Exceptions to the right to be informed

The controller does not need to furnish the data subject with information that the data subject *already has knowledge of*.[71] For example, if the data subject signed up for a service with the controller, and later signed up for another service – the data subject only needs to be provided with any new information or information that had changed in the meantime. The controller still has the obligation to provide any remaining information that the data subject did not receive. In accordance with the principle of accountability, the data controller must be able to demonstrate what information the data subject has already received, how it was received and whether the information had changed.[72]

Where the controller did not obtain the personal data from the data subject:

---

[66] Art 29 Working Party Guidelines on transparency under Regulation 2016/679, at 24.
[67] Art 29 Working Party Guidelines on transparency under Regulation 2016/679, at 24.
[68] Art 29 Working Party Guidelines on transparency under Regulation 2016/679, at 24.
[69] Art 29 Working Party Guidelines on transparency under Regulation 2016/679, at 24.
[70] Art 13(3) GDPR, Art 14(4) GDPR.
[71] Art 13(4) GDPR, Art 14(5) GDPR.
[72] Art 29 Working Party Guidelines on transparency under Regulation 2016/679, at 27.

Further exemptions arise where the personal data is not gathered from the data subject. In this instance, the controller is not required to provide the data subject with the information under the right to be informed if one of the following five situations are arise.[73]

1	Impossibility	It is impossible to fulfil the right to be informed i.e. the contact information is not available and it is not possible to provide the information in another way.
2	Disproportionate effort	Fulfilling the right to be informed would cause a disproportionate effort (in particular for ASHS purposes).[74] Recital 62 GDPR states that the number of data subjects, when the data was collected (the age of the data) and any appropriate safeguards would need to be taken into consideration. The WP29 provided the following examples of situations that would cause a disproportionate effort to fulfil the right to be informed:[75] o Where "next of kin" data is collected in a large hospital o Where historical research is taking place on a data set collected 50 years ago and there are no contact details
3	Impair purpose for the data processing	Fulfilling the right to be informed would make the achievement of the objectives of the processing impossible or seriously impair them. WP29 provided the example of when personal data may be processed to check for money laundering; informing the data subject would impair the money laundering assessment.[76]

73 Art 14(5) GDPR.

74 See Ch 4 on ASHS purposes — DPA 2018, s 42 states that controllers do not need to ensure the provision of data subject rights, as specified within Ch 8 of this book, if it would impair or render impossible the intended ASHS purposes.

75 Art 29 Working Party Guidelines on transparency under Regulation 2016/679, at 30.

76 Art 29 Working Party Guidelines on transparency under Regulation 2016/679, at 32.

4	Law	Where obtaining or disclosing the personal data is expressly laid down by law, the duty to inform need not be fulfilled if appropriate measures to safeguard the data subject's interests are in place. WP29 provided the example of when the national tax authority processes data.[77]
5	Confidentiality	Where the information must remain confidential, subject to an obligation of professional secrecy laid down by law, the right to be informed does not need to be carried out. WP29 provided the example of when a doctor collects personal data about medical family history from a patient – the doctor does not need to provide the information to every member of the family due to doctor client confidentiality.[78]

The WP29 noted that these exceptions to the right to be informed arise out of the circumstance caused by the fact that personal data was not collected directly from the data subject.[79] Thus, the need to use the exceptions must be caused in part by the fact that the personal data was not obtained from the data subject. For example, if it is merely a large effort due to the general circumstances of the data processing rather than a large effort due to the impediment caused by the fact that the personal data was collected from a source other than the data subject, the exemption may not be utilised.

In accordance with the principle of accountability, if the controller is relying on an exception to not fulfil the right to be informed, the controller must be able to *demonstrate* where one of the exceptions apply. In particular, a balancing exercise would need to take place to prove that there was a disproportionate effort or to show the processing objectives would be impaired, etc. If one of the exceptions are applicable, the controller *still needs to ensure the other rights of the data subject are fulfilled*.

Exemptions not absolute and must remain accountable: None of the exemptions to the right to be informed are absolute and are only applicable to the piece of information or the situation to which the exception applies. For example, where an exception ceases to

77 Art 29 Working Party Guidelines on transparency under Regulation 2016/679, at 32-33.

78 Art 29 Working Party Guidelines on transparency under Regulation 2016/679, at 33.

79 Art 29 Working Party Guidelines on transparency under Regulation 2016/679, at 30.

apply, the right to be informed must then be fulfilled, i.e. where it becomes possible, or the professional secrecy has ended.

Where it is not possible to provide one piece of information but possible to provide the other information, the *other information must still be provided*. For example, Recital 61 GDPR provides that where it is impossible to identify the origin of the personal data, general information may be provided instead.

Information must still be publicly available: Even where the information may not be provided directly to the data subject because an exception applies, where possible, the general information required under the right to be informed should be made publicly available, i.e. provided on the controller's website,[80] or where there is no website, a hard copy at the controller's premises or a statement in the local newspaper.[81]

2. Right to Access (Data Subject Access Request)

Relevant law: Recital 59, 63, 68 GDPR; Article 15 GDPR

In accordance with Article 15 GDPR the data subject may request access to the personal data concerning them that is being held by the controller. This is known as a data subject access request (DSAR). The data subject can utilise this right to check what personal data is being collected and to verify the lawfulness of the processing operations. Note that there is no obligation on controllers to retain personal data for longer than is necessary for the purposes of the right to access. The storage limitation principle takes precedence.[82]

What information should be provided in DSAR?

When an individual makes a DSAR, the controller must provide the data subject with all the personal data the controller retains concerning the data subject, i.e. all information the controller has on file or in a database in either electronic or hard-copy format. Where the data subject only requests specific personal data, only that personal data needs to be provided. Where the data subject does not specify what personal data they wish to have access to, and the controller retains a large amount of information on the

---

80 Art 29 Working Party Guidelines on transparency under Regulation 2016/679, at 29.

81 Art 29 Working Party Guidelines on transparency under Regulation 2016/679, at 31.

82 Recital 64 GDPR; Art 11 GDPR.

data subject, the controller is allowed to request that the data subject specifies what personal data they are seeking access to in particular, if any.

The controller must provide copies of the personal data to the data subject,[83] and where the DSAR is made electronically, such copies should be provided in a commonly used electronic format.[84] The copies of the personal data must be provided along with information on the following items:[85]

- The purpose of the processing;
- The categories of personal data that are collected;
- The recipients or categories of recipients to whom the personal data have been or will be disclosed (where the recipient is a public authority that may receive information in the context of a public inquiry under Irish law,[86] this does not need to be revealed);
- Where possible, the envisaged retention period for the personal data, or, if not possible, the criteria used to determine that period;
- The existence of the right to request rectification or erasure of personal data;
- The existence of the right to restriction of processing of personal data concerning the data subject or to object to such processing;
- The right to lodge a complaint with the supervisory authority;
- Any available information as to the source of the personal data where *not* collected from the data subject;
- The existence of automated decision making, including profiling as defined in the GDPR and at least meaningful information about the logic involved, as well as the significance and the envisaged consequences of said processing for the data subject;
- Where personal data is transferred outside the EU, information must be provided regarding the GDPR method used to enable the transfer i.e. binding corporate rules, standard contractual clause, certification, etc (see Part 3).

83 Under the old Directive, *Nowak v DPC and Institute of Chartered Accountants in Ireland* [2018] IEHC 118 (26 February 2018) ruled that the information does not need to be provided in its original form but in an "intelligible form".
84 Art 15(3) GDPR.
85 Art 15(1) GDPR.
86 DPA 2018, s 91(9)(b).

This information that needs to be provided alongside the requested information, must be provided in accordance with the principle of transparency, as detailed in Chapter 7. However, for any further copies of personal data beyond the initial copy that the controller provided to the data subject, the controller may charge a reasonable fee based on administration costs.[87]

Copies of the requested personal data, along with the associated information, must be provided as soon as possible and no later than one month after the date on which the request is made.[88] Further details on this and the requirement to verify the identity of the data subject are provided later in this Chapter.

Exceptions to the requirement to carry out a full DSAR

Note that in all instances where an exception arises, the controller is still obligated to respond to the data subject and provide the details of such exception and all remaining information not covered by the exception to the data subject, as applicable. Thus, the controller may withhold access to the relevant personal data covered by an exception but must still provide all remaining personal data and information.

The controller is not required to carry out a full DSAR in the following three instances:

1. Where disclosing the personal data would "adversely affect the rights and freedoms of others." [89] An example of this is where data concerning a person other than the data subject is included within the information, to the extent that it would adversely affect the rights of that other person, it is permissible for that information to be redacted i.e. giving the specific name of each employee that may have had access to the data. Furthermore, this covers instances relating to intellectual property rights, trade secrets,[90] national security, matters of public importance, defence, obstruction of justice and public security.
2. Where a controller has already complied with a DSAR, a controller need not comply with a subsequent identical

---

[87] Art 15(3) GDPR.

[88] Art 12(4) GDPR.

[89] Art 15(4) GDPR.

[90] Art 29 Working Party Guidelines on the right to data portability, adopted on 13 December 2016, at 12.

DSAR unless a reasonable interval has elapsed.[91] A reasonable interval should be determined by the controller, with consideration of the nature of the personal data processing operations and how often personal data regarding the data subject is altered.[92]

3. Where the personal data relates to an expression of opinion about the data subject by another person given in confidence, or on the understanding it would be treated as confidential.[93]

It is prohibited to require a data subject to make a DSAR

In accordance with s 4 of the DPA 2018, a person or entity may not require a data subject to make a DSAR or require them to provide the results of a DSAR where it is in connection with:

- The recruitment of the data subject as an employee i.e. a prospective employer cannot ask the data subject to request a DSAR from their previous employer;
- The continued employment of the data subject i.e. if a current employer thinks the data subject is using a social media site during work time, the employer cannot require the data subject to request a DSAR from the social media site;
- A contract for the provision of services to the data subject i.e. an insurance provider cannot ask the data subject to request a DSAR from a previous insurance provider or from their health practitioner, etc.

Prior to DPA 2018 coming into effect, the High Court required an ex-employee to make a DSAR as an alternative to non-party discovery because the information needed was in the data subject's (ex-employee's) *power* to obtain.[94] It was determined that a data subject may be compelled to make a DSAR in order to obtain needed information because it is within the data subject's *power* to obtain such information. Thus, it remains to be seen whether such use of DSAR will be permissible in consideration of the principle of fairness under the GDPR and DPA 2018. Section 4 of the DPA 2018 would not specifically outlaw the requirement for ex-employees to make a DSAR in the context of the above case.

---

[91] Recital 63 GDPR.

[92] Recital 63 GDPR.

[93] Art 15(4) GDPR and see *Nowak v DPC and Price Waterhouse Coopers* [2018] IEHC 117 (26 February 2018).

[94] *Susquehanna International Group Limited v Needham* [2017] IEHC 706.

3. Right to Data Portability

The right to data portability is provided for within Article 20 GDPR. The right to data portability has three elements:

1. A data subject has the right to receive the personal data, which they have provided to the controller, in a structured, commonly used and machine-readable format[95] (further details below);
2. A data subject has the right to transfer their personal data to another controller, without hindrance from the original controller;[96]
3. A data subject has the right to have their personal data transmitted directly from one controller to another,[97] where technically feasible. Note that the initial data controller is not responsible for the receiving controller's compliance with data protection law.[98] Further note that the receiving controller has to abide by data protection law, including the duty to inform and the principles of purpose limitation and data minimisation, etc.

It differs from the right to access, in that the purpose of the right to data portability is to enable a data subject to use their personal data or transfer their data from one controller to another. The reason for establishing this right was to facilitate the free flow of data, enable user choice and encourage competition between service providers in IT environments.[99] Thus, this right enables a data subject to transfer their data to different service providers. However, WP29 noted that the use of the right to data portability may not prejudice the data subject and does not automatically trigger an erasure of data by the original controller,[100]i.e. a service provider that is requested to transfer personal data to a competing service provider cannot automatically consider that the data subject no longer desires to be a customer and delete their data. There is no obligation on controllers to retain personal data for longer than is necessary in accordance with the storage limitation principle;[101]

---

95 Art 20(1) GDPR.

96 Art 20(1) GDPR.

97 Art 20(2) GDPR.

98 Art 29 Working Party Guidelines on the right to data portability, adopted on 13 December 2016, at 6.

99 Art 29 Working Party Guidelines on the right to data portability, adopted on 13 December 2016, at 3-4.

100 Art 29 Working Party Guidelines on the right to data portability, adopted on 13 December 2016, at 7.

101 Recital 64 GDPR; Art 11 GDPR.

however, where there is a continuing necessity, it must be retained i.e. if a data subject is still utilising a service.[102]

Conditions for applicability of the right to data portability

The right to data portability of personal data is only available when all four conditions are met:

1. Where the personal data concerns the data subject;
2. Where the personal data was provided by the data subject; WP29 recommended that this covers: [103]
   - Data knowingly and actively provided by the data subject and
   - Personal data generated from the observation of the activities of the data subject, i.e. activity logs, location data or website usage.

   Thus, this does not include data created by the data controller, using such personal data —right is limited only to the personal data that the data subject provided;
3. Where the personal data is processed on the legal basis of consent or contractual necessity, as detailed in Chapter 5 herein;
4. Where the processing activity is carried out by automated means (i.e. most paper files not covered)[104]

WP29 listed examples that will generally fall within the scope of this right, such as titles of books purchased by a data subject from an online store, or songs listened to via a music streaming service.[105]

How should personal data be transferred?

The data requested must be sent in a structured, commonly used and machine-readable format.[106] The purpose of the format is to enable "re-use" of the data, either by the data subject themselves or by another controller.[107] Recital 68 GDPR encourages the

---

[102] See Ch 8, see also Art 29 Working Party Guidelines on the right to data portability, adopted on 13 December 2016, at 6.

[103] Art 29 Working Party Guidelines on the right to data portability, adopted on 13 December 2016, at 3, 9-10.

[104] Art 29 Working Party Guidelines on the right to data portability, adopted on 13 December 2016, at 9.

[105] Art 29 Working Party Guidelines on the right to data portability, adopted on 13 December 2016, at 8.

[106] Art 20(1) GDPR.

[107] Art 29 Working Party Guidelines on the right to data portability, adopted on 13 December 2016, at 16-17.

development of interoperable formats to enable data portability.[108] It is best practice for controllers to enable data subjects to select data they wish to receive to ensure no unnecessary data is transmitted.[109] Furthermore, the size of the data requested may make transmission via the internet difficult, and thus, alternative methods may be considered such as transmission via the internet, CD, DVD or other medium.[110]

Regarding the technical feasibility, Recital 68 GDPR confirms that controllers are not obliged to operate or maintain a processing system just because it might make a future request technically feasible. However, an interoperable format is expected, as stated above. Where a technical issue arises and a data controller cannot transfer the data to the other data controller, the data controller must explain those impediments to the data subject.[111]

Exception to right to data portability — adversely affect the rights and freedoms of others

As with a DSAR, this right may not be carried out where it would "adversely affect the rights and freedoms of others".[112] An example of this is where data concerning a person other than the data subject is included within the information to the extent that the other person's rights would be impacted. In this instance it would be permissible to redact or separate out that information. This is because it would be impossible for that person referenced to exercise their rights under data protection law. WP29 gave the example of where data concerning a bank account is transferred to another bank, often information containing other persons is contained within such information i.e. who the data subject transferred money to; however, the rights and freedoms of those other persons are unlikely to be impacted by this transfer as it is to another bank for the same purpose.[113] Furthermore, if the transfer

---

[108] WP29 refers to the following definition of interoperability: ISO/IEC 2382-01 defines interoperability as "[t]he capability to communicate, execute programs, or transfer data among various functional units in a manner that requires the user to have little or no knowledge of the unique characteristics of those units."

[109] Art 29 Working Party Guidelines on the right to data portability, adopted on 13 December 2016, at 12.

[110] Art 29 Working Party Guidelines on the right to data portability, adopted on 13 December 2016, at 14.

[111] Art 29 Working Party Guidelines on the right to data portability, adopted on 13 December 2016, at 16.

[112] Art 20(4) GDPR; see section within the Chapter "exceptions to the requirement to carry out a full DSAR".

[113] Art 29 Working Party Guidelines on the right to data portability, adopted on 13 December 2016, at 11.

is only to facilitate the personal use (household exemption outlined in Chapter 4 herein), then the person's right and freedoms are not impacted, for example where it is to retain contact details of friends, etc.[114] The rights and freedoms of others also includes intellectual property and trade secrets.[115]

Inform data subject about right to data portability (again) prior to termination

WP29 stated that controllers should provide information on the right to data portability before a data subject closes any relevant account they may have.[116] WP29 noted that this would allow users to have a greater awareness of their data and enable them to transfer such data prior to termination. This supports the principle of fairness and transparency.

4. Right to Rectification

In accordance with Article 16 GDPR, a data subject may request from the controller the rectification of incorrect or incomplete personal data. The controller has the obligation to rectify such data without undue delay. It is the obligation of the controller to inform all recipients, including processors and joint controllers, that rectification must occur, unless this constitutes a "disproportionate effort".[117] Furthermore, the controller shall inform the data subject of those recipients where so requested.[118]

5. Right to Erasure (Right to be Forgotten)

In accordance with Article 17 GDPR, a data subject may request from the controller the deletion of their data. This right is also known as the right to be forgotten. The right to erasure is not absolute. The controller has the obligation to erase such data without undue delay, where so requested, if one of the following six situations apply:[119]

---

114 Art 29 Working Party Guidelines on the right to data portability, adopted on 13 December 2016, at 12.

115 Art 29 Working Party Guidelines on the right to data portability, adopted on 13 December 2016, at 12.

116 Art 29 Working Party Guidelines on the right to data portability, adopted on 13 December 2016, at 13.

117 Art 19 GDPR.

118 Art 19 GDPR.

119 Art 17(1) GDPR.

1. The personal data is no longer necessary for the purpose for which the personal data was collected;
2. The data subject withdrew consent and no other legal basis for retaining the data is valid;
3. The data subject objects to the processing (see right to object below) and no other overriding legitimate grounds are applicable;
4. The personal data was unlawfully processed;
5. The personal data needs to be erased for compliance with a legal obligation;
6. The personal data was collected about a child in relation to information society services, as specified Article 8 GDPR (see Chapter 6).

It is the obligation of the controller to inform all recipients, including processors and joint controllers that erasure must occur, unless this constitutes a "disproportionate effort".[120] Furthermore, the controller shall inform the data subject of those recipients where so requested.[121] Article 17(2) GDPR makes specific reference to the instance where the controller has made the personal data public, that other controllers must be informed if erasure is required for any links, copies or replications of the personal data. The concept of disproportionate effort can take into account available technology and cost.[122]

Exceptions to the right to erasure

The right to erasure as provided above does not apply where processing is necessary for one of the following seven reasons:[123]

1. To exercise the right to freedom of expression and information;
2. For compliance with a legal obligation;
3. For the performance of a task carried out in the public interested;
4. For the exercise of official authority vested in the controller i.e. an ombudsman;
5. For reasons of public interest regarding public health as specified by law;[124]
6. For ASHS purposes, where the ASHS purpose would

---

[120] Art 19 GDPR.
[121] Art 19 GDPR.
[122] Art 17(2) GDPR.
[123] Art 17(3) GDPR.
[124] See Ch 6 on special categories of personal data and Ch 4 on objectives of a general public interest.

be rendered impossible or seriously impaired if erasure was to occur;[125]

7. For the establishment, exercise or defence of a legal claim to which the personal data relates.

Recall that the principle of transparency requires that where an exception is relied upon, the controller must document why such exception is applicable.

6. Right to Restriction of Processing

In accordance with Article 18(1) GDPR the data subject has the right to request that the controller restricts their processing activity vis a vis the data subject's personal data. The right to restriction of processing is not absolute. The controller has the obligation to restrict their processing activity where one of the following four situations apply:[126]

1. The accuracy of the personal data is contested by the data subject and restriction of processing is required for the time period needed to verify any inaccuracies;
2. The processing is unlawful and the data subject opposes the erasure of the personal data and requests restriction of processing instead;
3. The controller no longer needs the personal data for the purposes of the processing, but the personal data needs to be retained for the data subject in relation to a legal claim;
4. The data subject has objected to processing (detailed below in right to object) and such request is pending.

It is the obligation of the controller to inform all recipients, including processors and joint controllers, that restriction of processing must occur, where applicable, unless this constitutes a "disproportionate effort".[127] Furthermore, the controller shall inform the data subject of those recipients where so requested.[128] Where a data subject could successfully utilise their right to restriction of processing, the data subject must be informed when the restriction ends.[129]

---

125 See Ch 4 on ASHS.
126 Art 18(1) GDPR.
127 Art 19 GDPR.
128 Art 19 GDPR.
129 Art 18(3) GDPR.

What processing may occur when there is a restriction of processing?

Restriction of processing means that where one of the above four situations apply the personal data may only be stored by the controller. No other processing on the personal data may occur unless one of the following four bases is established:

1. Consent is provided by the data subject;
2. Must be processed in relation to a legal claim;
3. To protect the rights of another individual;
4. For reasons of important public interest as specified in law.[130]

Note that in accordance with the principle of transparency, such justification for processing the restricted personal data must be documented and justified.

7. Right to Object

In accordance with Article 21 GDPR, the data subject has the right to object to processing of their personal data. The right to object is not absolute and there are three instances that give rise to the right to object.

1	Processing based on the legal basis of 'Public interest or exercising official authority' or 'Legitimate interest'	Where the data subject objects to data processing based on the legal basis of 'Public interest or exercising official authority' or 'Legitimate interest',[131] the controller may no longer process the personal data unless one of the following are applicable:[132] 1. The controller demonstrates "compelling legitimate grounds for the processing which override the interests". Thus, a balancing process needs to take place between the interests of the controller and the rights of the data subject, OR 2. The processing is necessary in relation to a legal claim

130 See Ch 4 on objectives of a general public interest.
131 See Ch 5 for an explanation of these legal bases.
132 Art 21(1) GDPR.

2	Direct marketing	The data subject has the right to object to the processing of their personal data for direct marketing purposes, which includes profiling for direct marketing.[133] Where a data subject objects to such direct marketing, the personal data may no longer be processed for direct marketing purposes.[134]
3	ASHS purposes	Where personal data is processed for ASHS purposes,[135] the data subject has the right to object to the data processing activity that concerns the data subject's personal data.[136] Where such an objection arises, the processing must stop unless it is demonstrated that the ASHS processing is necessary in the public interest.[137]

In all instances the data subject must detail the reasons for their objection, and such reasons must be directly related to their particular situation. Furthermore, in the context of an information society service, the right to object must be able to be exercised by automated means using technical specifications (i.e. via privacy settings).[138]

Right to object must be presented separately to the data subject

The right to object must be presented clearly and separately from other information that is to be provided in accordance with the right to be informed.[139] In particular, the data subject must be specifically informed of: [140]

- The right to object where the legal basis is 'Public interest or exercising official authority';
- The right to object to direct marketing.

8. Right to Not be Subject to Automated Decision Making

In accordance with Article 22 GDPR, the data subject has the right to not be subject to a decision based solely on automated processing. The circumstances of this right are detailed within Chapter 6.

[133] Art 21(2) GDPR.
[134] Art 21(3) GDPR.
[135] See Ch 4 for an explanation of ASHS purposes.
[136] Art 21(6) GDPR.
[137] See Ch 4 for an explanation of topics of a general public interest.
[138] See explanation of information society service in Ch 6 on p 30.
[139] Art 21(4) GDPR.
[140] Art 21(4) GDPR.

9. Right to Withdraw Consent

In accordance with Article 7(3) GDPR, where personal data is processed on the legal basis of consent, the data subject has the right to withdraw consent at any time. Where the data subject withdraws consent, the controller may not continue to process the personal data. Thus, such data should be deleted unless there is another legal basis on which such personal data may be retained. Article 7(3) GDPR specifies that it must "be as easy to withdraw as to give consent." This is why the option to unsubscribe is always clearly set out in each email when a data subject consents to be on a mailing list.

General

Time Limits and Form

The duty to inform must be provided at the time the personal data is obtained, or, where not collected from the data subject, at the latest within one month of obtaining the personal data, as stated above. All other rights must be carried out within a one-month period.

Requests from data subjects to exercise any of their rights may be received by the controller in many forms, i.e. via letter or email. The controller must have a process in place to ensure such requests reach the appropriate person and get carried out. In accordance with Article 12(3) GDPR the controller must carry out any data subject request without undue delay and at the latest within one month of receipt of a data subject request. The data subject must be informed when a request has been carried out and any action taken per a data subject request, including when any request has been carried out regarding rectification, erasure or restriction.

The one-month period may be extended by two months considering the complexity of the request or the number of requests. In this case the following information still needs to be provided within one month:

- Confirmation that the request was received;
- An explanation as to why such an extension is necessary;
- Any action taken thus far regarding the data subject request.

In accordance with Article 12(4) GDPR, if the controller does not take any action regarding a data subject request, the controller must inform the data subject within one month of:

- The fact that the controller is not carrying out the data subject request;
- The reasons for not carrying out the data subject request;
- Provide information on the possibility of lodging a complaint or seeking a judicial remedy.

Received request electronically: Where the data subject requests to exercise one of their rights and such a request was made by electronic means, any information that needs to be provided to the data subject should likewise be provided by electronic means.[141]

Cost

In accordance with Article 12(5) GDPR, all data subject requests must be carried out free of charge. However, where a data subject request is unfounded or excessive, the controller may:[142]

- Charge a reasonable fee, considering the administration costs;
- Refuse to act on the request.

The controller bears the burden of proving a data subject request was unfounded or excessive.[143] One instance provided within the GDPR, is that a request is excessive or unfounded if it is repetitive. Note that regarding a DSAR, for any further copies of personal data beyond the initial copy that the controller provided to the data subject, the controller may charge a reasonable fee based on administration costs.[144]

Identifying the Data Subject Making the Request

The controller is required to use "all reasonable measures" to verify the identity of the data subject that is seeking to exercise their rights.[145] In accordance with Article 12(6) GDPR, where the controller has doubts as to the identity of the data subject making the request, the controller may request the provision of additional information necessary to confirm the identity of the data subject. Such personal data requested may be cross referenced with personal data that is held by the controller to confirm the data subject's identity.

---

141 Art 12(3) GDPR.
142 Art 12(5) GDPR.
143 Art 12(5) GDPR.
144 Art 15(3) GDPR.
145 Recital 64 GDPR; Art 11(1) GDPR.

Particular attention is drawn to the fact that the controller must verify the identity of the data subject where information is requested to be provided orally.[146] There cannot be reliance on the fact that the person confirms their identity,[147] there must be an appropriate verification check, for example by verifying their address, phone number or any piece of information that the controller knows about them that only the true data subject would know.

Controller not obliged to carry out request where unable to identify data subject: A controller is not obliged to retain personal data solely for the purpose of being able to respond to data requests.[148] Where a data subject desires to exercise a right as against the controller and the controller is able to demonstrate that it is not in a position to identify the data subject, the controller is not obliged to fulfil the request. In these cases, where possible, the controller shall inform the data subject that they are unable to process their request.[149] However, the data subject may still exercise their rights as against the controller if the data subject provides additional information to make themselves identifiable.[150]

No verification needed re right to be informed: WP29 noted that there is no requirement to verify identity in the case of the right to be informed because the information that needs to be provided under that right must also be accessible to future users and customers.[151] Thus, even where a data subject requests such information to be provided orally, there is no need to verify identity.

Retain Record of Requests

For the purposes of accountability, outlined in Chapter 7, the controller must retain information on:

- How and when any information was provided;
- Any request received, including if it was requested that information be provided by oral means;[152]

[146] Art 12(1) GDPR.
[147] Art 29 Working Party Guidelines on transparency under Regulation 2016/679, at 12.
[148] Recital 64 GDPR; Art 11 GDPR.
[149] Art 11(2) GDPR, Art 12(2) GDPR.
[150] Art 11(2) GDPR.
[151] Art 29 Working Party Guidelines on transparency under Regulation 2016/679, at 12.
[152] Art 29 Working Party Guidelines on transparency under Regulation 2016/679, at 13.

- The method via which the data subject's identity was verified, where appropriate;
- The fact that the request was carried out and that the requisite information was provided to the data subject.

This is commonly known as a "data subject request log". This is in addition to the requirement to keep a record of any consent provided, where applicable, as detailed in Chapter 5. Furthermore, this is additional to the record of processing requirements detailed in Chapter 9.

Further Discussion

Article 29 Working Party Guidelines on transparency under Regulation 2016/679.

Article 29 Working Party Guidelines on the right to data portability, adopted on 13 December 2016.

Chapter 9

Ensure Security via Appropriate Technical and Organisational Measures

The essence of the right to data protection is to provide a mechanism to ensure a data subject's personal data is adequately protected. This chapter deals with the topic of security. New security technologies are constantly being released and are developed in response to constantly evolving security risks. In light of this ever evolving and changing topic, two inspirational quotes:

> *"Security is always excessive until it's not enough"*
> – Robbie Sinclair, Australian security expert

> *"The companies that do the best job on managing a user's privacy will be the companies that ultimately are the most successful"*
> – Fred Wilson, American businessman

The GDPR takes a pro-active risk based approach to force controllers to implement measures to minimise risks to personal data. In accordance with Article 24(1) GDPR, the controller is required to implement *appropriate* technical and organisational measures to ensure, and demonstrate, compliance with the GDPR. Such measures need to be reviewed and updated where necessary as data processing continues and develops.[1] Section 72(1) of the DPA 2018 provides that:

> In determining appropriate technical or organisational measures ... a controller shall ensure that the measures provide a level of security appropriate to the harm that might result from accidental or unlawful destruction, loss, alteration or unauthorised disclosure of, or access to, the data concerned.

There are the obvious technical and organisational measures; ensure software updates are installed, educate employees on how to identify a virus email, encrypt work laptops, lock the computer screen when leaving a work desk, etc. However, five items are detailed within the GDPR that are to aid in determining the required appropriate technical and organisational measures that may go beyond the obvious measures:

1. Security of processing;
2. Data protection by design and default;
3. Maintain records of processing activities (data inventory);
4. Data protection impact assessment;
5. Adherence to codes of conduct or certification.

Furthermore, there should be *policies and procedures* in place to support all such measures to ensure clarity among controller's employees and representatives.[2] The controller must take all reasonable steps to ensure persons that come into contact with the personal data are aware of and comply with the technical and organisational measures in place.[3]

1. Security of Processing

Relevant Law: Article 32 GDPR, Recital 76–77 GDPR

Article 32 GDPR provides for a general obligation of security of processing. It reiterates the requirement to implement "appropriate" technical and organisational measures. For such

---

[1] Art 24(1) GDPR.
[2] See Ch 20.
[3] S 72(2) DPA 2018.

measures to be "appropriate" the controller must ensure a level of security proportionate to:

- The available technology;
- Cost of implementation;
- Nature, scope and context of processing;
- Purpose of processing;
- Risks for the rights and freedoms of natural persons.

Thus, the GDPR places a large burden on the controllers to assess the appropriate technical and organisational measures proportionate to the current processing situation. A large emphasis is placed on the fact that security measures need to be appropriate given the risk.[4]

Assessment of risk

An assessment of the risk related to any personal data processing activity is an absolute requirement.[5] The risk assessment is beneficial to ensure that appropriate security measures are in place.[6] The risk assessment not only includes risks posed to the right to data protection and privacy, but also all other rights such as free speech and freedom of movement.[7] There are two requirements for the risk assessment, it must:

- Be an objective assessment; *and*
- Take account of the likelihood and severity of the risk; this includes an assessment of the risks that arises from the personal data processing itself, and any risks that would arise in the case of a potential breach.

Objective Assessment

In accordance with Recital 76 GDPR, risk should be evaluated on the basis of an objective assessment. In order for an objective assessment to take place, account needs to be taken of the characteristics of the processing activity, including the:[8]

- Origin of the personal data;
- Nature of the processing activity;
- Scope of the processing activity;

---

4 Art 32(1) GDPR.

5 Art 32(1)-(2) GDPR.

6 A list of the different risk assessments are provided in Annex A.

7 Art 29 Working Party, Statement on the role of a risk-based approach in data protection legal frameworks, at 4.

8 Recital 76-77 GDPR, Art 24(1) GDPR.

- Context of the processing activity;
- Purpose of the processing activity;
- Likelihood and severity of risks;
- Identification of best technical and organisational measures to mitigate such risk.

In consideration of these characteristics, it should be established in an objective manner whether the data processing operations involve any risk, including if it is a high risk.[9] Ideally a controller will maintain a record setting out each processing operation, the associated risks and the measures taken to address each risk. For example:

Record	
Processing operation/ Characteristics of the processing activity	Paying employees via external payroll service
Associated risk	External entity, may not have appropriate data protection procedures in place
Measures taken to address risk	Assessed data protection procedures of the external payroll service and they provide a high level of data protection
Conclusion	No apparent risk

This objective risk assessment would also form part of the information required for the record of processing activities (see section 3 on data inventory below).

Likelihood and Severity

The risk assessment must encompass an assessment of the likelihood and severity of risks that arise or might arise from the personal data processing itself. Recital 75 GDPR emphasises that physical, material or non-material damage can arise from the processing of personal data. The GDPR provides the examples that the likelihood and severity of risk may be apparent where:[10]

- "The processing may give rise to discrimination, identity theft or fraud, financial loss, damage to the reputation, loss of confidentiality of personal data protected by professional secrecy, unauthorised

---

9 Recital 77 GDPR, note that guidelines may be provided by the Board on what does not constitute a high risk.

10 Recital 75 GDPR.

reversal of pseudonymisation, or any other significant economic or social disadvantage";

- "Data subjects might be deprived of their rights and freedoms or prevented from exercising control over their personal data";
- "Personal data are processed which reveal racial or ethnic origin, political opinions, religion or philosophical beliefs, trade union membership, and the processing of genetic data, data concerning health or data concerning sex life or criminal convictions and offences or related security measures";
- "Personal aspects are evaluated, in particular analysing or predicting aspects concerning performance at work, economic situation, health, personal preferences or interests, reliability or behaviour, location or movements, in order to create or use personal profiles";
- "Personal data of vulnerable natural persons, in particular of children, are processed";
- "Processing involves a large amount of personal data and affects a large number of data subjects."

The risk assessment should encompass the risks and damages that could arise if a "hypothetical" data breach occurred.[11] Article 32(2) GDPR draws attention to the fact that an assessment of a potential data breach must take account of the severity of physical, material or non-material damages that could arise:[12]

- If accidental or unlawful destruction of the personal data occurs;
- If alteration to personal data caused by the loss of personal data occurs;
- If unauthorised disclosure of or access to the personal data occurs, including access to the equipment used for the processing.

In assessing these risks, the controller needs to consider the likelihood of each risk and the severity of each risk related to the processing activity. For example:

11 Within the risk assessment required when a data breach occurs, the assessment will be based on the actual breach, see Annex A.

12 See also Recital 83 GDPR and Recital 39 GDPR.

Record	
Processing operation/ Characteristics of the processing activity	Paying employees via external payroll service
Associated risk	External entity, may not have appropriate data protection procedures in place
Measures taken to address risk	Assessed data protection procedures of the external payroll service and they provide a high level of data protection
Current status	No apparent risk
Risk if data breach	Exposure of or alteration to employee's salary, bank details, name, address and PPS number, or loss of such data
Severity of risk if data breach	*High severity* – identity fraud, publicity of salary could lead to social stigma, etc
Safeguards to prevent breach	Use of encryption when details transferred between controller, external payroll service and employee
Likelihood of risk	*Low risk*–due to safeguards; however, need to undergo quarterly review

Thus, if the likelihood of the risk is high and the severity of the risk is high, then a high security measure is required in relation to that identified risk. The below diagram may be used as an indicator as to how much resources, including spending costs and search for most up-to-date technology, should be used:

High Risk **Low Severity**	**High Risk** **High Severity**
Low Risk **Low Severity**	**Low Risk** **High Severity**

High	
Medium	↑
Low	

Indicator on how much resources, including spending costs and latest technology, should be used to implement security measures.

Technical and organisational measures

When considering what technical and organisational measures to implement for the purpose of satisfying security of processing under Article 32 GDPR, be aware of the following:

Article 32(1) GDPR provides a list of measures that should be carried out, as appropriate	• Pseudonymisation and encryption • Ongoing confidentiality, integrity, availability and resilience of the processing systems and services • The ability to restore availability and access to personal data in a timely manner in the event of a physical or technical incident • A process for regular testing, assessing and evaluating the effectiveness of technical and organisational measures for ensuring the security of processing.
Irish Data Protection Commission provided list of measures that should be used, as appropriate[13]	• Access controls • Automatic screen savers • Firewalls • Antivirus software • Staff training • Policy development.
Additional security required when using new technology	Must be aware of security risks when using new technology. For example, the Irish Data Protection Commission published the five steps to secure cloud based environments:[14] 1. Access control and authentication 2. Review default security settings 3. Seek assurances from your provider 4. Clear policies and staff training 5. Know what data you hold and secure it.
Clear instructions to person accessing the personal data	A required measure is that the controller must ensure that any person under their authority may only access personal data on instructions from the controller, unless otherwise required by law. Furthermore, the controller must ensure that a processor only processes data on the basis of instructions provided to the processor – this will be dealt with in Part 3.

13 See Irish Data Protection, Data Security Guidance, at https://www.dataprotection.ie/en/organisations/know-your-obligations/data-security-guidance.

14 See Irish Data Protection, Five Steps To Secure Cloud-based Environments, see https://www.dataprotection.ie/en/guidance-landing/five-steps-secure-cloud-based-environments.

Know the industry	There may be particular security measures recommended for the type of processing in place. For example, the Payment Card Industry Security Standard provides the appropriate security standard to be held vis-a-vis payment card details.
Enabling data subject rights forms part of security considerations	WP29 recommended appropriate security measures for enabling data subject rights, including, but not limited to: • An automated tool that can allow for the extraction of relevant data for a DSAR or for the right to portability[15] • Personal information management systems to enable data subjects to exercise their rights (this is technology that puts the data subject in control of their personal data)[16] • Authentication measures to ensure any transfer of data is to the correct entity and end to end encryption to ensure any transfer of data occurs safely.[17]
Appropriate measures	Remember that for appropriate security of processing, as outlined at the beginning of this section, consideration needs to be had to cost and available technology, among others.

Where carrying out vulnerable processing activities, particular technical and organisational measures are required to be in place for the below processing activities:

Political opinions	Recital 56 GDPR specifically states that where compiling personal data on people's political opinions in the public interest, appropriate safeguards must be in place.
Children	Recital 38 GDPR states that children merit specific protection as they may be less aware of the risks and safeguards in place, thus the technical and security measures should reflect that.

15 Art 29 Working Party Guidelines on the right to data portability, adopted on 13 December 2016, at 16.

16 See European Data Protection Supervisor, Opinion 9/2016, EDPS Opinion on Personal Information Management Systems, Towards more user empowerment in managing and processing personal data, 20 October 2016.

17 Art 29 Working Party Guidelines on the right to data portability, adopted on 13 December 2016, at 19.

Automated individual decision making, including profiling	Where automated individual decision making may take place in accordance with Article 22 GDPR,[18] reference is made to the fact that "suitable measures" must be in place.[19] In particular Recital 71 GDPR states the controller should: • Use appropriate mathematical or statistical procedures for the profiling • Implement technical and organisational measures appropriate to ensure, in particular, that factors which result in inaccuracies in personal data are corrected and the risk of errors is minimised • Secure personal data in a manner that takes account of the potential risks involved for the interests and rights of the data subject and that prevents discriminatory effects on natural persons on the basis of racial or ethnic origin, political opinion, religion or beliefs, trade union membership, genetic or health status or sexual orientation, or that result in measures having such an effect.
Genetic, biometric or health data	The Health Research Regulations[20] reiterates that appropriate technical and organisational measures should to be in place to safeguard health research data, including risk assessments, appropriate transparency requirements, etc. Appropriate procedures outside of what is normally required include:[21] • Ethical approval of the health research by a research ethics committee • Specification of any person who provides funding for, or otherwise supports, the project • Controls to log whether and by whom personal data have been consulted, altered, disclosed or erased Furthermore, a controller is required to carry out a data protection impact assessment[22] where they are seeking a declaration to avoid the explicit consent requirement.

18 Where decision may have a significant or legal effect on the data subject; See s on automated individual decision making in Chapter 6 for further explanation of the concept.

19 Art 22(3) GDPR.

20 The Data Protection Act 2018 (s 36(2)) (Health Research) Regulations 2018 SI No 314 of 2018: For any health research that started prior to such date, a transition period until 30 April 2019 is provided. See Ch 6.

21 Reg 3(1)(b) – (c).

22 See section 4 below.

2. Data Protection by Design and Default

Relevant Law: Article 25 GDPR, Recital 78 GDPR

In addition to the obligation for security of processing, Article 25 GDPR puts an *absolute obligation* to have measures in place to ensure that the data processing activity is:

1) Designed with data protection in mind (data protection by design); *and*
2) Has data protection mechanisms in place by default (data protection by default).

These obligations on the controller exist both at the time of determining how the processing will take place and at the time of the processing itself; therefore, it is a continuing obligation. This means that the principles of data protection, including transparency and data minimisation, should be integrated from the outset of any new product or service development or any processing operation. For example, products or services should not only be designed so that it is easy for data subjects to adjust their privacy settings (design), but by default the highest privacy settings should be active at the outset.

Default: Data protection by default means that at the outset and by default the user is protected as much as possible from data protection risks i.e. a user has to actively do something in order for the settings to change from default to other higher risk functionalities. Article 25(2) GDPR specifies that the controller must implement measures to ensure that by default only the personal data that is necessary to be processed for the intended purpose is processed. This default principle applies equally to all stages of the data processing activity, from initially gathering the data to retaining the data. [23]

Thus, the following data protection principles are at the core of data protection by default:

- Data minimisation – amount of data collected should by default be as little as possible for the purpose intended;
- Purpose limitation – the extent of the processing should be limited by default to what is necessary;
- Storage limitation – the storage period of the personal data should be limited by default to what is necessary;

[23] Art 25(2) GDPR.

- Integrity and confidentiality (in terms of accessibility) – the accessibility of the personal data should be limited to what is necessary.

Design: Data protection by design means that the default mechanisms need to be enabled via the design of the processing activity and the principles of data protection should be integrated into any design. In this context, even processors should take this into account within the design of their products so that controllers can fulfil their data protection obligations.[24]

Design and default measures

The GDPR requires that the appropriate measures for data protection by default and design are in place. Similar to the requirements for security of processing, outlined in section 1 of this chapter, such measures must be proportionate to:

- The available technology;
- Cost of implementation;
- Nature, scope and context of processing;
- Purpose of processing;
- Risks to rights and freedoms of a natural persons posed by the processing.[25]

Thus, a balancing assessment must take place. For example, where the cost is high for the latest technological measure, but the risk is low, a less costly technology may be satisfactory. However, even if the risk is low, perhaps the severity of the risk is high due to the amount of data subjects, thus the greater technology would be required. The below diagram may be used as an indicator as to how much resources, including spending costs and search for new technology, should be used:

---

[24] Recital 78 GDPR.

[25] The risk assessment must be an objective assessment and take into account the likelihood and severity of the risk; Risks to rights and freedoms include other fundamental rights like freedom of speech, as well as the right to data protection and privacy. See Annex A.

High Risk **Low Severity**	**High Risk** **High Severity**
Low Risk **Low Severity**	**Low Risk** **High Severity**

High
Medium
Low

↑ Indicator on need for latest technology and increased spending to implement data protection by design and default.

Regardless of the level of risk of severity, data protection by design and default measures should include, where applicable:[26]

- Minimising the processing of personal data to what is necessary;
- Pseudonymising personal data as soon as possible;
- Adequate provision of information in line with transparency requirements;[27]
- Enabling the data subject to monitor / consistently be kept up to date with the data processing;
- Enabling the controller to create and improve security functions;
- By default personal data should not be accessible to an indefinite number of individuals without the data subject's authorisation.[28]

All measures taken to implement data protection by design and default must be done with three goals in mind:[29]

1. The measures are effective in implementing data protection by design and default;
2. The measures integrate the necessary safeguards into the processing in order to meet the requirements of the GDPR;

---

[26] Recital 78 GDPR.
[27] See Ch 5 and 6.
[28] Art 25(2) GDPR.
[29] Art 25(1) GDPR.

3. The measures protect the rights of the data subject.

To this extent, Recital 78 GDPR states that the principles of data protection by design and default should be taken into consideration within the context of public tenders. Thus, seeking to create a data processing operation that integrates data protection by design and default should be there from inception.

3. Maintain Record of Processing Activities (Data Inventory)

Relevant Law: Article 30 GDPR

Article 30 GDPR provides that the controller must maintain a record of processing activities concerning personal data for which it is the controller where *one* of the four below criteria are fulfilled:

The controller employs more than 250 people	If the controller employs more than 250 people there is an automatic obligation to maintain a record of processing.[30] This is to take account of the fact that micro, small and medium-sized enterprises would not be required to automatically maintain a data inventory unless they meet any of the other criteria.
The processing is likely to result in a risk to the rights and freedoms of data subjects	If the processing is likely to result in a risk to the rights and freedoms of data subjects there is an automatic obligation to maintain a record of processing. Similar to other risk assessments within the GDPR,[31] the focus is on the likelihood of the risk to data subject's rights. Such rights include the right to privacy and data protection, as well as all other fundamental rights, such as the right to freedom of speech.[32]

30 See Recital 13 GDPR.

31 See Annex A.

32 Art 29 Working Party, Statement on the role of a risk-based approach in data protection legal frameworks, at 4.

The processing occurs regularly	If processing of personal data occurs regularly, there is a requirement to maintain a record. WP29 provided the example that even in a small company employee data is regularly processed,[33] thus a record of processing activities should always be maintained for employee data. If the processing activity is not carried out regularly and occurs outside the regular course of business or activity of the controller,[34] then there is no requirement to maintain a record.
The processing includes special categories of personal data or personal data relating to criminal convictions and offences	If the controller's processing activity includes special categories of personal data[35] or personal data relating to criminal convictions and offences[36] then a record of processing must be maintained.

Content and form of the record

The record of processing must include:

- Name and contact details of the controller, and where applicable, the joint controller, the controller's representatives and the data protection officer;
- Purpose of the processing;
- Description of the categories of data subjects and of the categories of personal data;
- List of entities that have or will receive the personal data, including recipients outside the EU, processors and other controllers;
- Where transfers outside the EU occurred;
- The planned time limits for erasure of the different categories of data;
- A general description of the technical and organisational measures in place.

Such records must be in writing, including in electronic format.[37] Often an excel spreadsheet is used to keep track of the above

---

33 Working Party 29 Position Paper on the derogations from the obligation to maintain records of processing activities pursuant to Art 30(5) GDPR, at 2.

34 Working Party 29 Position Paper on the derogations from the obligation to maintain records of processing activities pursuant to Art 30(5) GDPR, at 2.

35 See Ch 6.

36 Art 10 GDPR.

37 Art 30(3) GDPR.

information. It is intended that such records are useful to indicate compliance with the GDPR.

4. Data Protection Impact Assessment

Relevant Law: Recital 84, 90–94 GDPR, Article 35–36GDPR

The controller is required to carry out a Data Protection Impact Assessment (DPIA) where processing is "likely to result in a *high* risk to the rights and freedoms of natural persons". As with other risk assessments, the reference to rights and freedoms of natural persons not only includes the right to data protection and privacy, but also all other rights such as free speech and freedom of movement.[38] The focus is on managing risks that the data subject may be exposed to, this includes:[39]

- The risks caused by the personal data processing planned;
- The potential risks that may arise if a personal data breach occured.

It should become apparent via the risk assessment required for security of processing within Article 32 GDPR (detailed earlier in section 1 of this chapter) whether there is a high risk, and thereby whether a DPIA is required. A DPIA enhances the risk based approach to data protection, by forcing controllers to assess high risks at the outset, prior to data processing commencing. This enables controllers to prepare for any risk exposure. However, even where a DPIA may not be necessary, controllers still must minimise and manage any risk exposure via the other measures outlined within this chapter.

Purpose of a DPIA

The purpose of a DPIA is to ensure that data subjects are not exposed to undue high risk and that the measures in place are appropriate considering the high risk. Furthermore, the DPIA is useful to:

---

38 Art 29 Working Party, Statement on the role of a risk-based approach in data protection legal frameworks, at 4; Art 29 Working Party, Guidelines on Data Protection Impact Assessment (DPIA) and determining whether processing is "likely to result in a high risk" for the purposes of Regulation 2016/679, at 6.

39 Guidelines on Personal data breach notification under Regulation 2016/679, at 23.

- Demonstrate accountability with the GDPR;
- Determine if appropriate security measures and policies are in place;
- Determine if data protection by design and default has been implemented;
- Determine whether activities regarding automated decision making are taking place, including profiling.[40]

When is a DPIA mandatory (high risk)

A DPIA is not mandatory for all processing activities, only those that pose a "high risk" to the rights of data subjects. As with the other risk assessments required within the GDPR, there are no absolute rules and the burden is on the controller to conduct a close assessment of each processing activity.

Article 35(3) GDPR outlines three specific instances where a DPIA will be *mandatory*, which are automatically by their nature "high risk":

a) "Systematic and extensive evaluation of personal aspects relating to natural persons which is based on automated processing, including profiling, and on which decisions are based that produce legal effects concerning the natural person or similarly significantly affect the natural person";
b) "Processing on a large scale of special categories of data..., or of personal data relating to criminal convictions and offences...";
c) "Systematic monitoring of a publicly accessible area on a large scale".

The controller must assess whether their processing activity falls into one of the above categories and are required to carry out a DPIA if it does. Even if the data processing does not fall exactly within one of these categories, a DPIA is still required where there is "high risk". There are nine criteria that may be used to determine whether there is a high risk:[41]

---

40 See above on security of processing; Further see Article 29 Working Party, Guidelines on Automated individual decision-making and Profiling for the purposes of Regulation 2016/679, At 21.

41 Art 29 Working Party, Guidelines on Data Protection Impact Assessment (DPIA) and determining whether processing is "likely to result in a high risk" for the purposes of Regulation 2016/679, at 9-10.

	Criteria	Explanation	Source of criteria
1	The evaluation or scoring of data subjects	This could include profiling or prediction of the performance of data subjects, for example concerning health data for insurance premiums or behavioural advertising.[42]	This is one of the elements for a required DPIA within Article 35(3) (a) GDPR.
2	Automated decision making with legal or similar significant effect	This means an automated decision that may have a significant effect on the data subject,[43] for example an automated recruitment process that determines automatically whether a data subject would be accepted for a job.	This is one of the elements for a required DPIA within Article 35(3) (a) GDPR.
3	Systematic monitoring	This means continuous or regular monitoring.[44] For example, continuously monitoring a public area via CCTV.	This is one of the elements for a required DPIA within Article 35(3) (c) GDPR.
4	Sensitive data or data of highly personal nature	This includes special categories of personal data, as well as data relating to criminal convictions; furthermore, there is data that would by its nature be sensitive, such as financial information, credit card information, location data, personal emails or diaries. Whether the data was made public would be a factor in determining any related risks.	This is one of the elements for a required DPIA within Article 35(3) (b).
5	Data processed on a large scale	Large scale includes large in the sense of number of data subjects, volume of data, duration of processing or geographical extent of the processing activity.[45]	This is one of the elements for a required DPIA within Article 35(3) (c).

42 See section on profiling in Ch 6.
43 See section on automated decision making in Ch 6.
44 See what is meant by monitoring in Ch 3 on p 57.
45 Recital 91 GDPR, see details on large scale.

6	Combining data sets	This means combining data sets from different data processing operations, in a context a data subject would be unaware of. Such combination could reveal much more data about an individual and increase related risks.	This is derived from Recital 30 GDPR where it is noted that where certain personal data is combined with other personal data larger profiles may be created about data subjects and it may be possible to identify data subjects more easily.
7	Data concerning vulnerable data subjects	This includes individuals that are in a vulnerable position in relation to the controller; this may include employees vis a vis their employer, children, elderly people, people with disabilities, etc.	This is one of the risks identified within Recital 75 GDPR.
8	Innovative use or applying new technological or organisational solutions	This is because new technologies could include non-common ways of data collection i.e. via facial recognition. It also could use data in new ways i.e. via the internet of things, where personal data would be transferred from device to device, without any reversion to a network centre.	Article 35(1) GDPR makes it clear that this is an important criterion.
9	Detriments to data subjects	If the processing prevents the data subject from exercising particular rights or using a service or entering into a contract.[46] For example, whether a person would be accepted for a job or not, or to receive a loan, etc.	Throughout the GDPR risk assessments are required, and at their core is an evaluation of the severity of the risks to which the data subject is exposed to.[47]

WP29 stated that a process that meets two of the criteria listed above would need a DPIA. Generally, the more criteria that are met, the more likely a DPIA is needed. However, there may be instances

46 Recital 91 GDPR.
47 See Annex A.

where even just meeting one criterion may require a DPIA if it presents a high enough risk. WP29 provided examples of where a DPIA would be required when the nine criteria are considered:

- Systematically monitoring employees, including internet activity (meets two criteria: systematic monitoring and data concerning vulnerable data subjects);
- Monitor driving behaviour on a busy road where license plates may be recognised (three criteria: systematic monitoring, large scale and new technology).

WP29 also provided a list of examples where a DPIA would not be required, considering the nine criteria:

- Sending out generic email to a mailing list (only one criteria: large scale);
- Processing of data by an individual practitioner i.e. doctor or lawyer (even though meet two criteria: sensitive data and data concerning vulnerable subjects it is not considered a high risk).

List from Irish Supervisory Authority of further situations in which a DPIA is mandatory: Article 35(4) GDPR provides that the supervisory authority of each Member State should create a public list of processing operations for which a DPIA is mandatory. The Irish Data Protection Commission published a final list, following an opinion from the EDPB.[48] The Irish Commission stated that it is good practice to carry out a DPIA prior to any major new project involving data processing. Furthermore, the Irish Commission stated that a DPIA is mandatory in the below circumstances and clarified that this list is non-exhaustive:[49]

---

48 EDPB, Opinion 11/2018 on the draft list of the competent supervisory authority of Ireland regarding the processing operations subject to the requirement of a data protection impact assessment (Art 35.4 GDPR), Adopted on 25 September 2018.

49 Data Protection Commission, List of Types of Data Processing Operations which require a Data Protection Impact Assessment, available at https://www.dataprotection.ie/en/guidance-landing/data-processing-operations-require-data-protection-impact-assessment.

	Circumstance in which DPIA is mandatory
1	Use of personal data on a large-scale for a purpose(s) other than that for which it was initially collected
2	Profile vulnerable persons, including children, for target marketing
3	Use of profiling or special category data to determine access to services
4	Systematically monitoring, tracking, or observing individuals' location or behaviour
5	Profile individuals on a large-scale
6	Process biometric data to uniquely identify an individual or enable identification AND carrying out one of the nine criteria listed by WP29
7	Process genetic data AND carrying out one of the nine criteria listed by WP29
8	Indirectly obtain personal data where GDPR transparency requirements are not being met
9	Combine, link or cross-reference separate datasets where such linking contributes to profiling or behavioural analysis of individuals
10	Processing personal data on a large scale based on legislative measure under the Data Protection Act 2018 where suitable and specific measures are required to safeguard the fundamental rights and freedoms of individuals

How to conduct a DPIA

A DPIA should take place prior to the intended processing activity and should be continuously updated when changes occur.[50] Regardless of changes, WP29 stated that it is best practice nevertheless to continuously review and re-assess a DPIA.[51]

In accordance with Article 35(7) GDPR, the DPIA is a three stage process:[52]

---

50 Art 35(11) GDPR.

51 Art 29 Working Party, Guidelines on Data Protection Impact Assessment (DPIA) and determining whether processing is "likely to result in a high risk" for the purposes of Regulation 2016/679, at 14.

52 Also see Art 29 Working Party, Guidelines on Data Protection Impact Assessment (DPIA) and determining whether processing is "likely to result in a high risk" for the purposes of Regulation 2016/679, at 16-17.

1	Assess context of processing activity	• A description of the envisaged processing operations, including the nature of the processing activity, the scope and context • The purpose of the processing • The legal basis of the processing • The legitimate interest pursued by the controller, where legitimate interest is the legal basis • An assessment of the necessity and proportionality of the processing operations in relation to the purposes
2	Assess risks	An assessment of the risks to the rights and freedoms of the data subjects[53]
3	Assess risk mitigation	• The measures envisaged to address the risks, including safeguards and security measures • Mechanisms in place to ensure protection of personal data • Mechanisms in place to demonstrate compliance with the GDPR

Consultation: Interested parties should be consulted and their responses documented on the proposed activity that is the subject of the DPIA. Where there is a DPO designated, the controller must seek the advice of the DPO when carrying out a DPIA.[54] Where appropriate, the controller must seek the views of the data subjects or their representatives on the intended processing.[55] WP29 stated that the following should therefore be documented:[56]

- If a controller does not seek the views of data subjects, there should be justification for such decision. Such justification may be that it would compromise the confidentiality of business plans, or it would have been a disproportionate and or impractical endeavour;
- If the controller sought the views of the data subjects, the controller should document how the views were sought (i.e. survey) and demonstrate the GDPR was complied with in gathering those views;
- If the controller's assessment differs from the views of

[53] This should have been done via the assessment required to establish whether a DPIA is necessary and also via the risk assessment needed for the security of processing, see "security of processing" within Ch 9.

[54] Art 35 (2) GDPR.

[55] Art 35(9) GDPR.

[56] See Art 29 Working Party, Guidelines on Data Protection Impact Assessment (DPIA) and determining whether processing is "likely to result in a high risk" for the purposes of Regulation 2016/679, at 15.

data subjects, reasons for the controller proceeding in a different manner need to be documented.

Use of a single DPIA: A single DPIA may be used to assess similar processing activities that pose similar high risks. Similarly, a single DPIA could occur for a group of entities that will be carrying out a similar activity,[57] i.e. where all entities intend to use the same new technology.

Form of a DPIA: There is no specific form required for a DPIA; therefore the burden is on the controller to assess the best method to conduct a DPIA.[58] WP29 provided many examples of methodologies that are in use.[59] Furthermore, WP29 provided a comprehensive criteria list for an acceptable DPIA under the GDPR.[60]

Contract out DPIA: The controller may request another entity to carry out their DPIA, but it must be remembered that the controller holds ultimate responsibility for the obligation.[61]

Exception to conducting a DPIA

Even where there is a high risk, no DPIA is required in four instances:

57 Art 35(1) GDPR, Recital 92 GDPR.

58 See Art 29 Working Party, Guidelines on Data Protection Impact Assessment (DPIA) and determining whether processing is "likely to result in a high risk" for the purposes of Regulation 2016/679, at 17–It is possible in the future that sector specific DPIA frameworks are developed.

59 See Annex 1, Art 29 Working Party, Guidelines on Data Protection Impact Assessment (DPIA) and determining whether processing is "likely to result in a high risk" for the purposes of Regulation 2016/679.

60 See Annex 2, Art 29 Working Party, Guidelines on Data Protection Impact Assessment (DPIA) and determining whether processing is "likely to result in a high risk" for the purposes of Regulation 2016/679.

61 Art 29 Working Party, Guidelines on Data Protection Impact Assessment (DPIA) and determining whether processing is "likely to result in a high risk" for the purposes of Regulation 2016/679, at 14.

1	The processing activity falls within a list made by the supervisory authority that specifies processing operations for which no DPIA is required.[62]	The Irish Commission has stated that a DPIA is not required where:[63] • No high risk to the rights and freedoms of individuals • DPIA already concluded that there was no risk • Authorised by a supervisory authority • Existing legal basis that is clear • DPIA formed part of an impact assessment already conducted by a national body.[64]
2	Activity necessary for certain purpose	A DPIA is not required if the processing activity is necessary: • For compliance with a legal obligation[65] OR • For the performance of a task carried out in the public interest[66] OR • In the exercise of official authority vested in the controller.[67]
3	DPIA formed part of an impact assessment already conducted under Article 35(10) GDPR	A DPIA is not necessary if the law regulates that processing activity and a general DPIA was already carried out as part of the formation of that law. Note a DPIA may still be necessary in this instance where the Member State states that such obligation is still necessary.
4	Checked under Article 20 of Directive 95/46/EC	A DPIA is not necessary if the processing activity was already checked under Article 20 of Directive 95/46/EC,[68] unless there has been a change that would require a current DPIA.

62 Art 35(5) GDPR.

63 Data Protection Commission, List of Types of Data Processing Operations which require a Data Protection Impact Assessment, available at https://www.dataprotection.ie/en/guidance-landing/data-processing-operations-require-data-protection-impact-assessment.

64 Under Art 35(10) GDPR.

65 Legal basis under Art 6(1)(c) GDPR.

66 Legal basis under Art 6(1)(e) GDPR.

67 Legal basis under Art 6(1)(e) GDPR.

68 Recital 171 GDPR.

Outcome of DPIA – Prior consultation with supervisory authority

A consultation with the supervisory authority, prior to beginning the data processing activity, is required where there is a residual high risk after a DPIA. If the controller considers the risks are sufficiently reduced after the DPIA, the processing can proceed without prior consultation with the supervisory authority. If there remains a residual high risk then a consultation with the supervisory will be necessary.[69] A residual high risk may be apparent when a controller, perhaps due to a technological block, cannot find sufficient measures to mitigate the high risk detailed in the DPIA. As part of the consultation procedure with the supervisory authority, the DPIA will need to be provided in full,[70] along with the following information:[71]

- The respective responsibilities of the controller, joint controllers and processors, where applicable;
- The purpose and means of the intended high risk processing activity;
- The measures and safeguards provided to protect the data subject's personal data;
- The contact details of the DPO, where applicable;
- Any other information requested.

Note that Article 36(4) GDPR requires such prior consultation to take place where a Member State is proposing legislation that concerns personal data processing.[72] Furthermore, Member States may outline other circumstances where prior consultation is required.[73]

Where the supervisory authority determines that the processing which is the purpose of the consultation would infringe the GDPR, the controller shall be informed of such within eight weeks of requesting the consultation.[74] The supervisory authority should also provide the controller with advice where there is a negative outcome.[75]

Publishing DPIA: There is no requirement to publish the DPIA to

69 Art 36(1) GDPR.
70 Art 36(3)(e) GDPR.
71 Art 36(3) GDPR.
72 For a list of ongoing legislative consultations, see Data Protection Commission, Annual Report, 25 May - 31 December 2018, at 58-60.
73 Art 36(5) GDPR.
74 Art 36(2) GDPR; that period may be extended by a further 6 weeks and any such period may be suspended pending the receipt of further information.
75 Art 36(2) GDPR.

the public; however, WP29 stated that parts or a summary of the DPIA should be published in order to abide by the principles of accountability and transparency.[76]

Implement appropriate measures found as a result of DPIA: Recital 84 GDPR states that the outcome of the DPIA should be used to determine the appropriate technical and organisational measures needed to comply with the GDPR. Thus, considering the high risk of the processing activity, sufficient mitigation measures to reduce the risks are required.

For an example of a thorough impact assessment, which is available to the public online, see the European Commission assessment on a regulation for identity cards.[77]

5. Adherence to Approved Codes of Conduct or Certification

Relevant Law: Article 40–43 GDPR

Adherence to approved codes of conduct or certification is not obligatory; however, it is useful to demonstrate compliance with particular sections of the GDPR and the GDPR as a whole:

- Article 24(3) GDPR states that adherence to approved codes of conduct or certification may be used as an element by which to demonstrate compliance with the obligations of the controller;[78]
- Article 25(3) GDPR states that adherence to certification in particular may be used to demonstrate compliance with data protection by design and by default;
- Article 32(3) GDPR states that adherence to approved codes of conduct or certification may be used as an element by which to demonstrate compliance with security of processing; [79]
- Article 35(8) GDPR states that adherence to approved

---

[76] Art 29 Working Party, Guidelines on Data Protection Impact Assessment (DPIA) and determining whether processing is "likely to result in a high risk" for the purposes of Regulation 2016/679, at 18.

[77] Commission Staff Working Document, Impact Assessment, Strasbourg, 17.4.2018, SWD(2018) 110 final, Accompanying the Document, Proposal for a Regulation Of The European Parliament And Of The Council on strengthening the security of identity cards of Union citizens and of residence documents issued to Union citizens and their family members exercising their right of free movement.

[78] Also see Recital 77 GDPR.

[79] Also see Recital 77 GDPR.

codes of conduct should be taken into account when assessing the risk for a DPIA.

Further information on approved codes of conduct and certification is provided within Chapter 17.

Further Discussion

Article 29 Working Party, Guidelines on Data Protection Impact Assessment (DPIA) and determining whether processing is "likely to result in a high risk" for the purposes of Regulation 2016/679.

Article 29 Working Party, Statement on the role of a risk-based approach in data protection legal frameworks.

Article 29 Working Party, Opinion on Purpose limitation 13/EN WP29 203.

Article 29 Working Party, Position Paper on the derogations from the obligation to maintain records of processing activities pursuant to Article 30(5) GDPR.

Data Protection Commission, List of Types of Data Processing Operations which require a Data Protection Impact Assessment, available at www.dataprotection.ie.

European Data Protection Supervisor, Opinion 9/2016, EDPS Opinion on Personal Information Management Systems, Towards more user empowerment in managing and processing personal data, 20 October 2016.

EDPB, Opinion 11/2018 on the draft list of the competent supervisory authority of Ireland regarding the processing operations subject to the requirement of a data protection impact assessment (Article 35.4 GDPR), Adopted on 25 September 2018.

Chapter 10

Ensure Data Breach Procedures in Place

Relevant Law: Recital 85–88 GDPR, Article 33–34 GDPR

The controller must notify the supervisory authority within 72 hours of a personal data breach. This requirement allows the controller to be held accountable where insufficient security measures were in place or where processes were taking place that risked personal data. This requirement forms part of the principle of transparency as it enables data subjects to be informed of personal data breaches so that data subjects themselves may also take active steps to mitigate risks. Note that notification requirements may additionally exist under other legislation.[1]

[1] Directive 2009/136/EC (the Citizens' Rights Directive) and Regulation 611/2013 (the Breach Notification Regulation), Directive (EU) 2016/1148 concerning measures for a high common level of security of network and information systems across the Union (NIS Directive), Regulation (EU) 910/2014 on electronic identification and trust services for electronic transactions in the internal market (eIDAS Regulation).

The controller has six obligations vis-a-vis personal data breaches; the controller must be in a position to:

1. Detect when a personal data breach occurs;
2. Assess the risk to the rights and freedoms of natural persons;
3. Mitigate the risk;
4. Notify the supervisory authority, where required;
5. Notify the data subject, where required;
6. Document everything.

These obligations are further detailed in this chapter.

1. Detect when a Personal Data Breach Occurs

The basic requirement, in accordance with the security of processing obligation, is to have a level of security proportionate to any risk. The controller must have all appropriate technological and organisational measures in place to be in a position to establish immediately whether a breach has taken place.[2] This includes organisational measures to make sure that within an entity there are clear directions on what to do in these circumstances, and who to inform within the entity when a security issue is suspected. It should be made clear that a data breach needs to be notified to the controller via the agreement between the processor and controller.[3]

Types of personal data breach

There are three main types of breaches:[4]

- The "confidentiality breach" — where personal data is disclosed or accessed in an unauthorised or accidental manner;
- The "integrity breach" – where personal data is altered in an unauthorised or accidental manner;
- The "availability breach" – where personal data is lost or destroyed in an unauthorised or accidental manner.

WP29 noted there are circumstances where all three of these breaches or a combination of them may occur at the same time.

---

2 Recital 87 GDPR.

3 See Ch 12.

4 Art 29 Working Party, Guidelines on Personal data breach notification under Regulation 2016/679, at 7; Art 29 Working Party, Opinion 03/2014 on Personal Data Breach Notification.

It is noted that availability breaches may be less obvious. Article 4(12) GDPR states that a personal data breach is one that leads to one or more of the following instances:[5]

- "Accidental or unlawful destruction" of personal data; this is where the data no longer exists, or no longer exists in a form that the controller may access (availability breach);
- "Loss" of personal data; this is where the controller has lost control or no longer has access to the personal data (i.e. where encrypted by ransomware or loss of encryption key), or the personal data is no longer in the controller's possession (availability breach);
- "Alteration" of personal data (integrity breach);
- "Unauthorised disclosure of, or access to, personal data"; this includes disclosure to recipients that are not authorised to receive the data (confidentiality breach).

Regarding availability, even where there is a temporary loss of availability, this still counts as a breach; for example WP29 even gave an example of an unplanned power failure.[6] This is because the lack of access to data can cause an impact to data subjects. For example, in a hospital the lack of data could impact on data subjects by operations being cancelled, etc.[7] Part of the requirement for security of processing is the ability to restore personal data in a timely manner. If it is a planned maintenance, this would not count as a breach. [8]

2. Assess the Risk to the Rights and Freedoms of Natural Persons

The reference to rights and freedoms of natural persons not only includes the right to data protection and privacy, but also all other rights such as free speech and freedom of movement.[9] The risk assessment is an assessment of the risks resulting from the personal data breach. Assessing the risk is necessary to *mitigate*

---

5 Guidelines on Personal data breach notification under Regulation 2016/679, at 7.

6 Guidelines on Personal data breach notification under Regulation 2016/679, at 8.

7 Guidelines on Personal data breach notification under Regulation 2016/679, at 8.

8 Guidelines on Personal data breach notification under Regulation 2016/679, at 8.

9 Art 29 Working Party, Statement on the role of a risk-based approach in data protection legal frameworks, at 4.

any risk and to determine whether there is a requirement to *notify* the supervisory authority and/or the data subject.[10]

Controllers should have already assessed potential risks to data subjects via the security of processing requirements and via a DPIA, where applicable, detailed within Chapter 9. Further assessment of the risk will be necessary once the breach occurs, so as to take account of the actual circumstances of the breach. Thus, the assessment of risk must be done in a timely fashion once a personal data breach is detected. The risk assessment must be an objective assessment and must determine the likelihood and severity of the risk.[11]

As part of the ePrivacy Directive,[12] the European Union Agency for Network and Information Security (ENISA) produced recommendations for a data breach severity assessment.[13] Within this the severity of three factors are to be considered:

- The type of data that was breached (A) – can have value between 1-4;
- The ease with which a data subject may be identified (Y) – can have a value of 1 or lower;
- The specific circumstances of the breach (Z) – can have a value of 0.5 or lower.

Based on the level of severity, each factor is provided with a corresponding value, the higher the value, the higher the risk. Thereafter the level of severity is determined by:

$$(A \times Y) + Z$$

The answer provides the level of severity of the breach, with the highest value possible being 4.5. While no assessment has been adopted for the GDPR the ENISA method may be useful to quantify the risk severity to some degree.

WP29 recommended the following to be considered as part of the risk assessment:[14]

---

10 See sections 4 and 5 below.

11 Art 29 Working Party, Guidelines on Personal data breach notification under Regulation 2016/679, at 24-25; See Annex A.

12 Privacy and Electronic Communications Directive 2002/58/EC on Privacy and Electronic Communications, as amended via Directive 2009/136/EC, see Ch 21.

13 European Union Agency for Network and Information Security, Recommendations for a methodology of the assessment of severity of personal data breaches, working document, v 1.0, December 2013.

14 Art 29 Working Party, Guidelines on Personal data breach notification under Regulation 2016/679, at 24-25.

What should consider as part of risk assessment	Details
Type of breach	This must consider the specific circumstances of the breach and whether it was one of availability, integrity or confidentiality, or a combination of such.
Nature, sensitivity and volume of personal data	Generally the more sensitive the personal data that was the subject of the breach, the higher the risk. Volume includes the amount and combination of data impacted. For example, the list of job applicants to a certain position would be sensitive to those that were currently working for a competitor. Likewise, the higher the volume of data subjects impacted, the higher the risk.
Ease of identification of individuals	The easier it is to identify individuals, the higher the risk, i.e. if the data was encrypted or pseudonimsed the risk may be lower.
Severity of consequences for individuals	Recital 85 GDPR lists the risks that could arise for data subjects, including physical, material or non-material damage such as: • Loss of control over their personal data or limitation of their rights • Discrimination (high risk) • Identity theft or fraud (high risk) • Financial loss (high risk) • Unauthorised reversal of pseudonymisation • Damage to reputation (high risk) • Loss of confidentiality of personal data protected by professional secrecy • Any other significant economic or social disadvantage to the data subject concerned The items flagged as high risk are examples of high risk consequences of a data breach. WP29 stated that where the breach involves personal data that reveals special categories of personal data[15] or personal data relating to criminal convictions and offences, the items above flagged as high risk should be deemed likely to occur.[16] Permanency of the impact

[15] See Ch 6.

[16] Art 29 Working Party, Guidelines on Personal data breach notification under Regulation 2016/679, at 23.

	should also be considered when assessing the severity.
Special characteristics of the individual	Depending on the characteristics of the data subject, there may be a higher risk; for example, where the data subject is a vulnerable person such as a child.
Special characteristics of the data controller	The type of controller may impact upon the risk; for example if the controller is a bank, any data breach may present a higher risk then for controllers that hold less sensitive personal data.
The number of affected individuals	Generally, the higher the number of affected individuals, the higher the impact a breach can have.

3. Mitigate the Risk

Controllers must be in a position to prevent a breach and if a breach occurs, the controller must have systems in place to react to a breach within a timely manner.[17] When a breach occurs, the controller must assess and carry out activities to limit the extent and severity of the breach, where possible. The need for remedial action is necessary due to the risks that may arise out of a data breach. For example, if user's passwords were compromised during a data breach, a mitigating action may be to immediately notify user's to change their password.

4. Notify the Supervisory Authority, Where Required

The requirement to notify the supervisory authority will depend on whether a risk is likely to occur to the data subject. The breach does not need to be notified if the controller is able to demonstrate that the breach is "unlikely to result in a risk to the rights and freedoms of natural persons".[18] This essentially means that a controller does not need to notify the supervisory authority if the controller can guarantee that a person's rights were not infringed. For example, a situation unlikely to result in a risk is where:

- The personal data breached was already publicly available;
- The personal data was encrypted and the encryption key was not affected by the breach; however, the controller

[17] Art 29 Working Party, Guidelines on Personal data breach notification under Regulation 2016/679, at 6.

[18] Art 33(1) GDPR.

must be aware of the quality of the encryption and if it is of a high enough standard to diminish risk.[19]

Lack of availability of the data subject's personal data after a breach would be considered as a risk to the rights of the data subject i.e. particularly where there are no adequate back-ups or the back-up would take a considerable time to access.

Note that where it is initially assessed that there is no risk, it would still need to be monitored as this may change over time and a risk may arise. If the likelihood of a risk becomes apparent at a later stage, notification would be required at that time. Where it is unclear that a risk is unlikely, it is best practice to nevertheless notify the supervisory authority and they will be in a position to advise. There is no detriment for reporting a breach that is unlikely to result in a risk.

Requirement to notify supervisory authority within 72 hours

Where it is determined that the breach needs to be notified, the supervisory authority must be notified as soon as reasonably feasible, and no later than 72 hours from the controller being "aware" of the data breach. WP29 stated that the time the controller is aware begins at the time when the controller has a reasonable degree of certainty that a security incident, in which personal data may have been compromised, has occurred.[20] Where the controller becomes aware that a security incident may have occurred, they have an obligation to investigate whether personal data was impacted by the breach to see if a personal data breach occurred i.e. if personal data was impacted by the breach.[21]

Information to be provided to the Supervisory Authority

The notification to the supervisory authority must include:[22]

- A description of the nature of the personal data breach, including where possible:
    - o the categories of data subjects impacted (i.e. employees, children)

---

[19] Guidelines on Personal data breach notification under Regulation 2016/679, at 19.

[20] Guidelines on Personal data breach notification under Regulation 2016/679, at 10-11.

[21] Guidelines on Personal data breach notification under Regulation 2016/679, at 11.

[22] Art 33(3) GDPR.

  - approximate number of data subjects impacted
  - categories of personal data records impacted (i.e. credit card information, email addresses)
  - approximate number of personal data
- The name and contact details of the data protection officer or other contact point where further information can be obtained;
- A description of the likely consequences of the personal data breach;
- A description of the measures taken or proposed to be taken by the controller to address the personal data breach, including any measures to mitigate possible adverse effects.

The above is the minimum information that must be provided, and further information may be provided where appropriate. For example, where the data breach arose out of the fault of a processor, it would be best practice to also provide details of the processor to the supervisory authority.[23] The supervisory authority may request further information as part of its investigation.

The controller should also update the supervisory authority if further investigation shows that there was no personal data affected by the breach, or other changing circumstances.[24] There is no detriment for reporting a breach that may turn out to not be a personal data breach.

Delay in notification

Where all the information is not available within the 72 hours, the supervisory authority must still be informed of the breach within 72 hours. The remaining information may be provided in phases.[25] The controller can come to an agreement with the supervisory authority on how and when any remaining information should be provided, given the circumstances.

If the supervisory authority is not notified of the personal data breach within 72 hours, the reasons for the delay should accompany the notification.[26] WP29 noted that while the GDPR may allow for a delay in notification in particular instances, it should not be

---

23 Guidelines on Personal data breach notification under Regulation 2016/679, at 15.
24 Guidelines on Personal data breach notification under Regulation 2016/679, at 16.
25 Art 33(4) GDPR.
26 Art 33(1) GDPR.

seen as a regular occurrence, but rather the exception.[27] WP29 gave an example where a delay may be permissible; where multiple breaches occur around the same time period, making it difficult for the controller to notify each individually.[28] In such instances, the controller may be able to submit a "bundled" notification covering all the different breaches where the same personal data was impacted. However, if different breaches occur that concern different personal data, each should be notified independently. This would be the same even within the 72-hour notification period.

Cross border situation

Where there is a cross border situation in which personal data from multiple Member States were impacted, the lead supervisory authority must be notified, rather than multiple local supervisory authorities.[29] The controller should notify the lead supervisory authority whether the breach involved establishments located in other Member States and in which Member States data subjects are likely to be affected by the breach.[30] If there is any doubt as to who the lead supervisory authority is, the local supervisory authority should be notified at the very minimum.

Where the controller does not have an establishment within the EU, but personal data within the scope of the GDPR was impacted by the breach, WP29 recommended that notification should be made to the supervisory authority in the Member State where the controller's representative in the EU is established.[31]

5. Notify the Data Subject, Where Required

The requirement to notify the data subject will depend on whether the risk is high. The breach must be communicated to the data subjects that were impacted if "the personal data breach is likely to result in a high risk to the rights and freedoms of natural persons".[32] Such communications to data subjects should be made as soon as reasonably feasible.[33] WP29 noted that it should be obvious in

---

27 Guidelines on Personal data breach notification under Regulation 2016/679, at 16.

28 Guidelines on Personal data breach notification under Regulation 2016/679, at 16.

29 See section on lead supervisory authority at Ch 18, Art 56 (6) GDPR.

30 Guidelines on Personal data breach notification under Regulation 2016/679, at 17.

31 See Ch 16.

32 Art 34(1) GDPR.

33 Recital 86 GDPR.

certain situations that data subjects need to be notified promptly, perhaps even prior to notifying the supervisory authority, i.e. if there is an immediate threat of identity theft.[34] The risk assessment should reveal whether a high risk is likely to occur; furthermore, the assessment of high risks within the context of a DPIA may be useful in identifying what is a high risk.[35]

Information to be provided to the data subject

The communication to the data subject must include:[36]

- The nature of the personal data breach;
- The name and contact details of the data protection officer or other contact point where further information can be obtained;
- A description of the likely consequences of the personal data breach;
- A description of the measures taken or proposed to be taken by the controller to address the personal data breach, including any measures to mitigate possible adverse effects;
- Recommendations to mitigate potential adverse effects i.e. change password. [37]

Form and method of notification

The main purpose of the communication is to inform the data subject of a breach in order for the data subject to take precautionary measures to minimise their risk exposure. Notifying the data subject should generally occur in close cooperation with the supervisory authority, in particular:[38]

- Where the controller did not take the initiative to inform the data subject, the supervisory authority may require the controller to do so or may conclude that the communication is not required;[39]
- Controllers may also consult with the supervisory authority on the appropriate method to contact data subject's.

---

[34] Guidelines on Personal data breach notification under Regulation 2016/679, at 15-16.
[35] See Ch 9.
[36] Art 33(3) GDPR.
[37] Recital 86 GDPR.
[38] Recital 86 GDPR.
[39] Art 34(4) GDPR.

In accordance with Article 12(1) GDPR, and in line with the principle of transparency, the communication to the data subject must be in clear, plain language.[40] This means that information should be provided:

Succinctly	No longer or more complicated than necessary.
Separately	Separate from non-data protection related information i.e. separate from a newsletter containing other non-data protection information.[41]
Directly	Where it is feasible, the data subject should be contacted directly about the data breach i.e. via email, direct messaging or phone. It should be clear to the data subject that the information is directed towards them.
With recognition of who data subject is	Alternative forms and languages of the information should be available, depending on who the data subject is i.e. a child.

WP29 recommended that the controller must use a method of providing the information in a manner that maximises the chance of informing the impacted data subjects.[42] In doing so, the controller may use more than one form of medium for communication in order to maximise the chance of communicating with data subjects. WP29 gave examples of forms of communication, including direct messaging, notification, post, prominent website banner and prominent advertisements in print media.

Recital 88 GDPR states that any notification to data subjects would need to take into account the interests of law-enforcement authorities. Thus, while the information should be provided as soon as reasonably feasible, the controller may be advised to delay the notification until a time when it may not prejudice an investigation, etc.[43] Such a delay would need to be justified and on the advice of the relevant law authority.

Unable to identify data subject

The controller does not need to retain or acquire data to identify

40 See Ch 5.

41 Guidelines on Personal data breach notification under Regulation 2016/679, at 21.

42 Guidelines on Personal data breach notification under Regulation 2016/679, at 21.

43 Guidelines on Personal data breach notification under Regulation 2016/679, at 21.

a data subject.[44] If the controller is unable to notify a data subject due to insufficient information held on the data subject, then this must be documented. Other methods of mass communication may be appropriate in this instance. If the controller receives further information in the future, to identify the data subject, the controller then has an obligation to inform the data subject at that time.[45]

Exception to notifying data subject

Even if the risk is high, communication to the data subject is not required if:

- The personal data impacted by the breach was safeguarded via appropriate technical and organisational protection measures, in particular if such measures rendered the personal data unintelligible to any person who is not authorised to access it, i.e. encryption;
- Mitigation measures were taken after the data breach to the extent that the high risk is unlikely to materialise;
- It would involve disproportionate effort to inform each data subject; in such cases there shall be a public communication or similar measure whereby the data subjects are informed in an equally effective manner.

Note that such determination should form part of a risk assessment that must take place after the breach occurred. If the controller wishes to rely on an exception, the controller needs to be in a position to demonstrate to the supervisory authority that one or more of the exceptions are met. Furthermore, if the controller makes the decision to not notify data subjects and the supervisory authority finds this was the wrong decision, the controller may be fined.[46] Where it is unclear whether the data subject should be notified, it is best practice to consult with the supervisory authority.

6. Requirement to Document

Regardless of whether the controller has an obligation to notify or not, the controller must still document any and all personal data breaches, such documentation must include:[47]

---

44 Art 11 GDPR.

45 Guidelines on Personal data breach notification under Regulation 2016/679, at 21-22; also see Art 11(2). GDPR.

46 See Ch 19 on liability.

47 Art 33(4) GDPR; also see Guidelines on Personal data breach notification under Regulation 2016/679, at 27.

- Facts relating to the personal data breach, including:
  - o Causes of the breach
  - o What happened when the breach occurred?
  - o The personal data affected by the breach
- Consequences of the personal data breach;
- Remedial action taken vis a vis the personal data breach;
- Reasons for the decisions taken in response to the personal data breach, including:
  - o Why a breach was notified to the supervisory authority or not
  - o Why a breach was notified to data subjects or not
  - o Justification for any delays in notification

This is normally retained in what has become commonly known as a *data breach log*. This documentation may be used by the supervisory authority to verify compliance with the notification obligations. Thus, controllers must ensure that they continue to document how personal data breaches are dealt with. Even if notification took place, the controller must continue to document any relevant information relating to the personal data breach, including any remedial action taken.[48] This forms part of the accountability principle.

The period for which such documentation should be retained is not specified. If the documentation contains any personal data, it must follow normal retention procedures (storage limitation principle). To ensure continuing compliance with the accountability procedure, documentation with personal data redacted should ideally be retained indefinitely.[49]

Even if it may not be likely to result in a risk and the supervisory authority was not notified, a breach must be documented; the WP29 gave an example of a power failure in a company, resulting in newsletters being unable to be sent out. The WP29 noted that even if the breach may not seem like it caused a risk – it is important to assess all consequences of the breach as it may require notification, particularly in the instance of ransomware.

According to the Irish Data Protection Commission over 4,000 data breaches were reported between May and December 2018.[50]

---

48 Art 33(5) GDPR.

49 See Guidelines on Personal data breach notification under Regulation 2016/679, at 27.

50 Data Protection Commission, Annual Report, 25 May – 31 December 2018, at 5.

Further discussion

Article 29 Working Party, Guidelines on Personal data breach notification under Regulation 2016/679.

Article 29 Working Party, Opinion 03/2014 on Personal Data Breach Notification.

PART 3

TRANSFERRING PERSONAL DATA

Guide: When Can Personal Data be Transferred?

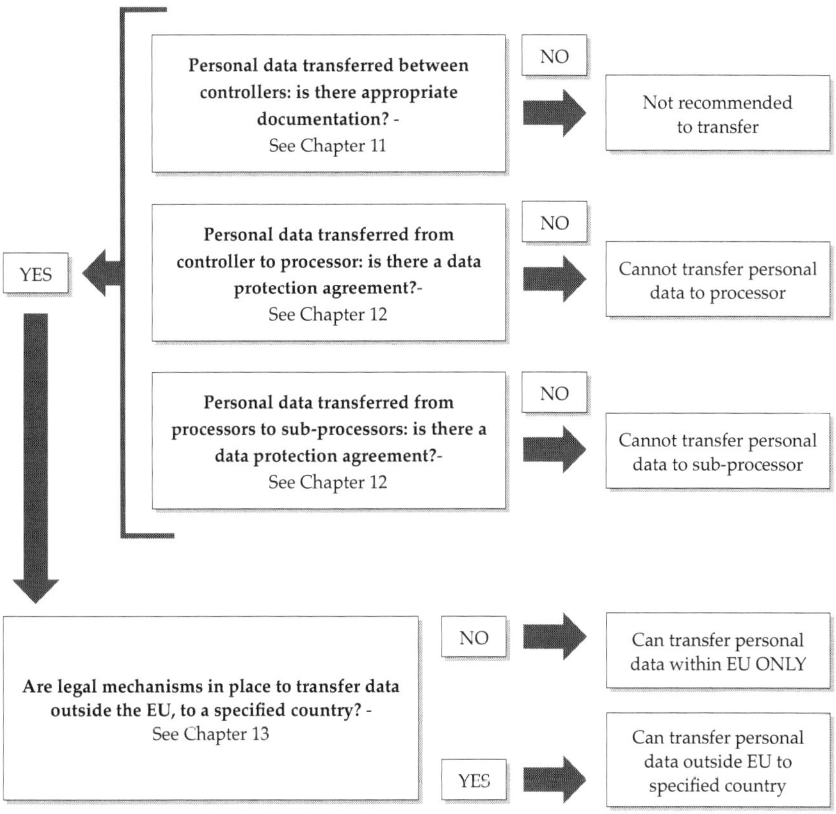

Chapter 11

Transferring Personal Data Between Controllers

This chapter deals with transfers from controller to controller. Personal data can be transferred from a controller to another controller in two capacities:

1. Where the other controller is a joint controller;
2. Where the other controller is a separate controller.

1. Joint Controller

In accordance with Article 26 GDPR, where a controller is transferring data to a "joint controller", there must be "a transparent manner" in which the respective responsibilities for compliance with the GDPR are made clear. This is generally done via an agreement.

As an example for such a "transparent manner" s 79 of the DPA 2018 (re law enforcement) requires a written agreement in this case. Section 79(2) of the DPA 2018 states that such agreement must include:

- A determination of the respective responsibilities of the joint controllers regarding how a data subject may exercise their rights (rights outlined in Chapter 8);
- In particular, a determination of the respective duties of joint controllers regarding the provision of the data subject's right to be informed (rights outlined in Chapter 8).

Furthermore, s 79(2) of the DPA 2018 specifies that the agreement may indicate a single point of contact for any matters relating to the processing activity concerning the data subject.

In addition, the GDPR and WP29 detail other items that are recommended to be contained in any such agreement:

- Details on which controller has the responsibility to take the lead for complying with the obligations for data breach notification (breach notification detailed in Chapter 10);[1]
- Process for carrying out data subject's rights between controllers, i.e. where a data subject requests erasure or rectification, such erasure or rectification must be carried out on the respective data held by both controllers.[2]

Note that where a request is received from a data subject, the controller needs to pass on the message to any processor or controller that has received the data "unless it proves impossible or involves disproportionate effort".[3] If appropriate agreements are in place and the controller is aware of the data flow, it should not cause a disproportionate effort to inform joint controllers.

Where data was made public, and an erasure request was made, the controller must "take reasonable steps, including technical measures, to inform controllers which are processing the personal data that the data subject has requested the erasure". There is no exception for disproportionate effort in this instance.

Remember requirement for transparency: Article 26(2) GDPR states that the "essence" of an arrangement between joint controllers shall be made available to the data subject. Thus, the data subject must be aware of the joint controller situation. It must be clear for a data subject who the data controllers are. To simplify this, the joint controllers may designate a contact point for data subjects.[4] Note that regardless of who has responsibility for which obligations, the data subject must be able to exercise the rights detailed in Chapter 8 as against each of the controllers.[5]

1 Guidelines on Personal data breach notification under Regulation 2016/679, at 13.
2 Art 29 Working Party Guidelines on the right to data portability, adopted on 13 December 2016, at 6.
3 Art 19 GDPR.
4 Art 26(1) GDPR; DPA, s 79(2).
5 Art 26(3) GDPR.

2. Separate Controller

As provided in Chapter 2, where there is no joint determination on how and why to process personal data, the controllers are deemed separate controllers. The example was given of employers and tax authorities; both entities process employee data for different reasons. Separate controllers fulfil and satisfy all the data protection requirements separately. Thus, no agreement is required between two separate controllers. However, the requirement to inform other controllers where there is a data subject request remains, where appropriate.[6]

The need to transfer data to a separate controller is likely to arise in the context of the right to data portability. Note that in the context of the right to data portability, the initial data controller is not responsible for the receiving controller's compliance with data protection law.[7]

---

6 Art 19 GDPR; Art 17(2) GDPR.

7 See Ch 8, see also Art 29 Working Party Guidelines on the right to data portability, adopted on 13 December 2016, at 6.

Chapter 12

Transferring Personal Data to Processors / Sub-Processors

Relevant law: Recital 81 GDPR, Article 28–29 GDPR

This Chapter deals with the following transfers that may occur:

- Controller to processor / processor to controller;
- Processor to another processor (sub-processor), etc.

In order for any of the above transfers to take place, there must be an agreement in place. Article 28(3) GDPR states that any processing conducted by a processor must be governed by a "contract or other legal act" that is binding on the processor vis-a-vis the controller. Article 28(9) GDPR specifies that such a contract should be in writing, in hard copy or electronic form, between a controller and a processor for any such transfer to occur. This agreement between the controller and processor has become known as a Data Protection Agreement (DPA).

The obligation for a DPA to be in place rests on both the controller and processor. A processor may not process personal data without a DPA and the controller may not transfer data to a processor without a DPA. Lack of a DPA, or an imperfect DPA, may result in liability to both the controller and the processor.[1]

The same obligations for an agreement are placed on any further processors (also known as sub-processors), which are contracted by the initial processor, as shall be outlined below.

[1] See Ch 19.

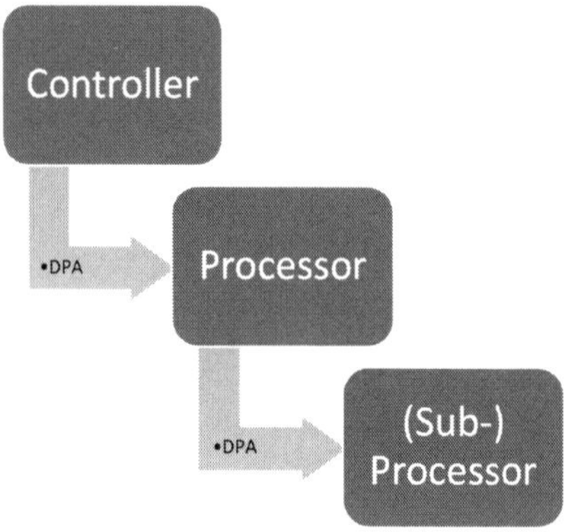

Data Protection Agreement (DPA)

As stated above, a DPA must be in writing to be valid, which includes electronic format.[2] A DPA can be presented in a variety of ways; it may be included as an addendum to a contract, the terms may be incorporated within the contract or it may form part of separate privacy terms.

Article 28(3) GDPR outlines ten mandatory terms that must be contained within a DPA. Such terms do not need to be written in any particular order, as long as the terms are clearly contained within the DPA. The ten terms are:

1. Details of the data processing activity;
2. Duties of the controller;
3. Processor only processes data on documented instructions, including re transfers outside the EU;
4. Duty of confidentiality;
5. Security;
6. Transferring data to other processors (sub-processors);
7. Duties of processor re data subject requests;
8. Duties of processor re compliance;
9. Retention;
10. Duties of processor re inspections and audits.

Due to the importance of these terms, a direct quote from Article 28(3) GDPR is provided vis-a-vis each required term, along with commentary on how it is usually dealt with in a DPA.

---

[2] Art 28(9) GDPR; DPA 2018, s 80(1)(a).

1	*Details of the data processing activity* Article 28(3) GDPR, first paragraph: "...subject-matter and duration of the processing, the nature and purpose of the processing, the type of personal data and categories of data subjects..."	A DPA will usually refer back to the underlying contract between the parties regarding the subject matter, where the specific tasks and responsibilities of the processor are outlined. The duration is generally stated to be for the duration of such contract. In addition, the information is usually provided within an Annex to the DPA, where for each type of personal data, the nature and purpose of processing is provided, as well as the category of data subject covered by that type and retention period. For example: <table><tr><td>Type</td><td>Email addresses</td></tr><tr><td>Nature of processing</td><td>Processing emails by sending out personalised emails at designated times in bulk</td></tr><tr><td>Purpose</td><td>Marketing</td></tr><tr><td>Categories</td><td>Current and potential customers of controller</td></tr><tr><td>Retention (duration of processing)</td><td>Until contract terminated or individuals unsubscribe</td></tr></table>
2	*Duties of the controller* Article 28(3) GDPR, first paragraph: "...the obligations and rights of the controller..."	This is generally not a very extensive clause within a DPA and will at the very minimum state that the controller accepts that they are the controller in line with the definition in Article 4 GDPR.

3	*Processor only processes data on documented instructions, including re transfers outside the EU* Article 28(3)(a) GDPR: The processor "processes the personal data only on documented instructions from the controller, including with regard to transfers of personal data to a third country or an international organisation, unless required to do so by Union or Member State law to which the processor is subject; in such a case, the processor shall inform the controller of that legal requirement before processing, unless that law prohibits such information on important grounds of public interest;"	A DPA must state that the processor will only process personal data on instructions from the controller; this is usually a term within one of the initial clauses of the DPA. The controller must provide instructions within the DPA on the circumstances in which transfers to third countries/ international organisations would be permissible. There may be a clause stating that transfers outside the EU are permissible to entities within the processors corporate group and to authorised sub-processors. Any such clause would also provide how this transfer outside the EU would be permissible under one of the safety mechanisms outlined in Chapter 13.
4	*Duty of confidentiality* Article 28(3)(b) GDPR: The processor "ensures that persons authorised to process the personal data have committed themselves to confidentiality or are under an appropriate statutory obligation of confidentiality"	Employees of the processor (or other people authorised) must be under a duty of confidentiality clause, usually found within their employment contract. Confirmation that such a clause is in place should be stated in the DPA.
5	*Security* Article 28(3)(c) GDPR: The processor "takes all measures required pursuant to Article 32"	A DPA must state that the processor has an appropriate level of security proportionate to the risk; details of the processor's security measures must be provided in detail and are generally provided within an Annex to a DPA. Any alterations to such security measures must be notified to the controller.

		Article 28(1) GDPR specifically states that the controller can only use processors providing sufficient guarantees to implement appropriate technical and organisational measures so as to meet the requirements of the GDPR. Furthermore, Recital 81 GDPR further emphasises that the processor must ensure security of processing. Article 28(5) GDPR states that adherence to an approved code of conduct or approved certification mechanism may go towards proof of such security measures. Therefore, it is beneficial for the processor to state within the DPA any adherence to such.
6	*Transferring data to other processors/ sub-processors* Article 28(3)(d) GDPR: The processor "respects the conditions referred to in paragraphs 2 and 4 for engaging another processor"	Article 28(2) GDPR states that the processor cannot engage another processor without specific prior or general written authorisation of the controller. General authorisation is usually provided when a processor provides a list of their sub-processes with an Annex to the DPA. Where general authorisation is provided, the processor must inform the controller of any intended changes concerning the addition or replacement of sub-processors, thereby giving the controller the opportunity to object to such changes. Article 28(4) GDPR states that the processor must impose the same obligations on any of their sub-processors as were imposed on them via the DPA with the controller. It particularly emphasises that the processor needs to ensure any sub-processor has appropriate security measures. Furthermore, it states that where the sub-processor fails to fulfil its obligations, the processor shall remain fully liable to the controller for the performance of sub-processor's obligations.

		This information is generally contained within a clause entitled sub-processors, stating that: • The processor will not engage another processor (sub-processor) without consent from the controller. If details of current sub-processors are provided in an Annex to the DPA, then such consent is provided via the DPA to the sub-processors listed in the Annex and the processor shall notify the controller of any changes to the Annex to enable the controller to object if needed • The processor must enforce the same DPA obligations on any further processor (sub-processor)
7	*Duties of processor re data subject requests* Article 28(3)(e) GDPR: The processor, "taking into account the nature of the processing, assists the controller by appropriate technical and organisational measures, insofar as this is possible, for the fulfilment of the controller's obligation to respond to requests for exercising the data subject's rights laid down in Chapter III"	The processor will aid the controller with responding to data subject requests, including: • How and what information is to be provided to the data subject • Enabling the data subject to access their personal data • Enabling the data subject to rectify their personal data • Enabling the data subject to erase their personal data • Enabling the data subject to restrict the processing of their personal data • Enabling the data subject to exercise their right to data portability • Enabling the data subject to object to processing and to automated individual decision making All the types of requests do not need to be listed within a DPA and reference to Chapter III is normal practice.

		It is also standard that there will be a separate clause that details what the processor should do when they receive a data subject request i.e. inform the controller of the data subject request.
8	*Duties of processor re compliance* Article 28(3)(f) GDPR: The processor "assists the controller in ensuring compliance with the obligations pursuant to Articles 32 to 36 taking into account the nature of processing and the information available to the processor"	This means that the processor will assist the controller in: • Maintaining appropriate levels of security (Article 32 GDPR) • Performing the relevant requirements when there is a personal data breach (Article 33-34 GDPR) • Conducting a data protection impact assessment (Article 35-36 GDPR) This obligation on the processor is largely one in which the processor must provide assistance in terms of the provision of information to the controller. Thereby the controller is in a position to request follow up information and perform the relevant obligations within Article 32 – 36 GDPR. The above does not need to be listed within the contract and reference to Article 32 to 36 in the DPA is common practice. A separate clause in the DPA is generally provided on security measures (see point on security above). However, any specific roles and responsibilities that the controller wishes to place on the processor must be contractually defined.
9	*Retention* Article 28(3) (g) GDPR: The processor "at the choice of the controller, deletes or returns all the personal data to the controller after the end of the provision of services relating to processing, and deletes existing copies unless Union or Member State law requires storage of the personal data"	It is imperative that the processor agrees to retention periods for the personal data.[3]

[3] Recital 81 GDPR further emphasises this.

10	*Duties of processor re inspections & audits* Article 28(3)(h) GDPR: The processor "makes available to the controller all information necessary to demonstrate compliance with the obligations laid down in this Article [28 GDPR] and allow for and contribute to audits, including inspections, conducted by the controller or another auditor mandated by the controller" Article 28(3), last paragraph GDPR: "With regard to point (h)...the processor shall immediately inform the controller if, in its opinion, an instruction infringes this Regulation or other Union or Member State data protection provisions."	This is usually a substantial clause within a DPA. It would generally detail: • When and how often audits may be conducted • Who should bear the cost of any audit • Time notice required to be provided to the processor prior to an audit • The time within which the processor has to provide information that is requested by the controller Furthermore, the clause shall provide that a processor has an obligation to notify the controller when the processor considers the controller's instructions to infringe the GDPR. Generally, all the duties of the processor are stated together within one clause in the DPA with several sub-sections.

The above ten items must be included within the DPA. As long as those items are specified, there is freedom to contract for additional terms. Generally, the following terms are also included within a DPA:

- Details of the respective data protection officers, or a contact point in the event a data protection issue arises, where applicable
- Distribution of liability, that may differ from Article 82 GDPR (see Chapter 19)

Furthermore, general contract terms may also be included, such as governing law, jurisdiction and a severability clause.

Instance where Processor Shall be Considered Controller

The processor may only act on documented instructions from the controller.[4] In accordance with Article 28(10) GDPR, the processor shall be considered to be a controller in respect of that processing where the processor acts outside the controller's instructions. Thus, where the processor determines the 'why' and 'how' of personal data processing, as detailed in Chapter 2, the processor is acting like a controller and will be treated like a controller. This means that the processor will have the obligations and liabilities of the controller.

Transferring Data from Processor to Another Processor (Sub-Processor)

The processor may only transfer personal data to another processor where the controller has authorised or given instructions to do so.[5] Article 28(4) GDPR states that the processor must impose the same obligations on any of their sub-processors. Thus, the processor must ensure that an equivalent DPA is in place with their sub-processor, which contains at a minimum the terms included within their DPA with the controller. It does not need to be in the same format, and it may contain further provisions, within the bounds of what is permissible by law.

GDPR Obligations on the Processor

The following seven items are GDPR obligations that are directly stated as against the processor, *these are in addition to any obligations set out in a DPA* and are applicable regardless of whether or not they are specified within the DPA. The seven obligations are:

1	May only process on instructions from the controller (Article 28-29 GDPR)	The processor has a duty under Article 28 GDPR to enter into a DPA with a controller prior to commencing any processing operations on personal data (see above re DPA). Article 29 GDPR makes it very clear that any person acting under the authority of the controller or of the processor, who has access to personal data, shall not process that data except on instructions from the controller, unless required to do so by law.

4 Art 28(3)(a) GDPR.
5 Art 28(2) GDPR.

2	May be required to retain a Data Inventory (Article 30(2) GDPR)	The criteria under which a record of processing must be maintained is the same for processors as for controllers (outlined in Chapter 9). However, the content of the record is slightly different for processors and includes: • The name and contact details of the processor and each controller on behalf of which the processor is acting, and where applicable, the respective representatives and the data protection officer • The categories of processing carried out on behalf of each controller • Where transfers outside the EU occurred • A general description of the technical and organisational measures in place Such records must be in writing, including in electronic format.[6]
3	Must cooperate with supervisory authority (Article 31 GDPR)	This provides that the processor must cooperate with the supervisory authority where required to do so.
4	Must ensure security of processing (Article 32 GDPR)	The requirements for security of processing in Article 32 GDPR are the same as that for the controller (see Chapter 9). Furthermore, Article 32(4) GDPR emphasises that processors must take steps to ensure that persons under their authority may only access personal data on instructions from the controller, unless otherwise required by law. This emphasises the need for processors to ensure any processor/ sub-processor they use maintains appropriate security measures.
5	Must cooperate when a data breach occurs (Article 33(2) GDPR)	While the controller has the ultimate duty to notify and document any data breach, Article 33(2) GDPR states that the processor must notify the controller, whose data may have been affected, without undue delay after becoming aware of a personal data breach. Where there are multiple controllers whose data may have been affected, all controllers must be notified.

6 Art 30(3) GDPR.

		The GDPR does not provide for any express time limit within which the processor needs to alert the controller. WP29 recommended that the controller is notified promptly and provided with further information as more information becomes available.[7] The DPA should specify how this notification should be met, this may include early notification within 72 hours. Such DPA could also provide the processor with authorisation to perform the relevant notification requirements to the supervisory authority and the data subject.
6	May require Data Protection Officer and or Data Protection Representative	The processor has an obligation to have a data protection officer and or data protection representative where the criteria within Chapter 15 and 16 are met.
7	May only transfer personal data to third countries if safeguards (Chapter V GDPR)	See Chapter 13 for safeguards that may be utilised when transferring data outside the EU. However, such transfer may still only occur under the instruction of the controller, as should be detailed within a DPA.

Note that these obligations are applicable even if the controller is established outside the EU and not subject to the GDPR.[8] If the processor is caught by the GDPR, as detailed in Chapter 3, the processor must comply with the above obligations, regardless of where the controller is established.

Standard DPA clauses

Article 28(6) GDPR states that standard clauses that are either adopted directly by the EU Commission,[9] or by a supervisory authority,[10] may be used for the DPA. As of yet no such clauses have been adopted.[11] These clauses may also form part of a code of conduct, or certification scheme, although currently no schemes have yet been approved.[12]

7 Art 29 Working Party, Guidelines on Personal data breach notification under Regulation 2016/679, at 13-14.

8 EDPB Guidelines 3/2018 on the territorial scope of the GDPR (Article 3)–Version for public consultation, Adopted on 16 November 2018, at 11.

9 Art 28(7) GDPR.

10 Art 28(8) GDPR.

11 As at February 2019.

12 See Ch 17.

Chapter 13

Transferring Personal Data Outside the EU

The GDPR provides for the free flow of personal data within the EU, subject to compliance with the relevant obligations.[1] Note that the GDPR is a text with EEA relevance,[2] thus it is also applicable for Iceland, Lichtenstein and Norway. Therefore, the free flow of data is also permissible with EEA countries. As noted in the introduction, any reference to the EU or EU Member States should also be taken as reference to the EEA.

For personal data to be transferred outside the EU or to an international organisation, there must be an additional *safeguard mechanism* to ensure that the obligations contained within the GDPR

1 Art 1 GDPR.

2 See European Economic Area, Decision of the EEA Joint Committee, No 154/2018 of 6 July 2018 amending Annex XI (Electronic communication, audiovisual services and information society) and Protocol 37 (containing the list provided for in Art 101) to the EEA Agreement [2018/1022]; See also Art 7(a), Agreement on the European Economic Area (OJ No L 1, 3.1.1994, p 3), as amended.

are guaranteed.[3] When personal data is transferred outside the EU, this is known as a transfer to a "third country". As safeguard mechanisms are also required for transfers to international organisations,[4] any reference herein to transfers to a third country shall also be taken to govern transfers to international organisations. There are seven safeguard mechanisms via which personal data may be transferred to a third country:[5]

1. Adequacy decision (detailed below);
2. Binding Corporate Rules (detailed below);
3. Standard data protection clauses (detailed below);
4. Legally binding and enforceable instrument between public authorities or bodies (detailed below);
5. An approved code of conduct (together with binding and enforceable commitments as to safeguards) – see Chapter 17;
6. An approved certification mechanism (together with binding and enforceable commitments as to safeguards) – see Chapter 17;
7. Authorised contractual clauses or administrative arrangements (must be authorised by relevant supervisory authority) (detailed below).

There are several derogations that may be utilised to transfer personal data outside the EU where none of the seven safeguard mechanisms may be utilised, which shall also be detailed below. In accordance with Article 44 GDPR, any transfers outside the EU must also meet all other relevant obligations within the GDPR, including the requirement for a legal basis. In any instance, a processor may not transfer personal data, regardless of the safeguard mechanism utilised, unless the processor has been authorised to do so by the controller.[6]

Note that there is provision within s 37 of the DPA 2018 for Ireland to restrict data to third countries without an adequacy decision; no country has as of yet been restricted. Further note that this does not cover personal data transfer within the context of criminal proceedings.[7]

---

3 Art 44 GDPR.

4 Art 4(26) GDPR defines international organisation as: "an organisation and its subordinate bodies governed by public international law, or any other body which is set up by, or on the basis of, an agreement between two or more countries".

5 See ch V GDPR.

6 Art 28(3)(a) GDPR.

7 See DPA 2018, s 96.

Adequacy Decision

Article 45(1) GDPR provides that a transfer of personal data to outside the EU may take place on the basis of an adequacy decision made by the EU Commission.[8] Article 45(9) GDPR provides that decisions adopted by the EU Commission under Article 25(6) of Directive 95/46/EC shall remain in force until amended, replaced or repealed by a Commission decision under Article 45 GDPR. The EU Commission has recognised the following countries/territories as providing adequate protection:

- Andorra[9]
- Argentina[10]
- Canada[11]
- Faroe Islands[12]
- Guernsey[13]
- Israel[14]
- Isle of Man[15]
- Japan[16]

---

8 Art 45(1) GDPR.

9 2010/625/EU: Commission Decision of 19 October 2010 pursuant to Directive 95/46/EC of the European Parliament and of the Council on the adequate protection of personal data in Andorra (notified under document C(2010) 7084) Text with EEA relevance OJ L 277, 21.10.2010.

10 2003/490/EC: Commission Decision of 30 June 2003 pursuant to Directive 95/46/EC of the European Parliament and of the Council on the adequate protection of personal data in Argentina (Text with EEA relevance) OJ L 168, 5.7.2003.

11 2002/2/EC: Commission Decision of 20 December 2001 pursuant to Directive 95/46/EC of the European Parliament and of the Council on the adequate protection of personal data provided by the Canadian Personal Information Protection and Electronic Documents Act (notified under document number C(2001) 4539) OJ L 2, 4.1.2002.

12 2010/146/: Commission Decision of 5 March 2010 pursuant to Directive 95/46/EC of the European Parliament and of the Council on the adequate protection provided by the Faeroese Act on processing of personal data (notified under document C(2010) 1130) (Text with EEA relevance) OJ L 58, 9.3.2010.

13 2003/821/EC: Commission Decision of 21 November 2003 on the adequate protection of personal data in Guernsey (Text with EEA relevance) (notified under document number C(2003) 4309) OJ L 308, 25.11.2003.

14 2011/61/EU: Commission Decision of 31 January 2011 pursuant to Directive 95/46/EC of the European Parliament and of the Council on the adequate protection of personal data by the State of Israel with regard to automated processing of personal data (notified under document C(2011) 332) (Text with EEA relevance) OJ L 27, 1.2.2011.

15 2004/411/EC: Commission Decision of 28 April 2004 on the adequate protection of personal data in the Isle of Man OJ L 151, 30.4.2004.

16 Commission Implementing Decision (EU) 2019/419 of 23 January 2019 pursuant to Regulation (EU) 2016/679 of the European Parliament and of the Council on the adequate protection of personal data by Japan under the Act on the Protection of Personal Information (Text with EEA relevance) OJ L 76, 19.3.2019, p 1–58.

- Jersey[17]
- New Zealand[18]
- Switzerland[19]
- Uruguay[20]
- United States of America (limited to the Privacy Shield framework, detailed below).

The EU Commission is required to monitor developments to ensure adequate protection continues to be provided.[21] Therefore, it is important to check that an adequacy decision has not been repealed due to future developments. Currently adequacy discussions are ongoing with South Korea.

Brexit

The UK has currently implemented the GDPR into their national law via their Data Protection Act, 2018 (c12). The Data Protection, Privacy and Electronic Communications (Amendments etc.) (EU Exit) Regulations 2019 was before the UK Parliament, which is part of the European Union (Withdrawal) Act 2018 but it was withdrawn from consideration.[22] Their act implementing the GDPR will also need to be amended. The EDPB has stated that if a no-deal Brexit occurs, the UK will be considered a third country for the purposes of the GDPR and one of the safeguard mechanisms for transfers outside of the EU will need to be used.[23] In this instance, where companies have Binding Corporate Rules (detailed below) and they detail the UK supervisory authority as the lead supervisory authority, then this will need to be changed to an EU

17 2008/393/EC: Commission Decision of 8 May 2008 pursuant to Directive 95/46/EC of the European Parliament and of the Council on the adequate protection of personal data in Jersey (notified under document number C(2008) 1746) (Text with EEA relevance) OJ L 138, 28.5.2008.

18 2013/65/EU: Commission Implementing Decision of 19 December 2012 pursuant to Directive 95/46/EC of the European Parliament and of the Council on the adequate protection of personal data by New Zealand (notified under document C(2012) 9557) (Text with EEA relevance) OJ L 28, 30.1.2013.

19 2000/518/EC: Commission Decision of 26 July 2000 pursuant to Directive 95/46/EC of the European Parliament and of the Council on the adequate protection of personal data provided in Switzerland (notified under document number C(2000) 2304) (Text with EEA relevance.) OJ L 215, 25.8.2000.

20 2012/484/EU: Commission Implementing Decision of 21 August 2012 pursuant to Directive 95/46/EC of the European Parliament and of the Council on the adequate protection of personal data by the Eastern Republic of Uruguay with regard to automated processing of personal data (notified under document C(2012) 5704) (Text with EEA relevance) OJ L 227, 23.8.2012.

21 Art 45(4) GDPR.

22 This would have brought the GDPR into domestic UK law when Brexit occurs.

23 EDPB, Information note on data transfers under the GDPR in the event of a no-deal Brexit, adopted 12 February 2019.

supervisory authority.[24] The UK government has made it clear that they want an adequacy decision.[25] The Information Commissioner's Office regularly updates information on the situation if a no deal Brexit arises.[26]

Privacy Shield

Note that the validity of the Privacy Shield, as adopted under Directive 95/46/EC, is being referred to the EU courts by the Irish High Court.[27]

The EU-US Privacy Shield decision was adopted on 12 July 2016 and the Privacy Shield framework became operational on 1 August 2016.[28] The Commission must annually review whether the findings related to the adequacy of personal data protection ensured by the US decision vis-a-vis the Privacy Shield are still valid.[29] The first review took place in 2017, with a report being published that determined that the Privacy Shield continues to provide adequate data protection.[30] Likewise a report on the second review was published in 2018 with the same determination.[31] The EU-US Privacy Shield provides for a number of principles,

---

24 EDPB, Information note on BCRs for companies which have ICO as BCR Lead Supervisory Authority, adopted 12 February 2019.

25 The progress of the UK's negotiations on EU withdrawal: Data, available at https://publications.parliament.uk/pa/cm201719/cmselect/cmexeu/1317/131702.htm.

26 Last updated December 2018, see Information Commissioner's Office, International data transfers, at https://ico.org.uk/for-organisations/data-protection-and-brexit/data-protection-if-there-s-no-brexit-deal/the-gdpr/international-data-transfers/.

27 The *Data Protection Commissioner v Facebook Ireland Limited & anor* [2017] IEHC 545 (known as 'Schrems II'); Furthermore, the Supreme Court has agreed to hear an appeal of the High Court decision, which may impact such referral: *Data Protection Commissioner & anor v Facebook Ireland Limited & anor* [2018] IESC 38

28 Commission Implementing Decision (EU) 2016/1250 of 12 July 2016 pursuant to Directive 95/46/EC of the European Parliament and of the Council on the adequacy of the protection provided by the EU-U.S. Privacy Shield (notified under document C(2016) 4176) (Text with EEA relevance) C/2016/4176, OJ L 207, 1.8.2016 (Privacy Shield Decision)

29 Recital 145, Privacy Shield Decision

30 European Commission, Brussels, 18.10.2017, COM(2017) 611 final, Report from the Commission to the European Parliament and the Council on the first annual review of the functioning of the EU–U.S. Privacy Shield {SWD(2017) 344 final}

31 European Commission, Brussels, 19.12.2018, COM(2018) 860 final, Report From the Commission to the European Parliament and the Council on the second annual review of the functioning of the EU-U.S. Privacy Shield {SWD(2018) 497 final}. See also European Data Protection Board, EU–U.S. Privacy Shield–Second Annual Joint Review, adopted on 22 January 2019

where transfers to entities that comply with these principles are permissible (Privacy Shield principles).

The US Department of Commerce maintains a website, which may be found at www.privacyshield.gov, with a list of all entities that have self-certified to the Privacy Shield (the Privacy Shield List). It is voluntary for entities to enter the Privacy Shield and self-certify. Once an entity self-certifies and informs the US Department of Commerce and declares their commitment to adhere to the Privacy Shield principles, the entity must be fully compliant with the Privacy Shield principles. The entity that self-certifies must annually affirm to the US Department of Commerce the commitment to continue to apply the principles. An entity will be removed from the list of self-certified entities where the entity:

- Voluntarily withdraws;
- Failed to complete the annual re-certification;
- Persistently failed to comply with the principles.

When removed from the list, the entity must return or delete the personal data that was obtained from the EU or provide adequate protection via another GDPR transfer mechanism. Entities removed from the list may not continue to claim that they are Privacy Shield compliant.

The EU Commission has flagged that there is a tendency for companies to publicly declare that they self-certify to the Privacy Shield, before the certification has been finalised by the Department of Finance.[32] Thus, in order to transfer personal data to an entity within the US under the Privacy Shield, the controller/processor should ensure that the entity is listed on the Privacy Shield List.

Privacy shield principles

The entity that wishes to self-certify to the Privacy Shield must abide by all Privacy Shield principles; these principles shall be referred to below, but shall not be dealt with substantively. The Privacy Shield principles include seven core principles, and sixteen supplemental principles. The seven core principles are:

32 Annual Review EU–U.S. Privacy Shield (SWD(2017) 344 final), at 4

	Principle	Details
1	Notice	This is essentially the right to inform and the requirement for transparency[33]
2	Choice	This requires the controller to offer data subjects the opportunity to opt out of the controller disclosing their data to a third party and to opt out of the controller using their data for purposes that are different to what was initially disclosed. In the case of sensitive personal data, express consent is required in those situations, rather than simply an opportunity to opt out. These requirements are not mandatory where the transfer is to a processor as it is assumed there will be a DPA or equivalent in place.
3	Accountability for onward transfer	Detailed below.
4	Security	This is similar to the security requirements under the GDPR.[34]
5	Data integrity and purpose limitation	This incorporates the principles of purpose limitation, data minimisation, accuracy, storage limitation, integrity and confidentiality.[35]
6	Access	This provides for the right to access, rectify and erasure.[36]
7	Recourse, enforcement and liability	This requires two main items: • A mechanism to verify compliance with the principles • The entity to respond promptly to data protection enquiries Annex I of the Privacy Shield provides the terms under which Privacy Shield organizations are obligated to arbitrate claims, pursuant to this principle. This arises where the data subject has invoked binding arbitration and where the data subject claims that there has been a violation of the principles.

The Privacy Shield also contains sixteen supplemental principles on:

33 See Ch 7 and Ch 8.
34 See Ch 9.
35 See Ch 7.
36 See Ch 8.

1. Sensitive data	10. Obligatory contracts for onward transfers (detailed below)
2. Journalistic exceptions	11. Dispute resolution and enforcement
3. Secondary liability[37]	12. Choice
4. Performing due diligence and conducting audits	13. Travel information
5. The role of the data protection authorities	14. Pharmaceutical and medical products
6. Access	15. Public record and publicly available information
7. Self-certification	16. Access requests by public authorities
8. Verification	
9. Human resource data	

Onward transfers

Core Principle 3 provides for the accountability of onward transfers, where the onward transfer is from a Privacy Shield entity to a controller or a processor. Onward transfers are only permissible from the Privacy Shield entity (the entity that self-certified to the Privacy Shield) to a *controller* (known as a recipient) where there is a contract in place that contains the following details:

- Data may only be processed for limited and specified purposes consistent with the consent provided by the individual;
- The recipient will provide the same level of protection as the principles;
- The recipient will notify the organisation if it makes a determination that it can no longer adhere to the principles;
- Where the recipient determines that it can no longer adhere to the principles, the recipient will cease processing or take other reasonable and appropriate steps to remediate.

Onward transfers are only permissible from the Privacy Shield entity to a *processor/sub-processor* (known as an agent), where all the below are fulfilled:

- Personal data is only transferred to the agent for limited and specified purposes;

[37] Entities that only transmit, route, switch, or store information on behalf of another organisation, such as telecommunication carriers, are not liable under the Privacy Shield Principles

- The agent provides at least the same level of protection as is required by the principles;
- The Privacy Shield entity takes reasonable and appropriate steps to ensure that the agent processes the personal information transferred in a manner consistent with the principles;
- The Privacy Shield entity requires the agent to notify them if the agent makes a determination that it can no longer adhere to the principles;
- Upon notice, the Privacy Shield entity takes reasonable and appropriate steps to stop and remediate unauthorised processing by the agent;
- The US Department of Commerce may request a summary or copy of the privacy provisions within the contract between the Privacy Shield entity and the agent.

In the context of an onward transfer to a processor (agent), Principle 7 states that the Privacy Shield entity remains responsible for the agent's compliance with the principles. As such, the Privacy Shield entity shall be liable if the agent breaches the principles, unless it can be proven that the Privacy Shield entity is not responsible for such breach.

In addition, Supplemental Principle 10 of the Privacy Shield provides further information regarding onward transfers:

- A DPA, as required under Article 28 GDPR (see Chapter 12), is still required where a Privacy Shield entity is receiving personal data as a processor/sub-processor from an EU entity;
- A contract as provided in Core Principle 3 may not be required where the transfer is between two controllers in a "controlled group" of entities and a different method to transfer data is used that is permissible under the GDPR, such as Binding Corporate Rules. In this instance the Privacy Shield entity remains responsible for compliance with the principles;
- Where the transfer is to a controller, the receiving controller need not be a member of the Privacy Shield; however, there must be a contract in place with such controller that provides the same level of protection as is provided within the Privacy Shield, apart from the independent recourse mechanism in Core Principle 7.

Binding Corporate Rules

Relevant Law: Recital 108–110 GDPR; Article 47 GDPR

Binding Corporate Rules (BCRs) may be used by a group of entities engaged in a joint economic activity, including their employees.[38] In order to utilise BCRs, the supervisory authority must approve the BCRs.[39] The process for approval shall differ between Member States.[40] Some Member States may require applicants to list the individual transfers that will take place from their jurisdiction to third countries. Furthermore, there is a consistent notification obligation on the entities that utilise BCRs:

- Any update to the BCRs must be notified; the notification must be immediate where:
    - o The change would affect the level of the protection offered by the BCRs, i.e. will be detrimental to the rights of the data subject, or;
    - o The change would significantly affect the BCRs, i.e. the extent to which the BCRs are binding.

  For other modifications, a communication once a year is required
- The Privacy Shield Ombudsperson in the US may need to be notified of the BCRs where the Privacy Shield is certified to.

Content of BCRs

The following are the terms that must be included in BCRs:[41]

BCRs details	• The structure and contact details of the group using the BCRs and a list of the entities using the BCRs • The data transfers that will take place and what third countries the personal data will be transferred to • The categories of personal data, the type of processing and the purposes for the processing and the type of data subjects that are impacted • How the BCRs are binding (details about approval from the supervisory authority and how the BCRs are enforced internally within the group)

38 Art 47(1)(a) GDPR
39 As part of this process the BCRs are also referred to the EDPB in accordance with Arts 63 and 64 GDPR.
40 No details within DPA 2018.
41 Art 47(2) GDPR

GDPR compliance	• The application of the data protection principles (see Chapter 7) • Mechanisms within the group to ensure compliance with the BCRs, including audits and remedial actions where applicable – any verification needs to be communicated to the DPO or person monitoring compliance • Data protection training for individuals that have permanent or regular access to personal data
Data subject rights	• BCRs must expressly provide for the rights of the data subject regarding the processing of their personal data[42] (see Chapter 8), including informing the data subject about the BCRs via the duty to inform • Must specify that there is a right to lodge a complaint on the face of the BCRs for a breach of the rules as a whole by any member of the group • Both the BCRs and the way to complain and seek a remedy for a breach of the rules should be easily accessible for the data subject[43] • Individuals are always entitled to bring a claim for breach of their rights under the BCRs before the supervisory authority and/or the courts without first having exhausted the company's internal complaint or alternative dispute resolution systems • Provide details on the complaint procedure; all BCRs should include a defined timeframe for the internal complaint procedure which is not expected to exceed two months[44] • *Note* WP29 stated that some companies have decided not to include these details on data subject rights in the core document of the BCRs but instead set the rights out in a separate document.[45] In those cases where the rights are in a separate document they should be made transparent and easily accessible to any data subject to whom the data processing relates

42 Art 47(1)(b) GDPR.

43 Art 47(2)(g) GDPR.

44 Art 29 Working Party, Working Document setting up a table with the elements and principles to be found in Binding Corporate Rules, As last Revised and Adopted on 6 February 2018, at 12.

45 Working Document WP 74: Transfers of personal data to third countries: Applying Art 26 (2) of the EU Data Protection Directive to Binding Corporate Rules for International Data Transfers, adopted on 3 June 2003.

Dealing with the supervisory authority	• Mechanisms for reporting and recording changes to the rules and reporting those changes to the supervisory authority • The cooperation mechanisms with the supervisory authority, including making compliance verifications available
Liability	• Must nominate an entity within the EU who accepts liability for any breaches of the rules by any member of the group outside of the EU.[46] WP29 envisaged that in most cases it would be the headquarters of the group, if EU based, that would accept liability.[47] WP29 noted that where it is not possible to place liability on a particular entity, the BCRs can place the liability on multiple members[48] • Where data subjects can demonstrate that they have suffered damage and establish facts which show it is likely that the damage has occurred because of the breach of BCRs, it will be for the member of the group in Europe that accepted liability to prove that no breach occurred or that the accused entity was not responsible for the breach[49] (reversal of burden of proof)
Miscellaneous	• Tasks of the data protection officer, where applicable, or other persons in charge of monitoring compliance

Note that the EU Commission may provide further specifications on the format and procedure for data transfers in future decisions.[50] Regarding the format, the BCRs should generally:

- Be in a single document;[51] however, sometimes the data subject rights are provided separately for ease of reference for data subjects;
- Be consistent with the wording and definitions of the GDPR.

46 Art 47(2)(f) GDPR.

47 Working Document WP 74: Transfers of personal data to third countries: Applying Art 26 (2) of the EU Data Protection Directive to Binding Corporate Rules for International Data Transfers, adopted on 3 June 2003.

48 Art 29 Working Party, Working Document setting up a table with the elements and principles to be found in Binding Corporate Rules, As last Revised and Adopted on 6 February 2018.

49 Art 47(2)(f) GDPR.

50 Art 47(3) GDPR.

51 Working Document WP 74: Transfers of personal data to third countries: Applying Art 26(2) of the EU Data Protection Directive to Binding Corporate Rules for International Data Transfers, adopted on 3 June 2003

According to the Irish Data Protection Commission 2018 report, 11 BCRs were in the process of being approved.[52]

Standard Contractual Clauses

Note that the validity of the SCCs referred to below, as adopted under Directive 95/46/EC, are being referred to the EU courts by the Irish High Court.[53]

The purpose of Standard Contractual Clauses (SCCs) is to provide sufficient safeguards to enable a transfer of personal data to take place to a third country not covered by an adequacy decision or other safeguard mechanism. Article 46(2) GDPR provides that SCCs may be adopted via two methods:

- SCCs adopted by an EU Commission decision in accordance with the examination procedure in Article 93(2) GDPR;[54]
- SCCs adopted by a supervisory authority and approved by an EU Commission decision pursuant to the examination procedure referred to in Article 93(2) GDPR.[55]

Article 46(5) GDPR provides that decisions adopted by the EU Commission on the basis of Article 26(4) of Directive 95/46/EC shall remain in force until amended, replaced or repealed via an EU Commission decision under Article 46(2) GDPR.

The decisions adopted under Directive 95/46/EC are still in use.[56] Two decisions were adopted vis-a-vis a transfer from a controller within the EU to a controller outside the EU:

52 Data Protection Commission, *Annual Report*, 25 May–31 December 2018, at 73.

53 The *Data Protection Commissioner v Facebook Ireland Limited & anor* [2017] IEHC 545 (known as 'Schrems II'); Furthermore, the Supreme Court has agreed to hear an appeal of the High Court decision, which may impact such referral: *Data Protection Commissioner & anor v Facebook Ireland Limited & anor* [2018] IESC 38.

54 Art 46(2)(c) GDPR.

55 Art 46(2)(d) GDPR.

56 Situation as at February 2019.

- Decision 2001/497/EC, [57] as amended by Article 1 of Decision 2004/915/EC (Set I SCCs);[58]
- Decision 2004/915/EC (Set II SCCs).

One decision remains valid vis-a-vis a transfer from a controller within the EU to a processor outside the EU:

- Decision 2010/87/EU (SCC(P)s),[59] replacing Decision 2002/16/EC.[60]

All the SCCs refer to the concept of a data exporter and data importer, where the data exporter is the entity that transfers the data outside the EU, and the data importer is the entity that receives the data from the EU.

All the obligations provided in the SCCs shall not be detailed here; however, the key obligations placed on the data importer are the same as that normally placed on a controller, including security, purpose limitation, restriction of onward transfers, ensuring data subject rights of access, erasure, rectification and objection. Regarding purpose limitation, the data importer may only process data for the purpose specified within the SCCs, as filled in by the parties.

Controller to controller

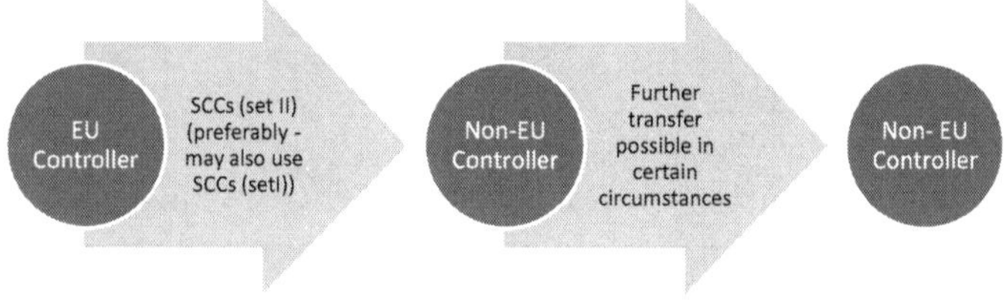

[57] 2001/497/EC: Commission Decision of 15 June 2001 on standard contractual clauses for the transfer of personal data to third countries, under Directive 95/46/EC (Text with EEA relevance) (notified under document number C(2001) 1539) OJ L 181, 4.7.2001.

[58] 2004/915/EC: Commission Decision of 27 December 2004 amending Decision 2001/497/EC as regards the introduction of an alternative set of standard contractual clauses for the transfer of personal data to third countries (notified under document number C(2004) 5271) OJ L 385, 29.12.2004.

[59] 2010/87/EU: Commission Decision of 5 February 2010 on standard contractual clauses for the transfer of personal data to processors established in third countries under Directive 95/46/EC of the European Parliament and of the Council (notified under document C(2010) 593) OJ L 39, 12.2.2010.

[60] Recital 25, and Art 7 Decision 2010/87/EU.

Both Set I and Set II SCCs may be used by controllers established in the EU.[61] It is up to the individual controller to choose which of the SCCs best suit their situation. [62] Both SCCs provide a substantive template that may be used, and the parties need to fill in the details and ensure the obligations provided therein are carried out. The parties are free to include any further clauses into the SCCs, as long as there is no contradiction with the model SCCs.[63] The actual clauses of the SCCs may not be amended as it is a model contract.[64]

Onward transfers: The data importer may only further transfer data outside the EU when it notifies the data exporter about the transfer and provides the legal safeguard on which the transfer is permissible, which may be one of the following:[65]

(i) Adequacy decision or EU Commission Decision[66] (as detailed above);

(ii) The entity to whom the personal data will be transferred (the third party data controller) becomes a signatory to the SCCs.[67] The data exporter signs SCCs with the entity with whom the data exporter wishes to transfer data to, thereby making it a new data importer;[68]

(iii) The data subject was informed and given the opportunity to object[69] OR in the case where the transfer includes sensitive data, unambiguous consent was provided by the data subject to the onward transfer.[70]

---

61 Recital 7, Decision 2001/497/EC.

62 Recital 3, Decision 2004/915/EC.

63 Recital 5, Decision 2001/497/EC.

64 Recital 3, Decision 2004/915/EC.

65 Set II SCCs, Part 2(i), Set I SCCs, Appendix 2, Part 6.

66 In accordance with Art 25(6) Directive 95/46/EC.

67 Appendix 2, Part 6(b), Decision 2001/497/EC.

68 FAQs in order to address some issues raised by the entry into force of the EU Commission Decision 2010/87/EU of 5 February 2010 on standard contractual clauses for the transfer of personal data to processors established in third countries under Directive 95/46/EC, adopted on 12 July 2010, at 5.

69 In accordance with Part 2(i)(iii), Set II SCCs The data subject must "been informed of the purposes of the transfer, the categories of recipients and the fact that the countries to which data is exported may have different data protection standards".

70 In accordance with Appendix 2, Part 6(a), Decision 2001/497/EC "The minimum information to be provided to data subjects must contain in a language understandable to them: — the purposes of the onward transfer, — the identification of the data exporter established in the Community, — the categories of further recipients of the data and the countries of destination, and — an explanation that, after the onward transfer, the data may be processed by a controller established in a country where there is not an adequate level of protection of the privacy of individuals".

Liability: Under Set I SCCs the data importer and data exporter are joint and severally liable. Under Set II SCCs, the data exporter is liable to the data subject to the extent that the data exporter failed to act with *due diligence* when engaging the data importer. Thus, to avoid liability the data exporter needs to use reasonable methods to ensure that the data importer is able to carry out the provisions within the SCCs, this may be done via a request for an audit or request for appropriate insurance cover, etc. Thus, a separation of responsibility is facilitated within Set II SCCs. There is a mutual indemnification clause, which enables the data exporter to recover any compensation that they may have to pay to the data subject as a result of the data importer's wrongdoing.

Under both SCCs, data subjects may bring an action either before the courts of the data exporter, or where the data subject is resident, and the data subject may claim compensation from either entity.

Controller to processor

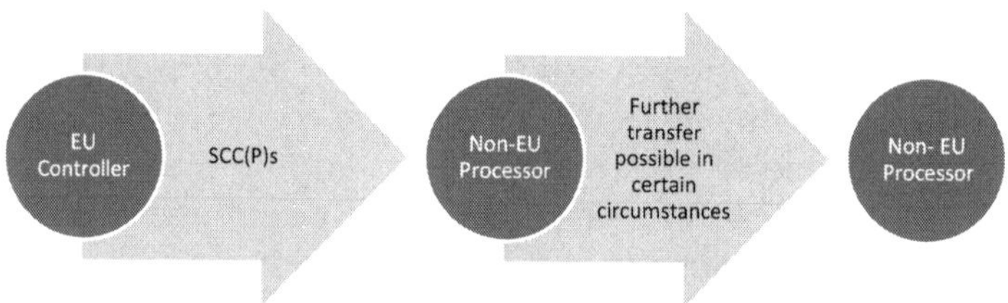

Decision 2010/87/EU provided for SCC(P)s that may be used by a data controller established within the EU[71] to transfer personal data to a non-EU processor.[72] This was developed in response to the trend of "global outsourcing" where more personal data is being transferred to processors outside the EU[73] and further transferred to sub-processes and sub-sub-processors. As such, it replaced the previous Decision 2002/16/EC.[74] Article 7(2) Decision 2010/87/EU provides that any SCCs entered into under the old Decision 2002/16/EC shall still remain in force, but where the parties wish to make changes or use sub-processors, they shall be required to enter into a new contract in line with the new SCC(P)s. The parties to the SCC(P)s are free to include any other clause as long as it does not

71 Recital 8, Decision 2010/87/EU.
72 2010/87/EU.
73 Art 29 Working Party, Opinion 3/2009 on the Draft Commission Decision on standard contractual clauses for the transfer of personal data to processors established in third countries, under Directive 95/46/EC (data controller to data processor), at 2.
74 Recital 25, and Art 7 Decision 2010/87/EU.

contradict the SCCs.[75] The following should be noted regarding SCC(P)s:

Onward transfers	The SCC(P)s do *not* apply to the situation where a processor established in the EU utilises a sub-processor outside the EU. [76] However, it does allow for processors outside the EU to transfer data onto further processors. See section on processor to processor.
Continuing need for DPA	A DPA in accordance with Article 28 GDPR should still be in place with any such processor, even if there may be repetition within the DPA and the SCC(P)s. It is recommended to still have a DPA in place because Decision 2010/87/EU was authorised under Directive 1995 and does not have all the elements as required within Article 28 GDPR; alternatively rather than having two documents the SCC(P)s could be amended to take into account the new GDPR obligations.
Security	Data importers may use the same technical and security measures where they provide processing services to multiple EU controllers, irrespective of the Member State.[77]
Governing law	The SCC(P)s should be governed by the law of the Member State where the data exporter is established, and the same law should govern any further sub-processor arrangement.[78]
Liability	The SCC(P)s are enforceable by the data subject.[79] The data subject should be allowed to take an action and receive compensation from the data exporter (the controller).[80] Where the controller has effectively ceased to exist in law or is insolvent, the data subject is allowed to take an action against the data importer (processor). Where the processor has also effectively ceased to exist in law or is insolvent, the data subject is entitled to take an action against further sub-processors. The liability of processors / sub-processors is limited to their own processing operations under the SCCs.

[75] Recital 4, Decision 2010/87/EU.
[76] Recital 23, Decision 2010/87/EU.
[77] Recital 13, Decision 2010/87/EU.
[78] Recital 22, Decision 2010/87/EU.
[79] Recital 19, Decision 2010/87/EU.
[80] Recital 20, Decision 2010/87/EU.

Processor to processor

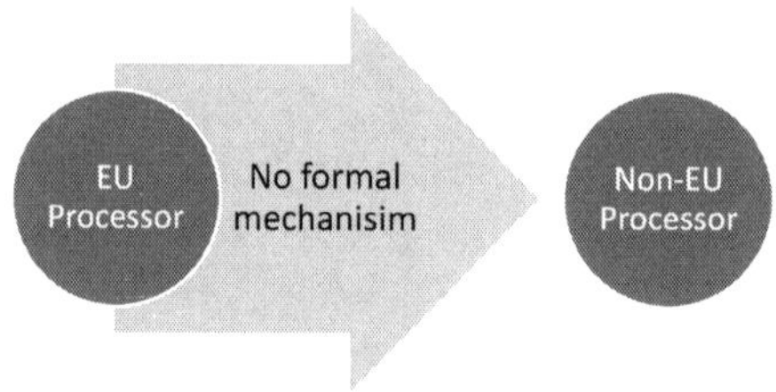

The SCC(P)s allow for processors outside with EU, which have SCC(P)s in place, to transfer data onto further processors. There are no particular SCCs for the situation of where a processor established in the EU wishes to utilise a sub-processor outside the EU. These two situations shall be discussed below.

Onward Transfers from non-EU Processor to non-EU Processors via SCC(P)s: Similar to the respective Article 28 GDPR requirements, the data importer may not disclose personal data to a third party without the prior written consent of the data exporter.[81] Transfers to further processors may occur in two instances:

1. If the new non-EU processor is engaged by the data exporter: In this case all the non-EU processors may sign the original SCC(P)s as data importers.[82] Footnote 9 of the Model Clause 2010/87/EU states that the sub-processor may co-sign the contract entered into between the data exporter and data importer, and that such co-signature satisfies the requirement for a written agreement between the data importer and the new sub-processor. The WP29 provides that in this case the parties must add in the signature section at the end of the contract a section "on behalf of the sub processor", which includes the "Name (written out in full)", "Position", "Address", "Other information necessary in order for the contract to be binding (if any)", "Signature", "(stamp of organization)".[83] In this case the data exporter would explicitly state how

[81] Recital 15, Decision 2010/87/EU.

[82] Clause 5(j) SCC(P)s; FAQs in order to address some issues raised by the entry into force of the EU Commission Decision 2010/87/EU of 5 February 2010 on standard contractual clauses for the transfer of personal data to processors established in third countries under Directive 95/46/EC, adopted on 12 July 2010, at 6.

[83] Clause 5(j) SCC(P)s; FAQs in order to address some issues raised by the entry into force of the EU Commission Decision 2010/87/EU of 5 February 2010 on standard contractual clauses for the transfer of personal data to processors

personal data may be transferred among such data importers.

2. If the new non-EU processors are engaged by the data importer: In this case the new non-EU processor must sign the SCC(P)s as a sub processor.[84] In this instance the following should be noted:

Liability	Where the data importer engages a further non-EU processor, the data importer is liable toward the data exporter for the activities of the sub-processor.[85]
Specific Instructions	As with the Article 28 GDPR requirements, the SCC(P)s with the sub-processor must specify that processing may only consist of processing permitted by the controller's original instructions.[86]
Consent to engage non-EU sub-processors	It is for the data exporter to decide whether the data importer must request consent on a case by case basis or whether the data exporter will provide general consent to the use of sub-processors by the data importer.[87]
Transparency	The data importer must send on the terms relating to the data protection elements of the sub-processing, to the data exporter.[88] Terms not relating to data protection do not need to be sent. Clause 11.4 SCC(P)s states that the data exporter must keep a list of such sub processing agreements that were received from the data importer. The data exporter must ensure that such list is available for the relevant supervisory authority.[89]

established in third countries under Directive 95/46/EC, adopted on 12 July 2010, at 7.

84 Recital 16-17, Decision 2010/87/EU, Clause 5(j) SCC(P)s; FAQs in order to address some issues raised by the entry into force of the EU Commission Decision 2010/87/EU of 5 February 2010 on standard contractual clauses for the transfer of personal data to processors established in third countries under Directive 95/46/EC, adopted on 12 July 2010, at 6.

85 Clause 11.1 SCC(P)s. Recital 18, Decision 2010/87/EU.

86 Recital 18, Decision 2010/87/EU.

87 FAQs in order to address some issues raised by the entry into force of the EU Commission Decision 2010/87/EU of 5 February 2010 on standard contractual clauses for the transfer of personal data to processors established in third countries under Directive 95/46/EC, adopted on 12 July 2010, at 5.

88 Clause 5(j) SCC(P)s; FAQs in order to address some issues raised by the entry into force of the EU Commission Decision 2010/87/EU of 5 February 2010 on standard contractual clauses for the transfer of personal data to processors established in third countries under Directive 95/46/EC, adopted on 12 July 2010, at 6.

89 Clause 5(j) SCC(P)s; Clause 8.1 SCC(P)s; FAQs in order to address some issues raised by the entry into force of the EU Commission Decision 2010/87/EU of 5 February 2010 on standard contractual clauses for the transfer of personal data to processors established in third countries under Directive 95/46/EC, adopted on 12 July 2010, at 8.

Data importer engages further non-EU processor to aid with several data exporter activities	It is not possible to make use of one single document for all sub-processors where a data importer engages such sub-processors to aid with multiple data exporter activities.[90] This is because Appendix 1 of SCC(P)s must always be different depending on the data exporter and the data processing activity. However, WP29 stated that the contract consisting of the details required for Appendix 1 may be signed with reference to the Model SCC(P)s and Appendix 2. Appendix 2 relates to the technical measures, as such if the measures change for each contract than Appendix 2 will need to vary.[91]

EU processor to non-EU processor: The SCC(P)s do not cover the situation of where a controller transfers data to an EU processor, and then the EU processor wishes to transfer data to a non-EU sub-processor.[92]

It is not possible to nevertheless use the SCC(P)s (without authorisation from the supervisory authority). This is because the definition of a data exporter within the SCC(P)s requires that the data exporter acts as a data controller within the EU, thus it would be inappropriate for an EU established data processor to act as the data exporter.

WP29 recognised the difficulty here. As such the WP29 urged the EU Commission to develop a solution to this. Furthermore, WP29 encouraged local supervisory authorities to recognise the use of clauses of a similar nature to the SCC(P)s as enabling adequate

90 Clause 5(j) SCC(P)s; FAQs in order to address some issues raised by the entry into force of the EU Commission Decision 2010/87/EU of 5 February 2010 on standard contractual clauses for the transfer of personal data to processors established in third countries under Directive 95/46/EC, adopted on 12 July 2010, at 7.

91 Clause 5(j) SCC(P)s; FAQs in order to address some issues raised by the entry into force of the EU Commission Decision 2010/87/EU of 5 February 2010 on standard contractual clauses for the transfer of personal data to processors established in third countries under Directive 95/46/EC, adopted on 12 July 2010, at 7.

92 FAQs in order to address some issues raised by the entry into force of the EU Commission Decision 2010/87/EU of 5 February 2010 on standard contractual clauses for the transfer of personal data to processors established in third countries under Directive 95/46/EC, adopted on 12 July 2010, at 1. Art 29 Working Party, Opinion 3/2009 on the Draft Commission Decision on standard contractual clauses for the transfer of personal data to processors established in third countries, under Directive 95/46/EC (data controller to data processor), at 2-3.

protection for personal data.[93] FAQs provided by WP29 provided for three possible solutions to this situation:[94]

Direct contract between the EU controllers and non-EU processors via SCC(P)s	This would imply that no contractual mechanism for the transfer would be needed between the EU processor and non-EU processor and such situation would be clarified via the DPA
Authorisation from the data exporter to contract with sub-processors on their behalf	Authorisation from the data exporter (EU controllers) to the EU-based processors to use SCC(P)s in their name and on their behalf; this could be provided for perhaps via the DPA. In this case the controller would still be the data exporter. Such consent may be provided by the data exporter on a case by case basis or on a general basis
Ad-hoc contracts	These would need to be assessed by the supervisory authority. Recital 23, Decision 2010/87/EU provides that data protection authorities (as they were then known) may take account the contents of the SCC(P)s as providing an adequate level of data protection. Thus, where the supervisory authority authorises the use of SCC(P)s in this instance, SCC(P)s do provide an adequate level of protection for contracts between EU processors and non-EU processors

Legal Instrument

Article 48 GDPR provides:

> "Any judgment of a court or tribunal and any decision of an administrative authority of a third country requiring a controller or processor to transfer or disclose personal data may only be recognised or enforceable in any manner if based on an international agreement, such as a mutual legal assistance treaty, in force between the requesting third

93 Art 29 Working Party, Opinion 3/2009 on the Draft Commission Decision on standard contractual clauses for the transfer of personal data to processors established in third countries, under Directive 95/46/EC (data controller to data processor), at 3.

94 FAQs in order to address some issues raised by the entry into force of the EU Commission Decision 2010/87/EU of 5 February 2010 on standard contractual clauses for the transfer of personal data to processors established in third countries under Directive 95/46/EC, adopted on 12 July 2010, at 4.

country and the Union or a Member State, without prejudice to other grounds for transfer pursuant to this Chapter."

Thus, the requirement to transfer personal data in accordance with a judgement or law of a third party should not be adhered to without a mutual treaty or appropriate safeguards for such a transfer as outlined herein.[95]

Air Passenger Name Record Data and Terrorist Finance Tracking Programme

A legal instrument is in place for passenger name record (PNR) data. PNR data is data that a data subject provides when they book and check in for an airline flight, such as passport numbers, names, addresses and flight details. Per Article 48 GDPR, the transfer of PNR data from the EU to non-EU countries can only be done via a bilateral agreement in which personal data is sufficiently protected. The EU has signed such bilateral PNR agreements with three countries:

- United States on transferring PNR data[96] and on transferring PNR data within the data terrorist and financing programme;[97]
- Canada;[98]

---

95 Recital 115 GDPR.

96 Agreement between the United States of America and the European Union on the use and transfer of passenger name records to the United States Department of Homeland Security OJ L 215, 11.8.2012; 2012/472/EU Council Decision of 26 April 2012 on the conclusion of the Agreement between the United States of America and the European Union on the use and transfer of passenger name records to the United States Department of Homeland Security OJ L 215, 11.8.2012.

97 The data terrorist and financing programme enables the US to request certain PNR data from the EU, it is the duty of Europol to decide whether to grant such requests based on an assessment of whether the requested data is necessary to be provided for the fight against terrorism and it's financing. See 2010/412/ Council Decision of 13 July 2010 on the conclusion of the Agreement between the European Union and the United States of America on the processing and transfer of Financial Messaging Data from the European Union to the United States for the purposes of the Terrorist Finance Tracking Program OJ L 195, 27.7.2010; Agreement between the European Union and the United States of America on the processing and transfer of Financial Messaging Data from the European Union to the United States for the purposes of the Terrorist Finance Tracking Program OJ L 195, 27.7.201; Staff Working Document Joint Review Report of the implementation of the Agreement between the European Union and the United States of America on the processing and transfer of Financial Messaging Data from the European Union to the United States for the purposes of the Terrorist Finance Tracking Program /* SWD/2014/0264 final */.

98 2006/230/EC: Council Decision of 18 July 2005 on the conclusion of an Agreement between the European Community and the Government of Canada

- Australia.[99]

The purpose of these bilateral agreements is to facilitate the investigation of serious crime and terrorism and such PNR data may only be processed for that purpose.

Authorised by Supervisory Authority

Transfers to outside the EU may take place where authorised by the supervisory authority. In particular, s 98(b) of the DPA 2018 re law enforcement provides that where no adequacy decision exists, a transfer may take place where the controller or processor has made an assessment on the circumstances of the transfer, and are thereafter satisfied that appropriate safeguards exist regarding the protection of the personal data that will be subject to the transfer.

Where the personal data is transferred on this basis, the controller or processor must:

- Inform the Irish supervisory authority;
- Create and maintain a written record of:
  - o Details of personal data transferred
  - o Date and time of the transfer
  - o Information about the entity in the third country
  - o Reasons for the transfer
- Maintain the record for possible inspection by the supervisory authority

Derogations from General Safeguard Rule

Article 49(1) GDPR provides several derogations from the general rule;[100] that in the case where no adequacy, or other safeguard

---

on the processing of API/PNR data and Agreement between the European Community and the Government of Canada on the processing of Advance Passenger Information and Passenger Name Record data OJ L 82, 21.3.2006.

99 Agreement between the European Union and Australia on the processing and transfer of Passenger Name Record (PNR) data by air carriers to the Australian Customs and Border Protection Service OJ L 186, 14.7.2012; Council Decision 2008/651/CFSP/JHA of 30 June 2008 on the signing, on behalf of the European Union, of an Agreement between the European Union and Australia on the processing and transfer of European Union-sourced passenger name record (PNR) data by air carriers to the Australian Customs Service and Agreement between the European Union and Australia on the processing and transfer of European Union-sourced passenger name record (PNR) data by air carriers to the Australian customs service OJ L 213, 8.8.2008.

100 Art 49 GDPR.

mechanisms exist, a transfer outside the EU may still take place in one of the below seven situations. Article 49 GDPR sets out a restriction to the general rule and, therefore, must be interpreted restrictively.[101] Thus, any derogation may only be used occasionally, i.e. not regularly.[102] In all cases the controller or processor must ensure that when using a derogation data subject's rights are still capable of being exercised.[103] Member State law may expressly limit the use of these derogations.[104] Where none of the seven derogations are applicable, there is a final resort option of a compelling legitimate interest that is detailed further below.

In all instances there is a requirement to *maintain a record*. Section 99 of the DPA 2018 governs derogations within Irish law re law enforcement. This requires that where data is transferred under the derogations that a record must be maintained of the following:

- Details of the personal data transferred;
- Date and time of the transfer;
- Information about the entity in the third country;
- Reasons for the transfer.

This record must be maintained for inspection by the Irish supervisory authority where requested.[105]

The seven derogations

The seven derogations are as follows:

---

[101] Art 29 Working Party, Guidelines on Art 49 of Regulation 2016/679, Adopted on 6 February 2018, at 3

[102] Recital 111 GDPR, see also Art 29 Working Party, Guidelines on Art 49 of Regulation 2016/679, Adopted on 6 February 2018, at 4.

[103] Recital 114 GDRP.

[104] Art 49(5) GDPR.

[105] DPA 2018, s 99(4).

	Derogation	Details
1	Consent	The transfer may occur with consent. The data subject must provide explicit consent to the actual transfer to a third country and the data subject must be informed of associated risks and appropriate safeguards. An explanation of consent is laid out in Chapter 5 – remember the data subject has the right to withdraw consent at any time. Note if all the information is not available prior to the transfer, the data subject still must be informed of the remaining information after the transfer.[106] Public authorities may *not* rely on explicit consent in the course of their duties.[107]
2	Contractual necessity between data subject and controller	The transfer must be necessary due to the contractual arrangements or pre-contractual arrangements between the data subject and the controller – for example if an employee has to occasionally meet a client in a third country and the employee's details need to be sent to book a hotel or transport, etc.[108]
3	Contractual necessity between controller and another entity in interest of data subject	The transfer must be necessary due to the contractual arrangements concluded in the interest of the data subject between a controller and another entity.
4	Public interest necessity	The transfer must be necessary for reasons of public interest. Only public interests recognised by Member State or EU law may be used.[109] For example competition law or tax purposes.[110]
5	Legal claim necessity	The transfer must be necessary for the establishment, exercise or defence of legal claims. Personal data may not be solely transferred on grounds that there is a possibility a legal claim may be brought in the future.[111]

106 Art 29 Working Party, Guidelines on Article 49 of Regulation 2016/679, Adopted on 6 February 2018, at 7

107 Art 49(3) GDPR.

108 Art 29 Working Party, Guidelines on Article 49 of Regulation 2016/679, Adopted on 6 February 2018, at 9

109 Art 49(4) GDPR – see items of general public interest in Chapter 4.

110 Recital 112 GDPR.

111 Art 29 Working Party, Guidelines on Article 49 of Regulation 2016/679, Adopted on 6 February 2018, at 12.

6	Vital interest necessity	The transfer must be necessary to protect the vital interests of the data subject or of other persons, where the data subject or other person is physically or legally incapable of giving consent. For example, a medical emergency or mental incapacity.[112] This also includes instances of legal incapability, for example in the case of a minor.[113]
7	Legal register	The transfer is made from a register that, according to EU or Member State law, is intended to provide information to the public. Furthermore, the register must be open to consultation either by the public in general or by any person who can demonstrate a legitimate interest. This derogation may be used by public authorities in the performance of their duties.[114] The personal data transferred under this derogation cannot involve the entirety of the personal data or entire categories of the personal data contained in the register.[115] Where the register is intended for consultation by persons having a legitimate interest, the transfer shall only be made where such person so requested.[116]

Necessity test: The requirement for necessity is required in many of the derogations. In such instances an evaluation needs to take place on whether a transfer of data may be considered necessary for the specific purpose for which the derogation is needed. There must be a *close and substantial connection* between the personal data in question and the reason for why it is necessary to transfer it to a third country.[117] WP29 noted that where anonymised or pseudonymised data is sufficient, then only such data should be transferred in line with the requirement for necessity and the principles of data minimisation.[118]

112 Art 29 Working Party, Guidelines on Article 49 of Regulation 2016/679, Adopted on 6 February 2018, at 13.
113 Art 29 Working Party, Guidelines on Article 49 of Regulation 2016/679, Adopted on 6 February 2018, at 14.
114 Art 49(3) GDPR.
115 Art 49(2) GDPR.
116 Art 49(2) GDPR.
117 See generally Art 29 Working Party, Guidelines on Art 49 of Regulation 2016/679, Adopted on 6 February 2018.
118 Art 29 Working Party, Guidelines on Article 49 of Regulation 2016/679, Adopted on 6 February 2018, 12-13.

Compelling legitimate interest

There is a *final resort* derogation from the general rule;[119] where personal data cannot be transferred under an adequacy or other safety measures laid out or under any of the seven derogations outlined above. The final derogation may only be used as a last resort. The final resort is that a transfer may take place on the grounds of a compelling legitimate interest pursued by the controller if the following criteria are met:[120]

- Transfer is not repetitive;
- Transfer concerns only a limited number of data subjects (determined on a case by case basis, i.e. cannot apply to all employees in a workplace – only to certain employees[121]);
- Transfer is necessary for the compelling legitimate interest pursued by the controller;
- The legitimate interest of the controller is not overridden by the rights of the data subject; (must consider likelihood and severity of risks to rights of data subject[122]);
- The controller has assessed the risk and has the appropriate safeguards in place;
- The controller has informed the supervisory authority of the transfer;
- The controller has provided the data subject with all the information required in accordance with the duty to inform and provide the data subject with information on the transfer and on the compelling legitimate interests pursued

A high threshold will apply in this regard, and in accordance with the principle of accountability the controller must be able to demonstrate all the above criteria.[123]

---

119 Art 29 Working Party, Guidelines on Article 49 of Regulation 2016/679, Adopted on 6 February 2018, 12-15.

120 Art 49 GDPR, last paragraph; Recital 113 GDPR.

121 Art 29 Working Party, Guidelines on Article 49 of Regulation 2016/679, Adopted on 6 February 2018, 12-16.

122 Recital 75 GDPR; see also Ch 9 re risk assessments.

123 Art 29 Working Party, Guidelines on Article 49 of Regulation 2016/679, Adopted on 6 February 2018, 12-15 – 16.

Further Discussion

Article 29 Working Party, Opinion 1/2001 on the Draft Commission Decision on Standard Contractual Clauses for the transfer of Personal Data to third countries under Article 26(4) of Directive 95/46 (draft distributed to the Working Party on 17 January, 2001) Adopted on 26 January 2001.

Article 29 Working Party, Opinion 7/2001 on the Draft Commission Decision (version 31 August 2001) on Standard Contractual Clauses for the transfer of Personal Data to data processors established in third countries under Article 26(4) of Directive 95/46 Adopted on 13 September 2001.

Article 29 Working Party, Opinion 8/2003 on the draft standard contractual clauses submitted by a group of business associations ("the alternative model contract").

Working Document WP 74: Transfers of personal data to third countries: Applying Article 26(2) of the EU Data Protection Directive to Binding Corporate Rules for International Data Transfers, adopted on 3 June 2003.

Article 29 Working Party, Opinion 3/2009 on the Draft Commission Decision on standard contractual clauses for the transfer of personal data to processors established in third countries, under Directive 95/46/EC (data controller to data processor).

FAQs in order to address some issues raised by the entry into force of the EU Commission Decision 2010/87/EU of 5 February 2010 on standard contractual clauses for the transfer of personal data to processors established in third countries under Directive 95/46/EC, adopted on 12 July 2010.

Article 29 Working Party, Adequacy Referential (updated), adopted 28 November 2017.

Article 29 Working Party, Guidelines on Article 49 of Regulation 2016/679, Adopted on 6 February 2018.

Article 29 Working Party, Working Document setting up a table with the elements and principles to be found in Binding Corporate Rules, As last Revised and Adopted on 6 February 2018.

Article 29 Working Party, Recommendation on the Standard Application form for Approval of Processor Binding Corporate Rules for the Transfer of Personal Data, Adopted on 11 April 2018.

Chapter 14

Transfers within a Non Traditional Network

As can be seen throughout Part 3 of this book, there are large obligations placed on entities when transferring personal data. Clear instructions must be in place. Chapters 11-13 looked at the following data transfer possibilities:

- Controller to controller;
- Controller to processor / processor to controller;
- Processor to sub-processor, sub-processor to sub-processor, etc.

Within this Chapter several scenarios shall be looked at that did not fit into the traditional categories.

Where Processor Requested by Controller to Transfer Data to Another Entity

What are the legal instruments that need to be in place where a processor is required to transfer data to a controller's other processor, i.e. not to their own sub-processor? The WP29 or EDPB have not explicitly advised on this situation to the knowledge of the author. The author makes the below assessment.

In accordance with Article 28(3) GDPR, a DPA is absolutely required to be in place for a processor to receive any personal data. If there is a DPA between the controller and each processor; is there a further obligation to have a DPA between processors if the processors are requested by the controller to transfer data between each other?

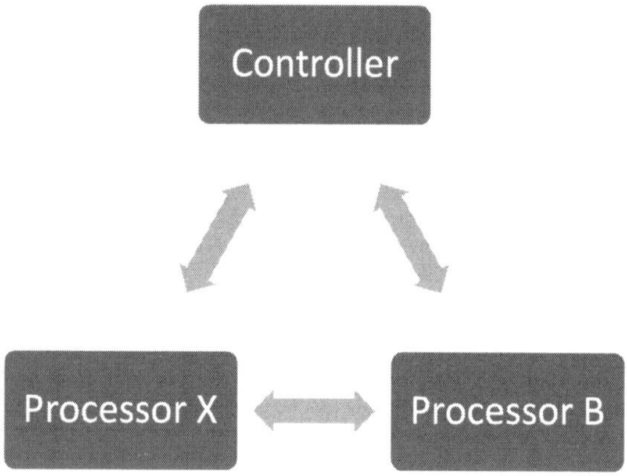

As a reminder, Article 28(4) GDPR states:

> "Where a processor engages another processor for carrying out specific processing activities on behalf of the controller, the same data protection obligations as set out in the contract or other legal act between the controller and the processor as referred to in [Article 28(3) GDPR] shall be imposed on that other processor by way of a contract or other legal act under Union or Member State law..."

Article 28(4) GDPR does not state that the contract must be between both processors, it simply states a DPA must be in place as against the processor with all the elements required for a DPA (see Chapter 12). If the controller has a DPA in place with both processors, in theory no further DPA would be required between the processors. The DPA is required to provide, among other items, that:

- A processor may only act on documented *instructions* from the controller;[1]
- A processor may not engage another processor without *consent*.[2]

Thus, where there is evidence that the controller requested a processor to transfer data to another processor, instruction and consent is provided. Thus, the processor may transfer personal data to another processor without the need for another DPA where:

- Both processors have a DPA in place with the same controller;
- There is a clear instruction and clear consent, from the

1 Art 28(3)(a) GDPR.
2 Art 28(2) GDPR.

controller, for the processors to transfer personal data between each other.

In order for the processors to safeguard themselves, it is recommended by the author that a processor faced with this situation sends a request to the controller to confirm:

- The transfer process that is being requested;
- That there is a DPA in place between the controller and the other processor;
- That all other GDPR requirements have been satisfied, including that the data subject is sufficiently aware of the data transfer arrangements, to the extent required under the GDPR.

Thus, clear categorisation of each entity as a controller and processor will be required. It must be remembered that while the controller has ultimate responsibility, the processor still has an obligation to act in compliance with the DPA and requisite GDPR obligations and principles. In the instance that the other processor is outside the EU, the processor must check that the safeguards are in place per Chapter 13. Article 46 GDPR states that a transfer outside the EU may only occur with appropriate safeguards. This situation is complicated where SCCs are in use, but one option outlined in Chapter 13 is for the controller to have SCCs with the non-EU processors. [3]

Where Controller Requests Processor to Collect Personal Data

Where a controller requests a processor to collect personal data on their behalf, this situation still carries the normal controller processor relationship. Recall that to collect personal data falls within the definition of processing.[4] Thus, in accordance with Article 28 GDPR there is no reason a controller cannot utilise a processor to also collect personal data, once a DPA is in place and the appropriate safeguards are carried out. As long as the processor is not acting outside the controller's instructions, the processor will not be considered a controller.

---

3 FAQs in order to address some issues raised by the entry into force of the EU Commission Decision 2010/87/EU of 5 February 2010 on standard contractual clauses for the transfer of personal data to processors established in third countries under Directive 95/46/EC, adopted on 12 July 2010, at 4.

4 Art 4(2) GDPR.

Where Controller is Established in a "Third Country"

Where the controller is established in a third country, this would be the type of situation in which the GDPR is applicable pursuant to Article 3(2) GDPR (see Chapter 3). The same requirement for appropriate safeguard mechanisms (as detailed in Chapter 13) would still apply where personal data is transferred outside the EU, even if it is to a controller outside the EU. Note that the SCCs can only be used in this instance where the data exporter is an EU controller. Where issues arise, the controller would need to coordinate with their EU representative (see Chapter 16), data protection officer (see Chapter 15) and their local supervisory authority (see Chapter 18).

Part 4

MISCELLANEOUS

Guide: Remaining Factors to Consider

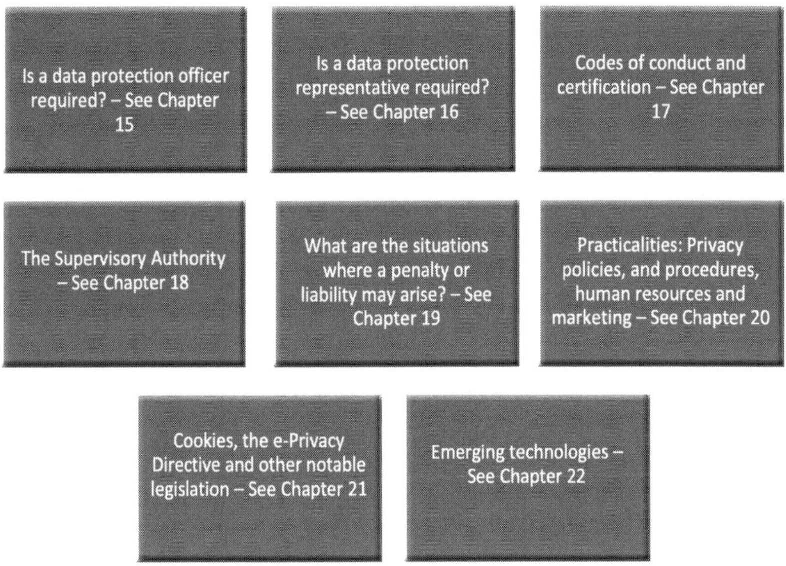

Chapter 15

Data Protection Officer

Relevant Law: Recital 97 GDPR, Article 37–39 GDPR

A Data Protection Officer (DPO) is an individual that aids with internal GDPR compliance. Controllers and processors are required to appoint a DPO where one of the following instances are met:[1]

1. Entity is a public authority or body, except for the courts acting in their judicial capacity;
2. It is a core activity of the entity to process personal data, which requires regular and systematic monitoring of data subjects on a large scale (detailed below);
3. Entity processes special categories of personal data or personal data relating to criminal convictions on a large scale.

Requirement to have a DPO

The second instance outlined above of "where it is a core activity ... to process personal data, which requires regular and systematic monitoring of data subjects on a large scale" is the most common instance in which a DPO will be required. Three elements need to be satisfied for a DPO to be required in this instance: It is a (i) core activity of the controller or processor to (ii) regularly and systematically monitor data subjects on a (iii) large scale.

1 Art 37 GDPR.

(i) Core activity

Recital 97 GDPR specifies that core activities should relate to the "primary activities" of the entity, and should not simply be "ancillary activities". For example, a company that makes chairs needs to employ people. As such, employee personal data is processed; however, this processing of personal data is not a core activity – it is simply required in order to facilitate the core activity of making chairs – the requirement for employees is ancillary, it supports the core activity. A core activity is one that is inextricably linked to the controller's or processor's purpose.[2] An example from WP29 is that of a private security company, whose primary purpose is to conduct surveillance: surveillance is inextricably linked to the processing of personal data. Therefore, processing personal data is a core activity of a security company.

(ii) Regular and systematic monitoring

Regular and systematic monitoring of data subjects is not defined in the GDPR. However, the concept of "monitoring the behaviour of data subjects" is mentioned in Recital 24 GDPR in relation to tracking and profiling. WP29 made the following interpretations:[3]

"Regular"	• Ongoing or occurring at particular intervals for a particular period of time • Recurring or repeated at fixed times • Constantly or periodically taking place
"Systematic"	• Occurring according to a system • Pre-arranged, organised or methodical • Taking place as part of a general plan for data collection • Carried out as part of a strategy
Examples of what may constitute "regular and systematic"	• All forms of tracking and profiling on the internet • Telecommunications network • Scoring for risk assessment i.e. insurance or credit scoring • Location tracking by mobile apps • Loyalty programs • Behavioural advertising • Closed circuit television

2 Art 29 Data Protection Working Party on the Guidelines on Data Protection Officers, at 7.

3 Art 29 Data Protection Working Party on the Guidelines on Data Protection Officers, at 8-9.

	• Monitoring of health or fitness via wearable devices • Connected devices i.e. smart meters, smart cars, home automation, etc.

(iii) Large Scale

The term large scale is undefined within the GDPR; however, Recital 91 GDPR states what would be included in the concept:

> Processing "a considerable amount of personal data at regional, national or supranational level and which *could affect a large number of data subjects* and which are likely to result in a high risk". [emphasis added.]

Thus, the term large scale is linked with the effect on data subjects.

To determine "large scale" WP29 recommended to assess:[4]

1. The number of data subjects concerned – either as a specific number or as a proportion of the relevant population;
2. The amount of personal data being processed and/or the range of different personal data items being processed;
3. The duration, or permanence, of the data processing activity;
4. The geographical extent of the processing activity.

WP29 provided the following examples of processing on a large scale:[5]

- Processing of patient data in the regular course of business by a hospital;
- Processing of travel data of individuals using a city's public transport system;
- Processing of real time geo-location data of customers of an international fast food chain for statistical purposes by a processor specialised in providing these services;
- Processing of customer data in the regular course of business by an insurance company or a bank;

[4] Art 29 Data Protection Working Party on the Guidelines on Data Protection Officers, at 7-8.

[5] Art 29 Data Protection Working Party on the Guidelines on Data Protection Officers, at 8.

- Processing of personal data for behavioural advertising by a search engine;
- Processing of data (content, traffic, location) by telephone or internet service providers.

WP29 also gave examples of personal data processing that would not be on a large scale, including the processing of personal data by an individual professional, like an individual physician or lawyer.

Variances within Member States

Note that the requirement to have a DPO differs between Member States. For example, in Germany it is required to have a DPO once a company employs more than ten employees. DPA 2018, s 34 provides that further regulations may be made on how to designate a DPO.

Requirements to be a DPO and Obligations of the DPO

In accordance with Recital 97 GDPR, in order to be a DPO, a DPO must:

- Have expertise on the GDPR and the requisite national data protection laws;
- Ensure that there is no conflict of interest that may impact on their DPO duties.

A DPO must be able to carry out their tasks independently. Article 39 GDPR sets out mandatory tasks for the DPO, as set out below:

Educate	• To inform and advise the controller and the processor and the respective employees about GDPR compliance
Monitor & Assist	• To monitor compliance with the GDPR and assist the controller or processor to monitor internal compliance with the GDPR; including, where appropriate, to collect information to identify processing activities, to analyse and check the compliance of processing activities and information, advise and issue recommendations to the controller or processor
Time	• Have reasonable amount of availability to deal with data subjects queries and requests • Where time is limited, focus on issues that present higher data protection risks first

Confidentiality	• Be bound by secrecy or confidentiality concerning the performance of his or her tasks, in accordance with Union or Member State law.[6] However, the obligation of secrecy/confidentiality does not prohibit the DPO from contacting and seeking advice from the supervisory authority
DPIA	• To provide advice where requested vis a vis a DPIA and monitor the performance of the DPIA
Interact with supervisory authority	• To cooperate with the supervisory authority • To act as the contact point for the supervisory authority

In addition to the above, the GDPR does not prevent further tasks to be allocated by the controller to the DPO, if appropriate, i.e., the DPO could also be tasked with maintaining data breach records.[7] In addition, the DPO usually acts as an intermediary between the relevant stakeholders.

Obligations on the Entity for which the DPO is Acting

When an entity (controller or processor) appoints a DPO, the entity is required to fulfil certain further obligations:[8]

Notify	• The contact details of the DPO must be published • The contact details of the DPO must be sent to the relevant supervisory authority
Integrate	• The DPO must be involved from the earliest stage possible in all issues relating to data protection • The DPO must be invited to participate regularly in meetings of senior and middle management • It is recommended for the DPO to be present where decisions with data protection implications are taken • All relevant information concerning data protection decisions must be passed on to the DPO in a timely manner in order to allow the DPO to provide adequate advice • The opinion of the DPO must be given due weight; in case of disagreement, the WP29 recommended, as good practice, to document the reasons for not following the DPO's advice

6 Art 38(5) GDPR.
7 Art 33(4) GDPR; also see Guidelines on Personal data breach notification under Regulation 2016/679, at 28.
8 Art 37-38 GDPR.

Protection	• The DPO must not be held personally responsible in case of non-compliance with the GDPR • The DPO must not be dismissed or penalised by the controller or the processor for performing their tasks
Resources and autonomy	• The DPO must be given sufficient autonomy and resources to carry out their tasks effectively and independently. As such the DPO must not receive any instructions regarding the exercise of their tasks • The DPO must be provided with sufficient time to fulfil their duties • The DPO must be supported with continuous training on data protection where needed/appropriate • There must be active support of the DPO's function by senior management
Data breach and DPIA	• The DPO must be promptly consulted once a data breach or another incident has occurred • The DPO must be consulted when a DPIA is being carried out[9]

The controller/processor must remember:

- According to Article 35(1) GDPR, it is the task of the controller, not of the DPO, to carry out, when necessary, a DPIA. However, the DPO should assist the controller;
- According to Article 30(1) and (2) GDPR, it is the controller or the processor, not the DPO, who is required to maintain a record of processing operations (data inventory). However, the DPO could be provided with the additional task of maintaining data breach records, etc.[10]

Appointing a DPO for a Group of Entities

The controller or processor may designate one DPO for a corporate group or group of entities, provided that the DPO is "easily accessible from each establishment"[11] i.e. easily contactable and quick to respond.

Designating a DPO When Not Required

When an organisation designates a DPO on a voluntary basis, the same requirements apply as specified above. The obligations are in no way lessened.

9 Art 35(2) GDPR.

10 Art 33(4) GDPR; also see Guidelines on Personal data breach notification under Regulation 2016/679, at 28.

11 Art 37(2) GDPR.

According to the Irish Data Protection Commission over 1,000 DPOs were appointed in Ireland between May and December 2018.[12]

Further Discussion

Article 29 Data Protection Working Party on the Guidelines on Data Protection Officers.

[12] Data Protection Commission, Annual Report, 25 May – 31 December 2018, at 5

Chapter 16

Data Protection Representative

Relevant Law: Recital 80 GDPR, Article 27 GDPR

Article 27 GDPR states that where an entity falls within the scope of Article 3(2) GDPR a representative within the EU must be set up. This is where a non-EU controller or processor processes the personal data of EU individuals for (1) the offering of goods or services or (2) monitoring purposes. See Chapter 3 for an explanation of these terms. The representative should be established in a Member State where the EU data subjects are:

(1) Offered the goods and or services, or
(2) Where the EU data subjects are monitored.

If the activities occur in multiple Member States, the Member State with the most activities may be chosen. The purpose of the representative is to have an easily accessible entity for EU data subjects to exercise their rights and also for the controller or processor to have an entity to aid with GDPR compliance. Note that under the right to be informed, the data subject must be informed of the representative.[1]

There are two exceptions to the requirement for a representative:[2]

- The processing is occasional (except in cases where the occasional processing is on a large scale, concerns special categories of personal data or personal data relating to criminal convictions and offences, and or is likely to result in a risk to the data subject); or
- The controller is a public authority or body.

Furthermore, if the relevant entity has a pre-existing establishment[3] within the EU, another representative will not be necessary.

Where a representative is required, the representative must be explicitly designated via a written mandate to act on behalf of

1 See Chapter 8.
2 Art 27(2) GDPR.
3 See explanation of establishment in Ch 3.

the controller or processor regarding the GDPR obligations,[4] and the representative may only act within the scope of that mandate. The controller or processor still retains liability and no liability is transferred to the representative.[5] However, the representative may be contacted by the supervisory authority and may be subject to enforcement proceedings.[6]

The EDPB notes that a representative should not also act as a DPO as a conflict of interest may arise.[7]

Further Discussion

Part 4, EDPB Guidelines 3/2018 on the territorial scope of the GDPR (Article 3)–Version for public consultation, Adopted on 16 November 2018.

4 Recital 80 GDPR.
5 Recital 80 GDPR. Art 27(5) GDPR.
6 Recital 80 GDPR.
7 EDPB Guidelines 3/2018 on the territorial scope of the GDPR (Article 3) – Version for public consultation, Adopted on 16 November 2018, at 20-21.

Chapter 17

Codes of Conduct and Certification

Relevant Law: Recital 98 GDPR, Article 40–43 GDPR

As stated throughout the book, codes of conduct and certification are useful to demonstrate compliance with particular sections of the GDPR and the GDPR as a whole:

Adherence to approved codes of conduct or certification:	
May be used as an element by which to provide proof that the controller is complying with their GDPR obligations[1]	Art 24(3) GDPR
May be used to demonstrate compliance with the requirement for data protection by design and by default	Art 25(3) GDPR
May be used as an element by which to demonstrate compliance with the requirement for security of processing [2]	Art 32(3) GDPR
Should be take into account when assessing the processing operations as part of a DPIA	Art 35(8) GDPR
Is a factor that may be taken into consideration when considering matters of liability, in particular it can be a factor when deciding a fine amount	Art 83(2)(j) GDPR

The GDPR encourages the drawing up of codes of conduct, the establishment of certification mechanisms and data protection seals and marks to aid processors and controllers with establishing and demonstrating GDPR compliance. In particular, the GDPR emphasises certain common elements vis-a-vis codes of conduct and certification:

- They can take into account the activities of certain

1 Also see Recital 77 GDPR.
2 Also see Recital 77 GDPR.

sectors, in particular the needs of micro, small and medium enterprises;[3]

- They can aid with the accountability requirement for controllers,[4] i.e. to demonstrate compliance with the GDPR;
- They can aid processors in proving to controller's that they have sufficient data protection guarantees in place as is required within Article 28 GDPR;
- Businesses, as well as data subjects, can assess the level of data protection compliance of other companies;[5]
- Any adherence to codes of conduct or certification is completely voluntary.[6]

Codes of Conduct

It should be noted that no codes of conduct have been approved under Articles 40 and 41 GDPR within Ireland.[7] The Irish Data Protection Commissioner under Directive 95/46/EC had approved several codes for Ireland.[8] These previously approved codes are no longer valid and would need to be revised in line with the GDPR. Within Irish law there is a specific reference to codes within s 32 DPA 2018, which specifically encourages the drawing up of codes of conduct vis-a-vis children.

It is a designated task of the EDPB[9] and the supervisory authority[10] to encourage the drawing up of codes of conduct. It is up to the supervisory authority to issue an opinion on and approve draft codes of conduct.[11] The supervisory authority shall register and publish the code where it is relating to processing activities only within their Member State.[12] Where the code relates to activities within more than one Member State, the supervisory authority must submit it to the EDPB,[13] who shall in turn submit their opinion on the code to the EU Commission.[14] If the EU Commission

3 Art 40 GDPR, Art 42(1) GDPR, Recital 98 GDPR.
4 Art 42(1) GDPR.
5 Recital 100 GDPR; Art 42(1) GDPR.
6 Art 42(3) GDPR.
7 As of 1 February 2019.
8 Personal Data Security Breach Code of Practice and specific codes for Garda Síochána (police force), Injuries Board, Insurance Sector, Department of Education and Skills, Revenue Commissioners, Vocational Education Committees, The Probation Service and Department of Health.
9 Art 70(1)(n) GDPR.
10 Art 57(1)(m) GDPR.
11 Art 58(3)(d); Art 40(5) GDPR.
12 Art 40(6) GDPR.
13 Art 40(7)-(8) GDPR.
14 Art 40(9) GDPR.

deems the code valid, they must ensure appropriate publicity for the approved code.[15] Furthermore, the EDPB shall ensure all approved codes are kept in a register and made publicly available by appropriate means.[16]

The GDPR encourages the production of codes of conduct to aid with GDPR compliance, particularly vis-a-vis:[17]

- Fair and transparent processing;
- The establishment of legitimate interests as a basis of processing;
- How personal data is collected;
- Pseudonymisation of personal data;
- Information that should be provided to the public and to data subjects;
- How data subject rights should be facilitated;
- How the personal data of children should be handled;
- Security of processing;
- Notification of personal data breaches to supervisory authorities and the communication of such personal data breaches to data subjects;
- Transfer of personal data to third countries or international organisations;
- Handling out of court disputes between controllers and data subjects.

The monitoring of compliance with a code of conduct may be carried out by a body that has an appropriate level of expertise and is accredited by the supervisory authority.[18] It is also up to the supervisory authority to draft and publish accreditation criteria for a body to qualify as such,[19] as well as to organise the accreditation of the body.[20] The GDPR provides some guidance, in that a body may be accredited if it has:[21]

- Demonstrated independence and expertise in the subject matter;
- Established procedures that allow the body to assess whether controllers or processors are adhering to the code;

---

15 Art 40(10) GDPR.
16 Art 40(11) GDPR.
17 Art 40(2) GDPR.
18 Art 41(4) GDPR.
19 Art 57(1)(p) GDPR; Art 41(3) GDPR.
20 Art 57(1)(q) GDPR.
21 Art 41(2) GDPR.

- Established procedures to facilitate complaints about non-compliance and ensure those procedures are transparent to the data subject;
- Show that there is no conflict of interest in the body carrying out its duty.

Note that the EDPB adopted guidelines on codes of conduct at the seventh plenary session of the EDPB on 12 February 2019, which will first be subject to public consultation.[22]

Certification

As with codes of conduct, no certification is approved within Ireland.[23] EDPB notes that a certificate is a statement of conformity, and a seal or mark can be used to signify the successful completion of a certification procedure.[24] As stated by the EDPB, the GDPR does not define certification and it is the International Standards Organisation (ISO) who provide a universal definition of certification:[25]

> "the provision by an independent body of written assurance (a certificate) that the product, service or system in question meets specific requirements."

Certification may be issued by certification bodies or by the supervisory authority or by the EDPB.[26] Any certification body must be accredited, and this accreditation must be in accordance with EN-ISO/IEC 17065/2012 and any criteria provided by the supervisory authority or the EDPB.[27] The EDPB has issued an opinion on the accreditation of certification bodies.[28]

---

22 Guidelines 1/2019 on Codes of Conduct and Monitoring Bodies under Regulation 2016/679, Adopted on 12 February 2019 (version for public consultation).

23 As of February 2019.

24 European Data Protection Board, Guidelines 1/2018 on certification and identifying certification criteria in accordance with Arts 42 and 43 of the Regulation 2016/679, Adopted on 23 January 2019, at 6.

25 European Data Protection Board, Guidelines 1/2018 on certification and identifying certification criteria in accordance with Arts 42 and 43 of the Regulation 2016/679, Adopted on 23 January 2019, at 6.

26 Art 42(5) GDPR.

27 European Data Protection Board, Guidelines 1/2018 on certification and identifying certification criteria in accordance with Arts 42 and 43 of the Regulation 2016/679, Adopted on 23 January 2019, at 6.

28 European Data Protection Board, Guidelines 4/2018 on the accreditation of certification bodies under Art 43 of the General Data Protection Regulation (2016/679), Adopted on 4 December 2018. Also see Guidelines 4/2018 on the accreditation of certification bodies under Art 43 of the General Data Protection

Where a certification is approved by the EDPB this may result in a common certification, the European Data Protection Seal.[29] The EDPB emphasises that any such achievement of certification still requires the controller or processor to comply with the GDPR.[30]

The controller or processor will need to submit and or provide access to its relevant processing activities in order to be successful in a certification procedure.[31] Any certification should be issued for a maximum period of three years and may be renewed.[32] Certification may be withdrawn at any point where the requirements for certification are no longer met.[33] The EDPB shall put all certification mechanisms, including data protection seals and marks, in a register and make them publicly available by the appropriate means.[34]

The EDPB has stated that they will publish separate guidelines to address the identification of criteria to approve certification mechanisms as transfer tools to outside the EU in accordance with Article 42(2) GDPR.[35] Also note that the EDPB has issued an Annex 2 for public consultation detailing a review and assessment of certification criteria.[36]

Regulation (2016/679)–Annex 1, Version for public consultation, Adopted on 4 December 2018 which provides specifications on additional accreditation criteria.

29 Art 42(5) GDPR.

30 Art 42(4) GDPR.

31 Art 42(6) GDPR.

32 Art 42(7) GDPR.

33 Art 42(7) GDPR.

34 Art 42(8) GDPR.

35 European Data Protection Board, Guidelines 1/2018 on certification and identifying certification criteria in accordance with Arts 42 and 43 of the Regulation 2016/679, Adopted on 23 January 2019, at 5.

36 Annex 2 on the review and assessment of certification criteria pursuant to Art 42(5) to the Guidelines 1/2018 on certification and identifying certification criteria in accordance with Articles 42 and 43 of the Regulation 2016/679, Version for public consultation, Adopted on 23 January 2019.

Further discussion

Guidelines 1/2019 on Codes of Conduct and Monitoring Bodies under Regulation 2016/679, Adopted on 12 February 2019 (version for public consultation)

European Data Protection Board, Guidelines 1/2018 on certification and identifying certification criteria in accordance with Articles 42 and 43 of the Regulation 2016/679, Adopted on 23 January 2019

European Data Protection Board, Guidelines 4/2018 on the accreditation of certification bodies under Article 43 of the General Data Protection Regulation (2016/679), Adopted on 4 December 2018

Chapter 18

Supervisory Authority

Relevant Law: Recital 117–144 GDPR; Article 51–78 GDPR

The supervisory authority is the authority within each Member State that facilitates compliance with the GDPR. Part of the EDPB's duties is to promote the consistent application of the GDPR, including among supervisory authorities.[1] As stated in the Introduction, in Ireland the Data Protection Commission (Irish Commission) is the supervisory authority for the purposes of the GDPR. Other Member States may have more than one supervisory authority to reflect their state structure.[2] For example Germany, as a federation, has several supervisory authorities. However, there is a requirement for such Member States to designate one supervisory authority that may act as the single point of contact for communication with other supervisory authorities, the EDPB and the EU Commission.[3]

A key facet of a supervisory authority is that it must be independent.[4] Thus, it is a requirement that the supervisory authority is provided with sufficient resources to carry out their tasks effectively.[5] Members of a supervisory authority must ensure independence, in particular, they should:[6]

---

1 Recital 139 GDPR.
2 Recital 117 GDPR.
3 Recital 119 GDPR.
4 See recital 118 GDPR supervisory authorities may still be subject to financial review and judicial review.
5 Recital 120 GDPR.
6 Recital 121 GDPR.

- Act with integrity;
- Refrain from any action that is incompatible with their duties;
- Not engage in any incompatible occupation, whether or not there is a financial and or other benefit.

Competence of Supervisory Authority

Every supervisory authority has several key tasks:

1. To be competent within their territory to handle complaints lodged by data subjects, conduct investigations on compliance with the GDPR and promote awareness of the GDPR;[7]
2. To cooperate with other supervisory authorities to facilitate the free flow of data within the EU, to monitor compliance with the GDPR[8] and provide mutual assistance in performing their tasks;[9]
3. Respond quickly and appropriately to established risks, and where appropriate, utilise urgency procedure (see below);
4. Enable the consistency mechanism (see below);[10]
5. To exercise powers to ensure compliance with the GDPR appropriately, fairly and within a reasonable time.[11]

Regarding point 3, Article 66 GDPR provides that there may be instances where an urgent act is required to mitigate risks to data subjects.[12] In this instance a supervisory authority may adopt a measure within its territory for a period of validity that may not exceed three months.

Regarding point 4, the *consistency mechanism* ensures that the GDPR is implemented consistently throughout the EU. This requires that measures adopted are consistent with other supervisory authorities. In this regard, the EDPB is also capable of adopting legally

---

[7] Recital 122 GDPR.
[8] Recital 123 GDPR, Art 60 GDPR.
[9] Recital 133-134 GDPR, Art 61 GDPR.
[10] Art 63 GDPR.
[11] Recital 129 GDPR. Note: "Each legally binding measure of the supervisory authority should be in writing, be clear and unambiguous, indicate the supervisory authority which has issued the measure, the date of issue of the measure, bear the signature of the head, or a member of the supervisory authority authorised by him or her, give the reasons for the measure, and refer to the right of an effective remedy."
[12] Recital 137 GDPR.

binding decisions where there are disputes between supervisory authorities.[13] Any decision of the EDPB may have an action for annulment brought against them.[14]

Note that a decision of a supervisory authority may be subject to judicial review.[15]

Communication with the EDPB

The supervisory authority must communicate a draft decision with the EDPB where it concerns:[16]

- List of processing operations for which a DPIA is required;
- A draft code of conduct being authorised;
- Certification being authorised;
- Standard data protection clauses (for transferring personal data) being authorised;
- Contractual clauses (for transferring personal data) being authorised;
- Binding corporate rules being authorised.

The EDPB may adopt a binding decision regarding the above matters.[17] Any decision of the EDPB may have an action for annulment brought against it.[18]

Obligations on Controller and Processor vis-a-vis the Supervisory Authority

The GDPR provides for specific obligations on the controller or processor vis a vis the supervisory authority. The major obligations are that the controller/processor must:

- Make records of processing (data inventory), required under Article 30 GDPR,[19] available to the supervisory authority on request;

---

[13] Recital 136 GDPR, Art 65 GDPR.
[14] Recital 143 GDPR.
[15] Recital 129 GDPR, Recital 141 GDPR.
[16] Art 64 GDPR.
[17] Art 65 GDPR.
[18] Recital 143 GDPR.
[19] See Ch 9.

- Cooperate with the supervisory authority on the performance of tasks relating to GDPR compliance;[20]
- Notify data breaches[21] to the supervisory authority (or lead supervisory authority where the controller has several establishments throughout the EU); where the controller does not have an establishment within the EU, the WP29 recommended that notification should be made to the supervisory authority in the Member State where the controller's representative in the EU is established.[22]

Lead Supervisory Authority

Relevant Law: Recital 36, 125–127, Article 4(16) and Article 56 GDPR

The Lead Supervisory Authority (LSA) needs to be identified where a controller or processor is carrying out cross-border processing of personal data i.e. where data is transferred between entities in different countries. Article 56(6) GDPR states that the LSA shall be the only point of communication for the controller or processor for cross border processing carried out. The LSA provides a one stop shop mechanism, in that an LSA streamlines the process to avoid the need to deal with multiple supervisory authorities. Only the LSA needs to be dealt with. This is largely beneficial for the notification procedure vis-a-vis a personal data breach.[23] Note that LSAs are not relevant for public authorities.[24]

According to Recital 36 GDPR, where disputes arise involving both the controller and the processor, the competent LSA should be the *LSA for the controller*.

In accordance with Recital 127 GDPR, each supervisory authority not acting as the LSA is still competent to handle local cases where the subject matter only concerns processing within the territory of that supervisory authority, i.e. regarding employees employed in that territory.

Identifying LSA – Main establishment

Article 56(1) GDPR states that the LSA is the supervisory authority of the *main establishment* or single establishment. The single establishment is where the only location of the controller

---

20 Art 31 GDPR.
21 See Ch 10.
22 See Ch 16.
23 See Ch 10.
24 Recital 128 GDPR.

or processor is. Where the controller or processor have several establishments, the main establishment must be identified. Article 4(16)(b) GDPR provides a definition of 'main establishment':

> "as regards a processor with establishments in more than one Member State, the place of its central administration in the Union, or, if the processor has no central administration in the Union, the establishment of the processor in the Union where the main processing activities in the context of the activities of an establishment of the processor take place to the extent that the processor is subject to specific obligations under this Regulation"

Therefore, the main establishment is where the central administration within the EU is located, or, failing that, where the main processing activities are carried out within the EU.

Where the processor or controller is established in several Member States and it is unclear where the main establishment is or where the main establishment is outside of the EU, an LSA cannot be randomly chosen. WP29 made it very clear that forum shopping is not permitted. There has to be clear proof and evidence that a chosen LSA is indeed where the main establishment or single establishment is. WP29 recognised that borderline instances may arise.[25] In such instance WP29 recommended to simply designate an establishment that will act as the main establishment. In order for any establishment to be categorised as a main establishment, it must be able to implement decisions on GDPR compliance and accept liability for failure to comply. WP29 warned that if it is not possible to designate a main establishment, an LSA may not be designated and as such every supervisory authority will need to be dealt with. WP29 stated that supervisory authorities will always be able to investigate further if a certain LSA is not appropriate.

The Internal Market Information system enables supervisory authorities throughout the EU to share information confidentially. Since 25 May 2018 until February 2019, 642 procedures were initiated within the EU to identify the LSA (306 of which have been concluded and an LSA identified). Furthermore, within the same time period, 281 cases were registered as having a cross border element, 45 "one-

[25] Art 29 Working Party, Guidelines for identifying a controller or processor's lead supervisory authority, Adopted on 13 December 2016, As last Revised and Adopted on 5 April 2017, at 8.

stop-shop" procedures were initiated, of which six are at a final decision.[26]

Data Subject Lodging Complaint with Supervisory Authority

In accordance with Article 77 GDPR the data subject has the right to lodge a complaint with the supervisory authority where a data subject feels their data protection rights have been adversely impacted by an entity. The data subject may contact the supervisory authority of their usual place of residence or work or where the offending entity's office is located.[27] A data subject should be able to lodge a complaint via a complaint submission form, which may be provided electronically.[28]

The supervisory authority must acknowledge, in writing, that the complaint was received and inform the data subject of their associated rights to an effective judicial remedy (detailed in Chapter 19).[29]

The supervisory authority must inform the data subject of the progress and the outcome of the complaint within a reasonable period of time.[30] Within Ireland such period of time is 3 months.[31] Where further investigation is required or coordination with other supervisory authorities is needed, information should be provided to the data subject as to the ongoing status of their complaint.[32] If the case requires further investigation or coordination with another supervisory authority, intermediate information should be given to the data subject.

If the data subject does not lodge the complaint to the requisite LSA for the controller, the supervisory authority that was notified must cooperate with the LSA.[33]

Where a complaint has been rejected or dismissed by a supervisory authority, the complainant may bring proceedings before the courts

---

26 European Data Protection Board, First overview on the implementation of the GDPR and the roles and means of the national supervisory authorities, (EDPB LIBE report on the implementation of GDPR), 26 February 2019, at 2-4.
27 Further see Recital 141 GDPR.
28 Recital 141 GDPR.
29 S 108, DPA 2018.
30 Recital 141 GDPR.
31 S 108, DPA 2018.
32 Recital 141 GDPR.
33 Recital 130 GDPR.

where the supervisory authority is established.[34] Furthermore, the complainant may bring proceedings before said court if the supervisory authority does not handle the complaint within three months (or provide details on the progress or outcome of the complaint within that time).[35]

A not-for-profit body, organisation or association, that is permissible within the law of the Member State, may lodge a complaint on behalf of the data subject.[36] Member States may allow such body to lodge a complaint independently of the data subject where it is considered that the rights of the data subject under the GDPR have been infringed;[37] note, the ability for such a body to act independently has not been provided for within Ireland. However, Ireland allows for data subjects to mandate such a body. Section 120 of the DPA 2018 provides for the conditions to qualify as such a body (re law enforcement) that data subjects may mandate to lodge a complaint on their behalf; the body must:

- Provide its services on a not-for-profit basis;
- Be properly constituted / formed in accordance with Irish law or the law of another Member State;
- Have objectives in the public interest;
- Be active with regard to the protection of data subject rights and freedoms, including protection of their personal data.

According to the Irish Data Protection Commission over 2,846 complaints were received between May and December 2018.[38] The most common complaint was over data subject access rights (detailed in Chapter 8).

Further Discussion

Article 29 Working Party, Guidelines for identifying a controller or processor's lead supervisory authority, Adopted on 13 December 2016, as last revised and adopted on 5 April 2017.

34 Recital 143 GDPR, Art 78 GDPR.
35 Art 78 GDPR.
36 Art 80 GDPR.
37 Art 80(2) GDPR.
38 Data Protection Commission, Annual Report, 25 May – 31 December 2018, at 13.

Chapter 19

Liabilities, Penalties and Orders

Relevant Law: Recital 142–152 GDPR; Article 79–84 GDPR

There are four potential consequences where a controller or processor breaches the GDPR:

1. Civil claim brought by data subject;
2. Civil claim brought by the controller or processor;
3. Penalties, including orders, reprimands and administrative fines;
4. Criminal penalties.

The law and procedures relating to these four areas shall be dealt with below. The GDPR states that any penalties must be effective, proportionate and dissuasive.[1]

1. Civil Claim Brought by Data Subject

Article 79 GDPR provides the data subject with the right to an effective judicial remedy as against a controller or processor where the data subject's GDPR rights were infringed.[2] This means a data subject may bring a claim to court for damages, an injunction or other remedy. This right is still in effect even if the controller or processor already had an administrative fine imposed on them or if the data subject has lodged a complaint with the supervisory authority. The data subject's claim will be that their rights under the GDPR were infringed due to non-compliance with the GDPR.

---

1 Recital 152 GDPR.
2 Reiterated in s 117 DPA 2018.

The data subject may bring this claim where they live.[3] However, where the claim is against a public authority, the claim must be brought in the country where the public authority is established.[4] The data subject also has the right to bring a claim at the location where the controller or processor has an establishment.[5]

Where an action is brought within the jurisdiction of Ireland, a data protection action shall be considered an action founded on tort.[6] The Circuit Court,[7] along with the High Court, shall have jurisdiction to hear such data protection actions. The court has the power to grant one or more of the following reliefs:[8]

- Relief by way of injunction, where the controller or processor will be prevented from continuing the breaching activity;[9]
- Relief by way of declaration, where it will be declared that the controller or processor breached data protection law;
- Relief by way of compensation for damage suffered by the data subject as a result of the breached data protection law.[10]

The controller or processor should be found liable to pay full compensation for the damage which a person suffered due to an infringement of the GDPR (or national data protection law).[11] The

3 This is known as the data subject's habitual residence, see Art 79(2) GDPR; Recital 145 GDPR. Regarding the term habitual residence, see chapter 12(2), The Law Reform Commission Working Paper on Domicile and Habitual Residence (supplemental to the Report on Domicile and Habitual Residence (LRC 7 – 1983)). See *In the Matter of A* [2013] UKSC 60 (*'Re A'*); *In the matter of KL (A Child)* [2013] UKSC 75 and *In the matter of LC (Children)* [2014] UKSC 1; *Tv O* [2007] IESC 55 (2007); *Coventry City Council v S* [2010] IEHC 303 (2010).

4 DPA 2018, s 117(9) emphasises that an action may not be brought within Ireland against another Member State's public authority.

5 Art 79(2) GDPR; Recital 145 GDPR; s 117(7) DPA 2018.

6 DPA 2018, s 117(2).

7 In accordance with DPA 2018, s 117(4), the circuit may likewise be determined by the habitual residence of the data subject or where the controller or processor has their establishment; In accordance with Part 3 of the Courts and Civil Law (Miscellaneous Provisions) Act 2013 the monetary jurisdiction of the Circuit Court is €75,000; where it is envisaged the compensation will be above this amount, the proceedings should be issued in the High Court.

8 DPA 2018, s 117(4).

9 In accordance with DPA 2018, s 117(10) such injunction includes interim injunction, interlocutory injunction or an injunction of indefinite period.

10 In accordance with DPA 2018, s 117(10), damages include material and non-material damage.

11 Recital 146 GDPR.

controller or processor should be exempt from liability if it is proven that it is not in any way responsible for the damage.[12]

Where more than one controller or processor is responsible for the breach of the GDPR, each controller or processor can be held liable for the entire damage.[13] This means, if the data subject only brought an action as against one of the entities, the data subject can still receive full compensation. Where the entities are joined within the same judicial proceedings, either by the data subject or via third party procedure,[14] compensation may be apportioned according to the responsibility of each controller or processor for the requisite damages, so long as the data subject receives full compensation.[15]

A data subject may mandate a not-for-profit body, organisation or association that is permissible within the law of the Member State, to bring the claim on their behalf.[16] Such an entity can also receive compensation on their behalf, but only with the explicit mandate of the data subject.[17] Such entity is the same as the entity that may lodge a complaint on behalf of the data subject to the supervisory authority (see Chapter 20).

2. Civil Claim Brought by Controller or Processor

Article 82(5) GDPR provides that where a controller or processor paid full compensation to a data subject, the controller or processor is entitled to claim for the amount of damages for which the other controller or processor was liable. In addition, the controller or processor may claim for damages for which the other is liable. In this regard, note:

- Article 82(2) GDPR provides that a controller is liable for damage caused via an infringement of the GDPR;
- Article 82(2) GDPR provides that a processor is liable for damages caused via an infringement of the DPA;
- Article 28(4) GDPR states that where a processor engages a further processor, the initial processor shall remain fully liable to the controller for the performance of that other processor's obligations.

---

12 Recital 146 GDPR.
13 Recital 146 GDPR.
14 See Ord 7 of the Circuit Court Rules (where claim brought in Circuit Court) or Ord 16 of the Rules of the Superior Court (where claim brought in High Court).
15 Recital 146 GDPR.
16 Art 80(1) GDPR; Recital 142 GDPR; DPA 2018, s 117(7).
17 Recital 142 GDPR.

As such the controller or processor may initiate recourse proceedings against the other controller or processor to recover any amounts paid in full compensation for which the other controllers and or processors are liable.[18]

3. Penalties (Including Orders, Reprimands and Administrative Fines)

Section 115 of the DPA 2018 provides that the Irish Commission may either impose an administrative fine on the controller or processor or exercise a corrective power specified in Article 58 GDPR, which includes carrying out investigations and issuing warnings.[19] Furthermore, s 115 of the DPA 2018 provides that the Irish Commission may issue an enforcement notice (detailed below). The purpose of fines and corrective measures is to enforce compliance. Fines may be imposed in addition to or instead of appropriate measures imposed by the supervisory authority.[20]

In providing a penalty, the supervisory authority must take into consideration:[21]

- The nature, gravity and duration of the infringement;
- The intentional character of the infringement;
- Actions taken to mitigate the damage suffered;
- Degree of responsibility;
- Any relevant previous infringements;
- The manner in which the infringement became known to the supervisory authority;
- Compliance with measures ordered against the controller or processor;
- Adherence to a code of conduct;
- Any other aggravating or mitigating factor.

Where penalties are imposed, there must be appropriate procedural safeguards in accordance with the law, including effective judicial protection and due process.[22]

---

18 Recital 146 GDPR.

19 Irish Commission may conduct inquiry into data protection infringements in accordance with s 110, DPA 2018. For more detailed description see Data Protection Commission, Annual Report, 25 May–31 December 2018, at 28–29.

20 Recital 148 GDPR.

21 Recital 148 GDPR, Art 83 GDPR.

22 Recital 148 GDPR.

There are two instances in which the GDPR states that a reprimand may be issued instead of a fine: [23]

- In a case of a minor infringement of the GDPR; or
- If the fine likely to be imposed would constitute a disproportionate burden.

Enforcement notice

Where it is determined that a controller and or processor is breaching data protection law, the Irish Commission or an authorised officer acting on behalf of the Irish Commission,[24] may issue an enforcement notice requiring the controller and or processor to take remedial steps.[25] An enforcement order may order the controller or processor to stop or remedy breaching activity. Furthermore, the Irish Commission may make an application to the High Court to suspend or restrict data processing where an enforcement order does not satisfy the urgency of the matter. [26]

Fines

Where a controller or processor is fined, they have 28 days within which to appeal to the court as against the decision.[27] In any regard, the Irish Commission must refer the matter to the Circuit Court for confirmation of the decision if no appeal is made.[28] In this case, the Circuit Court must confirm the decision unless the Circuit Court has "good reason not to do so". Therefore, it is good practice for the offending entity to issue an appeal as it appears a more substantive review would occur rather than a semi-automatic approval.

In accordance with Article 83(4) GDPR administrative fines of up to 10 million euro or 2% or the offending entities worldwide annual turnover may be imposed where there was a breach in the GDPR obligations. In accordance with Article 83(5) GDPR administrative fines of up to 20 million euro or 4% or the offending entities worldwide annual turnover may be imposed:

---

23 Recital 148 GDPR.
24 Appointed in accordance with DPA 2018, s 129.
25 DPA 2018, s 133.
26 Art 134 GDPR.
27 DPA 2018, s 142 the appeal shall be brought to the Circuit Court where the fine is less than €75,000, where the amount is higher the appeal should be brought to the High Court.
28 DPA 2018, s 143.

- Where there was a breach of the basic principles of processing – see Chapter 7;
- Where there was a breach regarding the legal basis of the processing, including consent – see Chapter 5;
- Where there was a breach regarding processing of vulnerable person's data, in particular children and special categories of personal data – see Chapter 6;
- Where there was a breach in providing data subject's rights – see Chapter 8;
- Where there was a breach regarding the transfer of personal data to a third country – see Chapter 13;
- Where there was a breach regarding Member State law on items detailed in Chapter IX GDPR, including processing for ASHS purposes;
- Where there was non-compliance with an order of the supervisory authority.

There are two instances in DPA 2018 where an administrative fine is specifically identified as the appropriate measure:

- Section 30 of the DPA 2018 – direct marketing, micro targeting and profiling children;
- Section 133(9)(a) of the DPA 2018 – failure to comply with an enforcement notice.

Examples of fines that have been imposed

A hospital in Portugal received a €400,000 fine largely due to a breach of the data minimisation principle. All doctors were able to access all patient data, which was not necessary as such access to data was not required for the functioning of the hospital.

A social network company in Germany was fined €20,000 for storing unencrypted passwords. This fine was relatively low due to the fact the entity was very cooperative.

One of the largest fines, thus far, was against the search engine company, Google. They were fined €50 million in France, for inadequate transparency and consent mechanisms.

In Austria, a fine of €5,000 approx. was imposed due to the use of an un-signposted CCTV that surveyed public areas outside an establishment. This breached the necessity and transparency principle, among others. The owner of the establishment was fined a relatively small amount because their earnings were taken into consideration.

4. Criminal Penalties

Member States are allowed to lay down rules for criminal penalties for infringements of the GDPR and associated national legislation.[29] However, it is emphasised in Recital 149 GDPR that national law may not punish controllers and or processors for the same crime twice.[30] DPA 2018 provides for a series of criminal penalties, listed below. Section 147 of the DPA 2018 provides that the Irish Commission may bring and prosecute summary proceedings for an offence as listed below and such proceedings may be brought within three years from the date on which the offence was alleged to have been committed.[31] In the majority of instances detailed below "without reasonable excuse" is specified. Thus, where a reasonable excuse exists, such penalties may be avoided.

Instance where penalty can be incurred	Details	Penalty
Breach of DPA 2018, s 4.	Where data subject is forced to make a DSAR – see Chapter 8	(i) On summary conviction, to a class A fine or imprisonment for a term not exceeding 12 months or both, or (ii) On conviction on indictment, to a fine not exceeding €50,000 or imprisonment for a term not exceeding 5 years or both

29 Recital 149 GDPR.

30 This is the principle known as *ne bis in idem.*

31 Note DPA 2018, s 147(2)(b) details that where the subject of proceedings is outside the state, proceedings may be brought when the person is next within the state, provided that no proceedings may be commenced more than 5 years from the date on which the offence was alleged to have been committed.

Instance where penalty can be incurred	Details	Penalty
Breach of DPA 2018, s 26	Where a person discloses confidential information obtained while carrying out processing operations and or obligations under data protection law	Liable on summary conviction to a class A fine
Breach of DPA 2018, s 55	This relates to the processing of personal data relating to criminal offences and convictions, which is not dealt with in this book	(i) On summary conviction to a class A fine or imprisonment for a term not exceeding 12 months or both, or (ii) On conviction on indictment, to a fine not exceeding €50,000 or imprisonment for a term not exceeding 5 years or both
Breach of DPA 2018, s 130(7)-(8) .	Where an authorised officer (appointed by the Commission under DPA 2018, s 129 to check for data protection compliance) is obstructed	(i) On summary conviction, to a class A fine or imprisonment for a term not exceeding 12 months or both, or (ii) On conviction on indictment, to a fine not exceeding €250,000 or imprisonment for a term not exceeding 5 years or both
Breach of DPA 2018, s 132.	Where a controller or processor fails to comply with an information request issued by the Irish Commission	(i) On summary conviction, to a class A fine or imprisonment for a term not exceeding 12 months or both, or (ii) On conviction on indictment, to a fine not exceeding €250,000 or imprisonment for a term not exceeding 5 years or both

Instance where penalty can be incurred	Details	Penalty
Breach of DPA 2018, s 133.	Where a controller or processor fails to comply with steps required to be taken in accordance with an enforcement notice	(i) On summary conviction, to a class A fine or imprisonment for a term not exceeding 12 months or both, or (ii) On conviction on indictment, to a fine not exceeding €250,000 or imprisonment for a term not exceeding 5 years or both
Breach of DPA, s 135.	Where a controller or processor fails to provide the Irish Commission with a report demonstrating compliance with data protection law, when requested to do so	(i) On summary conviction, to a class A fine or imprisonment for a term not exceeding 12 months or both, or (ii) On conviction on indictment, to a fine not exceeding €250,000 or imprisonment for a term not exceeding 5 years or both
Breach of DPA 2018, s 138.	Where the controller or processor refuses to provide information requested in the course of an investigation or otherwise hinders an authorised officer (appointed by the Irish Commission under s 129 of the DPA 2018 to check for data protection compliance) from performing their duties	(i) On summary conviction, to a class A fine or imprisonment for a term not exceeding 12 months or both, or (ii) On conviction on indictment, to a fine not exceeding €250,000 or imprisonment for a term not exceeding 5 years or both

Instance where penalty can be incurred	Details	Penalty
Breach of DPA 2018, s 144.	Where the processor "knowingly or recklessly" discloses personal data to another entity without the authorisation of the controller (See Chapter 12 for a description on the requirement of a processor to only act on instructions of controller)	(i) On summary conviction, to a class A fine or imprisonment for a term not exceeding 12 months or both, or (ii) On conviction on indictment, to a fine not exceeding €50,000 or imprisonment for a term not exceeding 5 years or both
Breach of DPA 2018, s 145(1).	Where a person, without the authority of the controller or processor, obtains personal data and discloses it to another person	(i) On summary conviction, to a class A fine or imprisonment for a term not exceeding 12 months or both, or (ii) On conviction on indictment, to a fine not exceeding €50,000 or imprisonment for a term not exceeding 5 years or both
Breach of DPA 2018, s 145(3).	Where a person who received personal data unlawfully then sells the personal data	(i) On summary conviction, to a class A fine or imprisonment for a term not exceeding 12 months or both, or (ii) On conviction on indictment, to a fine not exceeding €50,000 or imprisonment for a term not exceeding 5 years or both

Instance where penalty can be incurred	Details	Penalty
Breach of DPA 2018, s 145(4).	Where a person offers to sell personal data obtained without the prior authority of the controller or processor	(i) On summary conviction, to a class A fine or imprisonment for a term not exceeding 12 months or both, or (ii) On conviction on indictment, to a fine not exceeding €50,000 or imprisonment for a term not exceeding 5 years or both.
Breach of DPA 2018, s 202(d).	This relates to an amendment of the Disability Act 2005, where genetic data is processed contrary to s 42 of the Disability Act 2005 – see Chapter 6 for details on s 42 of the Disability Act 2005	(i) On summary conviction, to a class A fine, or (ii) On conviction on indictment, to a fine not exceeding €100,000

Further Discussion

Article 29 Working Party, Guidelines on the application and setting of administrative fines for the purposes of the Regulation 2016/679

Chapter 20

Policies & Procedures to be in Place, Human Resources and Marketing

Policies and Procedures

Under the GDPR a policy is required per the duty to inform (see Chapter 8). A cookies policy is also required, this is dealt with in Chapter 21.

Where appropriate, policies are an important organisational tool to ensure employees and representatives of the controller are aware of their requirements under the GDPR.[1] Recital 78 GDPR states that the controller should adopt internal policies that meet in particular data protection by design and default requirements.[2] Below are the main internal policies that should be in place:

Policy/ Procedure	Key details
Data Protection Policy – see Chapter 8	The details required for a privacy policy can be found under the right to be informed. A different privacy policy may be required for different groups of people, for example: • Employees • Clients • Subscribers to mailing lists
Procedure for a DPIA – See Chapter 9	• Process to determine whether DPIA is needed • Who to notify within the company when it is considered a DPIA is needed • At what stage to consult with the DPO

1 Art 24(2) GDPR.
2 See Chapter 9.

Policy/ Procedure	Key details
	• At what stage, if any, to consult with data subject • Where it is necessary to obtain external advice i.e. lawyers, security experts • Determine a methodology to carry out the DPIA • How often the DPIA should be reviewed • When the supervisory authority needs to be consulted
How to handle a request from a data subject, including a DSAR – See Chapter 8	• Raise awareness that requests can be received in any form • Who is in charge of responding to the data subject request • How will it be ensured that the request is processed in a timely manner • System to remind data subjects on the right to data portability before a data subject closes any relevant account they may have[3] • Authentication procedures to verify a data subjects' identity when a data subject is making a request
How to handle a data breach[4] – See Chapter 10	• What constitutes a data breach • How to react in a breach situation[5] • How to contain, manage and mitigate risks (risk assessment) • How to recover any lost data • Who is in charge of notifying the breach to the supervisory authority • What supervisory authority needs to be notified
DPO – See Chapter 15	• When should the DPO be consulted • How to avoid conflict of interests that the DPO may be presented with
Retention Policy – See Chapter 7	• When each data set is deleted or anonymised or reviewed for deletion • Who is in charge of each data set regarding retention

3 Art 29 Working Party Guidelines on the right to data portability, adopted on 13 December 2016, at 13.

4 Art 29 Working Party, Guidelines on Personal data breach notification under Regulation 2016/679, at 6.

5 Art 29 Working Party, Guidelines on Personal data breach notification under Regulation 2016/679, at 27.

Policy/ Procedure	Key details
Acceptable use policy (general information for employees for security purposes – see Chapter 9)	• Explain what personal data is • How personal data may be handled • What is considered as risky activity regarding personal data • How to handle devices that may contain personal data

Human Resources

Human resources must look at the issue of data protection from two aspects:

1. Ensure that the employer complies with data protection law in protecting employees data;
2. Ensure employees are educated about data protection and are under a confidentiality clause so that the employer is not exposed to liability from a personal data breach caused by an employee.

Protect employee's data protection rights

The legal basis upon which employee personal data may be processed is generally considered to be that of contractual necessity.[6] The employer-employee relationship means that the employer needs to be able to pay the employee, as well as satisfy the corresponding tax and leave requirements. Thus, the employer must process employee personal data in order for the employment relationship to function. Consent should not be used as the legal basis to process personal data within the employment context, unless there is no other option. Due to the disparity in power between the employer and employee, consent will generally not be recognised unless it is true consent that would not impact on the employee's prospective within their employment. There must be the ability for the employee to say no. The employee data protection clause/policy must include all the information contained within the right to be informed,[7] including but not limited to:

- What personal data the employer collects;
- That the employee personal data shall only be used for the employee relationship (legal basis);
- Whether employee personal data shall be transferred to

[6] See Chapter 5.
[7] See Chapter 8.

another entity: i.e. if third parties are used, for example for payroll;
- Whether employee personal data shall be transferred outside the EU;
- That the employer will store and process personal data in a confidential and secure manner and in a manner compliant with the GDPR;
- If the employer wants other personal data that is not necessary for the employment relationship to be collected or further processed, the legal basis for this needs to be set out (for example employee photos are generally not necessary for the employment relationship and consent will need to be gathered);
- Details on the retention policy for employee personal data.

Furthermore, the employee must be informed of all their rights under the GDPR. Note that the right to object must be set out separately from the other rights. [8] Often employers require a medical certificate for sick leave, and sometimes employers retain the right to request employees to undergo a medical examination; as this information is a special category of personal data, the employer must ensure that the appropriate legal basis and safeguards are in place.[9]

All details regarding data protection must be provided to the employee *prior* to the commencement of the employment relationship/ prior to signing the contract of employment in accordance with the right to be informed.

Systematically monitoring employees, including internet activity (systematic monitoring and data concerning vulnerable data subjects) requires a DPIA[10] and the employees must be explicitly informed of the monitoring operations. Furthermore, often internal infrastructure means employee email accounts may be accessed – it is important that the procedure for accessing employee emails is made very clear.

---

8 Art 21(4) GDPR, see Right to object in Chapter 8 for details.

9 See Chapter 6.

10 Art 29 Working Party, Guidelines on Data Protection Impact Assessment (DPIA) and determining whether processing is "likely to result in a high risk" for the purposes of Regulation 2016/679, at 11.

Protect liability exposure of employer

The controller or processor must take all reasonable steps to ensure employees that may handle personal data are aware of and comply with the technical and organisational measures in place.[11] Employers should keep track of whom in the company has access to what personal data.

Ensure a confidentiality clause is in place for employees – this should form part of the contract of employment. Ensure the confidentiality clause is valid and enforceable.[12] The wording must be clear and unambiguous, and what is considered confidential information needs to be specifically defined. Ensure all the policies outlined above are clear and provided to the appropriate employees.

It is common practice for employers to request that the employee sign to confirm that they have read and understood their own employee privacy policy, as well as all related internal policies. This can go towards demonstrating that the employer made steps towards ensuring their employees were informed. However, the employer should be encouraged to think of multiple impactful forms via which the information may be conveyed.

Marketing

Current marketing practices may include the utilisation of personal data. As such, below are items that should be kept in mind for the purposes of marketing specifically, this list is not exhaustive:

Remember GDPR principles — see Chapter 7	Everything must be transparent, only data that is necessary may be collected and data may only be retained for as long as it is needed. For example, if a company decides to stop using a mailing list because they are focusing more on social media advertisements — the mailing list is then no longer needed and should be deleted. Retention of data for longer than is necessary is not compliant with the GDPR.

[11] See Ch 9.

[12] Confidentiality is largely governed by common law in Ireland, for an overview see *Apex Fire Protection Ltd v Murtagh* [1993] ELR 201; *Mahon v Post Publications* [2007] IESC 15, *The Pulse Group Limited & Anor v O Reilly & Anor* [2006] IEHC 50, *Net Affinity Ltd v Conaghan & Ors* [2011] IEHC 160.

Be aware of children	Recital 38 GDPR specifically makes it clear that children may be less aware of risks and require particular protection, specifically with regard to marketing. Thus, marketing personnel must be aware of their audience.
Direct Marketing	Section 30, DPA 2018 prohibits direct marketing and micro targeting children. Within Ireland, children are data subjects under 16 years of age. Regarding the Article 22 GDPR prohibition against making decisions based solely on automated decisions (see Chapter 6), this may include certain marketing manoeuvres. WP29 gave the example of an advertising company targeting a data subject in financial difficulty with advertisements on high interest loans.[13] This would have a high enough effect to constitute a 'similar legal effect' to satisfy Article 22 GDPR. As stated in Chapter 5, legitimate interest may be used as a legal basis for communications where there is a reasonable expectation to receive such communications, for example in a business to business scenario.
Mailing lists	Opt out mechanisms (generally in the form of unsubscribe buttons) are required for all marketing mailing lists. All emails must have the following items within the signature: 1. To unsubscribe to that type of marketing communication 2. To unsubscribe to all marketing communications (if multiple) 3. To contact a return email address, i.e. there must an email address provided that they can contact if they have an issue 4. Link to Privacy Policy Ensure that when a data subject opts out of a mailing list that it is synchronised with other mailing lists that are retained or other back-ups of the list.
Privacy Policy must govern marketing communications too	Privacy policy should detail (as part of the requirements within the right to be informed): • Retain email address until unsubscribe; • Whether use a third-party emailing system to create mailing lists and prepare campaigns;

[13] Art 29 Working Party, Guidelines on Automated individual decision-making and Profiling for the purposes of Regulation 2016/679, at 22.

	note that many of these services also collect IP addresses and time stamps, so the fact that other personal data may be collected must also be informed. The privacy policy must also include how data is handled on social media platforms, etc.
Avoid buying mailing lists	Buying mailing lists is not advised unless there is full confirmation that consent from the data subject was obtained and the data subject is informed of its use, etc.
Consent must be verifiable	Sometimes emails are gathered organically, i.e. at a conference; however, consent still needs to be verifiable — so it is best practice to send a follow up email requesting consent to be on the mailing list.

Further Discussion

Article 29 Working Party, Opinion 2/2017 on data processing at work, adopted on 8 June 2017

Chapter 21

Cookies, e-Privacy and other Notable EU Laws and Proposals

This chapter is intended as a brief summary of related data protection issues that can be found in EU laws and proposals other than the GDPR, and this is intended to be non-exhaustive.

e-Privacy Directive and Proposed Regulation

Privacy and Electronic Communications Directive 2002/58/EC on Privacy and Electronic Communications (as amended),[1] otherwise known as the e-Privacy Directive, was implemented into Irish law via Statutory Instrument No 336 of 2011. There is a proposal to repeal that Directive and enforce a regulation.[2]

The key element in the e-Privacy Directive is that of confidentiality

---

1 Privacy and Electronic Communications Directive 2002/58/EC on Privacy and Electronic Communications, as amended via Directive 2009/136/EC.

2 Proposal for a Regulation of the European Parliament and of the Council concerning the respect for private life and the protection of personal data in electronic communications and repealing Directive 2002/58/EC (Regulation on Privacy and Electronic Communications) 2017/0003 (COD).

of communications, beyond GDPR requirements. It is prohibited to process the content of electronic communications beyond what is actually necessary for the provision of the service. Narrow exceptions are provided to this prohibition, including that processing of communications may be conducted on the basis of *consent*. Thus, no other legal basis will be able to be used to process data within electronic communications. Protection of terminal equipment is also an obligation on the communication provider, this includes the use of a user's terminal equipment. Transmission services used for the provision of machine to machine services are in the scope of the current e-Privacy Directive.

The main issue with the current e-Privacy Directive is that 'Over-the Top' (OTT) services are not covered within its scope, such as services like Skype, Facebook or WhatsApp. These OTT services provide essentially the same services as traditional communication entities. The proposed Regulation will bring these OTT entities within the scope of the above stated prohibition against processing the content of communications.

The EDPB notes that increased use of digital communication platforms creates the risk that more special categories of personal data may be collected directly or indirectly by the mere volume of personal data that can be collected about the data subject due to the use of these platforms.[3] Thus, the EDPB supports the approach of the proposed Regulation to include OTT entities.

The EDPB notes that data from electronic communications that has been anonymised may still be processed without restrictions under the proposed Regulation.[4]

Cookie Consent

The most publicised section of the e-Privacy Directive is that of Article 5(3). This requires prior informed consent for storage or for access to information stored on a user's terminal equipment. This includes cookies. A cookie is a text file stored on a user's (data subject's) device. [5] In other words, the user is required to agree to

3 S 1, Statement of the EDPB on the revision of the ePrivacy Regulation and its impact on the protection of individuals with regard to the privacy and confidentiality of their communications, 25/05/2018.

4 S 1, Statement of the EDPB on the revision of the ePrivacy Regulation and its impact on the protection of individuals with regard to the privacy and confidentiality of their communications, 25/05/2018

5 A cookie is a text file that may be stored on a user's device when the user visits a website or App. Cookies are used for many reasons, that are often beneficial

the use of cookies and similar technologies (e.g. web beacons, Flash cookies, etc.) before a website may use them.

Within the e-Privacy Directive consent to cookies was able to be obtained explicitly (i.e. tick the box to accept cookies) or via implication (i.e. by continuing to use the site, you agree to the use of cookies). The key aspect is that the notice was prominent and required a positive action to remove it.

Within the proposed Regulation the consent that must be obtained is to have the same meaning as in the GDPR (detailed in Chapter 5).[6] Thus, consent via implication is not permissible, i.e. a pre-ticked box. Access to a service may not be made conditional on consent, as is described within Chapter 5. Explicit, freely given, consent is required. Thus, the need to obtain freely given consent means that "cookie walls" will become impermissible. Cookie walls prevent a user from accessing a website until they accept the cookies.

Article 10 of the proposed Regulation sets out that the preference of the user must be recognised. The hope is that the user will be able to set their cookie and privacy settings for their device, which must be recognised. Currently there is no obligation for entities to comply with "Do Not Track" browser requests. This will be interpreted under the proposed Regulation as a signal indicating that the user does not accept tracking cookies. Note that there has been a proposal to delete Art 10.[7]

Cookies that are essential to deliver a service do not require consent.[8] In particular:

- Cookies necessary to transmit a communication;
- Cookies necessary to enable an online service to which the user wanted i.e. use of a website.

For example, cookies that keep track of the storage of items in an online shopping cart do not require consent as it is necessary for the performance of the website. Such necessary cookies are generally

for the user, such as to remember language preferences. Cookies are stored for a period of time so that, for example, the language preference does not need to be continuously re-set. Thus, the website can remember your preferences. Some cookies are more intrusive, for example, certain cookies track user's movements across the internet.

6 See Art 8 of proposed legislation; however, note that it is subject to debate, see draft revision of 10 July 2018, 10975/18.

7 Para 3, draft revision of 10 July 2018, 10975/18.

8 Art 5(3) e-Privacy Directive; See Art 29 Data Protection Working Party, Opinion 04/2012 on Cookie Consent Exemption, Adopted on 7 June 2012.

only stored for the duration of the session. However, even necessary cookies must be informed within the cookie statement. Necessary cookies may not be used for other purposes for which consent would be required, i.e. tracking.[9]

Cookies and the GDPR

Cookie identifiers are items that cookies reveal about a user (data subject). Such cookie identifiers can be considered personal data. Cookie identifiers are mentioned within Recital 30 GDPR, stating that cookie identifiers may be used in combination with other information to identify an individual. Therefore, if cookie identifiers can be linked to an identifiable individual, as provided in Chapter 1, the cookie identifier is personal data. Often cookie identifiers utilise pseudonymous identifiers in the form of numbers or letters; however, as is stated within Chapter 1, even where personal data undergoes pseudonymisation, it is still personal data and the GDPR must be complied with.

Thus, if cookies already fall within the scope of the GDPR, consent as required within the GDPR may already be necessary as a required legal basis. WP29 made it clear that if the use of cookies generates personal data, both data protection law and the e-Privacy Directive will apply.[10]

Third party cookies — joint controller

When third party cookies are utilised, both the website operator and the advertising network are generally categorised as joint controllers. The website operator chose to host the third party cookies and the advertising network is deciding to advertise on such website.[11]

Cookie policy

In a cookie policy, certain information is required in accordance

9 Art 29 Data Protection Working Party, Opinion 04/2012 on Cookie Consent Exemption, Adopted on 7 June 2012, at 6.

10 Art 29 Data Protection Working Party, Opinion 2/2010 on online behavioural advertising, 22 June 2010, at 171. See also EDPB, Opinion 5/2019 on the interplay between the ePrivacy Directive and the GDPR, in particular regarding the competence, tasks and powers of data protection authorities, Adopted on 12 March 2019, at 11.

11 Art 29 Data Protection Working Party, Opinion 2/2010 on online behavioural advertising, Adopted on 22 June 2010, at 11-12.

with the ePrivacy Directive. The following information should be included in a cookie statement:

1. An explanation of what cookies are;
2. Information on the cookies (see below);
3. An explanation that cookies will not be used for any purpose other than the ones stated
4. An explanation on how consent to cookie use may be withdrawn and how cookies may be managed and controlled, including:
   - o How cookies stored on their device may be deleted;
   - o How to set the browser to prevent cookies from being placed. Note that user's should be warned that if this is done, some functionalities on certain webpages may not function.

Below is a table of the information required on each cookie/ set of cookies in accordance with point 2 above.

	Information	*Comments/ Questions to consider*
1	Name of cookie in plain language	State the name of the cookie i.e. necessary cookie or third party cookie
2	Purpose/ reason for why those cookies are being used	Is a cookie used to remember the user's language preference? Is a cookie used to remember pre filled data? Is a cookie used for targeted advertising? Is a cookie used for web analytics?
3	Whether the cookies are essential for the website or not	Are the cookies necessary for the website to function? Are the cookies only necessary for a certain feature to function? Are the cookies simply to enhance the performance of the website?
4	Explanation of the types of cookies used	Is a cookie in use a permanent cookie stored on the user's device? Is a cookie in use a session cookie, only stored for the duration of an individual session? Is a cookie in use a third party cookie, for example when enable an analytics company to place a cookie on the user's device to provide information on the performance of a website?

	Information	*Comments/ Questions to consider*
5	Expiry dates of cookies used	State when or the criteria for when the cookies will be deleted

Generally, this information is provided under separate headings within the policy reflecting each type of cookie, for example: (1) "necessary/functional cookies"; (2) "preference cookies"; (3) "analytics cookies" "behavioural cookies", etc.

Net Neutrality

The Open Internet Regulation (EU) 2015/2120 brought rules on net neutrality into the EU as of 30 April 2016. This provided the right for users to access internet content and services of their choice, Furthermore, discrimination on traffic management is prohibited i.e. internet service providers cannot enable access to certain internet services over others. Most importantly there can be no differentiation based on the user i.e. on the basis of their internet plan or the type of laptop they own. This formed part of the Digital Single Market strategy.

e-Commerce Directive

Recital 21 GDPR specifies that the GDPR is "without prejudice" to the e-Commerce Directive,[12] which regulates "information society services" (defined in Chapter 6, p 57 herein). This means that the GDPR should not impact on the effectiveness of the Directive. This Directive provides for further security and additional information that must be provided to the user of such services, among other things.

Public Sector Information Directive

The Directive on the re-use of public sector information (PSI Directive),[13] as amended,[14] allows for Member States to make as

[12] Directive 2000/31/EC of the European Parliament and of the Council of 8 June 2000 on certain legal aspects of information society services, in particular electronic commerce, in the Internal Market ('Directive on electronic commerce') (OJ L 178, 17.7.2000, p 1). Brought into Irish Law via SI No 68/2003.

[13] Directive 2003/98/EC.

[14] Directive 2013/37/EC, see SI No 279/2005, SI No 103/2008, and SI No. 525/2015, and related Circulars issued by the Department of Finance (Circular 32/05), and Department of Public Expenditure and Reform (Circular 16/15 and Circular 12/16).

much public sector information available for re-use as possible. This includes use of data from government, museums, libraries and related archives. Such PSI data includes funded research projects and geographical information, etc. Recital 154 GDPR provides that:

> "Public access to official documents may be considered to be in the public interest. Personal data in documents held by a public authority or a public body should be able to be publicly disclosed ... [in accordance with law] .... Such laws should reconcile public access to official documents and the reuse of public sector information with the right to the protection of personal data ... ."

Therefore, access is determined via Member State law. Recital 154 GDPR provides that the PSI Directive should not apply:

- To documents or parts of documents to which access is limited on grounds of the protection of personal data;
- To documents or parts of documents to which the re-use of personal data therein has been determined incompatible with data protection law.

Note that in April 2018 there was a proposal for a revision of the PSI Directive.[15]

Clinical Trials Regulation

Where processing for an ASHS purpose, Recital 156 and 161 GDPR specify that any related clinical trials laws must also be complied with. Specific reference is made to the Clinical Trials Regulation.[16] The EDPB issued an opinion on the GDPR vis a vis the new regulation.[17] As stated in Chapter 6, under the Clinical Trials Regulation, consent is required. However, the EDPB questions the validity of such consent for the purposes of the GDPR and recommends that another legal basis should be established for satisfaction of the GDPR. WP29 stated that the consent needed under the Clinical Trials Regulation may be considered as an additional safeguard, rather than as the legal basis under the

---

15 Proposal for a Directive of the European Parliament and of the Council on the re-use of public sector information (recast) Brussels, 25.4.2018, COM(2018) 234 final.

16 Clinical Trial Regulation EU No. 536/2014, which will replace EU Clinical Trial Directive (EC) No. 2001/20/EC.

17 EDPB Opinion 3/2019 concerning the Questions and Answers on the interplay between the Clinical Trials Regulation (CTR) and the GDPR.

GDPR.[18] The processing required under the regulation is considered to occur under the legal basis of a "legal obligation to which the controller is subject to" in accordance with Article 6(1)(c) GDPR.[19] However, processing related to purely research activities will likely require another different legal basis.[20] Where further processing occurs the presumption of compatibility may apply where it is for an ASHS activity;[21] however, the EDPB notes that this shall require specific attention in future.[22]

Proposal for a Regulation on Promoting Fairness and Transparency for Business Users of Online Intermediation Services

The EU Commission has formulated a proposal for a regulation on promoting fairness and transparency for business users of online intermediation services (OIS).[23] The term OIS includes information society services,[24] including online platforms and search engines, that provide services to businesses established in the EU, where those businesses offer goods or services to consumers in the EU.[25] Examples of an OIS are Google or Amazon. The purpose of the regulation is to recognise the control an OIS has in enabling and facilitating businesses to access their customers in an online environment. Recital 20 and Article 7 of the proposed regulation establishes a requirement on the OIS to include a description in their terms and conditions about the access to personal data (and other data) that business users or consumers provide to the OIS or which are generated through the OIS. Article 3 states that the online intermediation service must provide a 15-day minimum notice period for changes to their terms and conditions. Article 6 describes that information must be provided by the OIS on how businesses are treated differently within their OIS (in terms of ranking, etc), including whether it is due to personal data available.

---

18 See Art 29 Working Party, Guidelines on consent under Regulation 2016/679, as last Revised and Adopted on 10 April 2018, at 28.

19 See Ch 5 on legal basis; EDPB Opinion 3/2019 concerning the Questions and Answers on the interplay between the Clinical Trials Regulation (CTR) and the GDPR, at 4-5.

20 EDPB recommends consent, public interest, legitimate interest, see Chapter 5 for details on these legal bases.

21 See Ch 5.

22 EDPB Opinion 3/2019 concerning the Questions and Answers on the interplay between the Clinical Trials Regulation (CTR) and the GDPR, at 8.

23 Proposal for a Regulation of the European Parliament and of the Council on promoting fairness and transparency for business users of online intermediation services (Text with EEA relevance) Brussels, 26/4/2018, COM(2018) 238 final.

24 See Chapter 6, p 57 for definition on information society service.

25 Art 1, Proposed online intermediation services Regulation.

It is emphasised that the GDPR must still be complied with in these contexts.[26]

Cyber Security Directive and Proposed Regulation

Directive on security of network and information systems (2016/1148) (commonly known as the NIS Directive or cyber security Directive) requires Member States to set up a framework to prevent and respond to cyber-attacks. The Directive was transposed in Ireland via SI No 360 of 2018.[27] This also requires applicable entities to have appropriate security measures in place and to notify the requisite authority where a security incident occurs (in Ireland this is the National Cyber Security Centre). Such applicable entities include operators of essential services (i.e. providers of energy, transport, banking, finance, health, water and digital services) and digital service providers. It is for the Member State to identify operators of essential services and digital service providers must self-identify. Note that micro and small enterprises (as defined in the Directive) do not constitute a digital service provider.[28] Thus, when a data breach occurs, there may be a parallel notification requirement under this Directive and under the GDPR.

Separate from the NIS Directive, there is a (soon to be approved) Regulation on the EU Cybersecurity Agency, which contains a certification framework for information and communication technologies.[29] This certification is not compulsory and is purely voluntary; the framework involves safety certification and labelling for different types of products, including internet of things devices. The aim of this regulation is to enable a high level of cybersecurity in the digital single market and it notes that the GDPR aids in the achievement of this aim.

European Electronic Communications Code

There are likewise security obligations, separate from the

[26] Recital 20, Proposed online intermediation services Regulation.

[27] SI No 360 of 2018, European Union (Measures for a High Common Level of Security of Network and Information Systems) Regulations 2018.

[28] See art 16(11) NIS Directive; Micro, small and medium-sized enterprises mean enterprises which employ fewer than 250 persons and which have an annual turnover not exceeding €50 million, and/or an annual balance sheet total not exceeding €43 million.

[29] Proposal for a Regulation of the European Parliament and of the council on ENISA, the "EU Cybersecurity Agency", and repealing Regulation (EU) 526/2013, and on Information and Communication Technology cybersecurity certification ("Cybersecurity Act") COM/2017/0477 final, 2017/0225 (COD).

GDPR, for entities under Directive on the European Electronic Communications Code.[30] Member States have two years in which to transpose the Directive. It is relevant for, among others, entities providing electronic communication services, as defined in Article 2 therein, including machine to machine communications and "over the top" services such as Skype.[31] The Directive also reiterates that the processing of personal data by electronic communications services, whether a paid service or not, must comply with the GDPR.

EU Payment Services Directive

The EU Payment Services Directive[32] (PSD2) requires consent from payment service users.[33] The EDPB emphasised that the PSD2 and the GDPR have their own separate requirements.[34] Where consent is provided under the PSD2 this should not also be considered satisfaction for the purposes of the GDPR; a GDPR legal basis must be separately established. The PSD2 consent can be considered as an additional safeguard to ensure awareness for the data subject. In addition, the EDPB emphasised that any use of third party providers for payment services must be in line with the GDPR principles.

Further Discussion

EDPB, Opinion 5/2019 on the interplay between the ePrivacy Directive and the GDPR, in particular regarding the competence, tasks and powers of data protection authorities, Adopted on 12 March 2019

Statement of the EDPB on the revision of the ePrivacy Regulation and its impact on the protection of individuals with regard to the privacy and confidentiality of their communications, 25/05/2018, at <https://edpb.europa.eu/our-work-tools/our-documents/other/edpb-statement-eprivacy-25052018_en>.

---

30 Directive (EU) 2018/1972 of the European Parliament and of the Council of 11 December 2018 establishing the European Electronic Communications Code (Recast)Text with EEA relevance. PE/52/2018/REV/1 OJ L 321, 17.12.2018, p 36–214.

31 Communication services that are ancillary to a service and not the primary objective are excluded, for example in-game conversations.

32 EU Payment Services Directive (2015/2366) (PSD2); Implemented in Ireland via the European Union (Payment Services) Regulations 2018 (Statutory Instrument No 6 of 2018)

33 Art 94(2) PSD2

34 EDPB reply Sophie in 't Veld, Brussels, 5 July 2018, EDPB-84-2018

Article 29 Data Protection Working Party, Opinion 04/2012 on Cookie Consent Exemption, Adopted on 7 June 2012.

Article 29 Data Protection Working Party, Opinion 2/2010 on online behavioural advertising, Adopted on 22 June 2010.

Chapter 22

Emerging Technologies

This chapter is intended as a brief summary of the main GDPR issues to be aware of for popular emerging technologies, and is in no way exhaustive. Note from Chapter 9 that any assessment of appropriate security measures requires particular attention where it involves novel technologies and automated decision making.

Currently, the most popular emerging technologies are internet of things devices, cloud computing, 3D printing, biometrics and blockchain. These technologies often utilise interdependent connection and automated decision making. Thus, it is important that GDPR is taken into consideration at the outset of development for products and services that utilise these emerging technologies, especially in light of the obligation for data protection by design and default.[1]

It is recommended that any service or product that incorporates these elements designs a fully traceable product[2] that integrates GDPR principles from the outset (data protection by design). It is particularly imperative with these technologies to integrate GDPR principles at the outset because, given the complexity of the technologies, it would be very difficult to integrate privacy at any late stage. Furthermore, due to the interconnected nature of these technologies, it must be clear where responsibilities lie within the chain of developers and suppliers.[3] In particular, responsibilities

1 See Chapter 9.
2 Para 2.10, European Economic and Social Committee, INT/846 Opinion on Trust, privacy and security for consumers and businesses in the Internet of things (IoT).
3 Para 3.1, European Economic and Social Committee, INT/846 Opinion on Trust, privacy and security for consumers and businesses in the Internet of things (IoT).

regarding security, safeguarding personal data and anticipating data breaches. Furthermore, there needs to be a high level of education along such chain about GDPR principles, in particular privacy by design and default. As such, accountability, transparency and security need to be at the core of any development process.

Biometrics

Biometrics is being increasingly used for identification purposes. The EDPS released an opinion regarding the use of such data in EU identity cards and other documents.[4] The EU proposed the collection of individual's images and fingerprints for the ID cards. The EDPS noted that the proposal from the EU did not sufficiently justify the need to process two types of biometric data (facial images and fingerprints). It was particularly concerning as biometric data is considered a special category of personal data.[5] As such, the EDPS called for close scrutiny; requiring an assessment on the necessity of such measures. Thus, the EDPS showed that collecting unnecessary biometric data will not be permissible.

Internet of Things

Internet of Things (IoT) devices will naturally gather a lot of personal data on data subject's location, preferences and even health data. In accordance with the GDPR, it must be transparent to the data subject how such data is used and who has access. WP29 identified three types of IoT devices to which the GDPR shall be the most relevant:[6]

1. Wearable devices, such as fit-bits and smartglasses;
2. Devices and applications that track user's habits/ lifestyles, such as sleep monitors, activity counters;
3. Home automation devices, such as connected light bulbs or heating systems.

WP29 noted that it will be difficult for data collected via IoT devices to remain anonymous because data sets may be combined.[7] For

4 EDPS Opinion 7/2-18 on the Proposal for a Regulation strengthening the security of identity cards of Union citizens and other documents, 10 August 2018.

5 See Chapter 6.

6 Art 29 Working Party, Opinion 8/2014 on the on Recent Developments on the Internet of Things, adopted on 16 September 2014, 5-6.

7 Art 29 Working Party, Opinion 8/2014 on the on Recent Developments on the Internet of Things, adopted on 16 September 2014, 8.

example, the data recorded by a fit-bit may be combined with the device's unique identifier or the WiFi access point, thereby making it personal data. The more information that is gathered, the more it is capable of being attributable to an identifiable individual.[8] The EDPS advised on smart glasses;[9] these are considered an IoT device as they may be linked to multiple devices i.e. if the glasses receive updated information on the weather, a notification may pop up telling the wearer. The EDPS noted that increasing technological capabilities and the integration of alternative reality technology may increase the use of these glasses. As such, given the amount of data that may be collected by these glasses, the EDPS advised that the use of these glasses should be monitored and more robust laws may be needed.

The concept of IoT devices is that decisions will be made automatically without human input as the devices communicate with each other i.e. a device reads that you are cold and turns on your heating system. Thus, it is the goal that more automated decision making will occur and it is imperative safeguards are in place to minimise associated risks.

Geolocation Services and Smart Devices

WP29 issued an opinion on geolocation services, such as maps and navigation, geo-personalised services (including nearby points of interests), augmented reality, geotagging of content on the internet, tracking the whereabouts of friends, child control and location based advertising.[10] WP29 focused on the main three types of infrastructure used to provide geolocation services:

- GPS (GPS receiver within a device can determine the location of the device);
- GSM base stations (device can link with several telecommunication operator's base stations and via triangulation determine the location of the device);
- WiFi (WiFi access points can be used to determine location).

As provided for within Chapter 1 on the definition of personal data

---

8 See Chapter 1; Article 29 Working Party, Opinion 8/2014 on the on Recent Developments on the Internet of Things, Adopted on 16 September 2014, 8-9.

9 European Data Protection Supervisor, Technology report No 1, Smart glasses and data protection, Brussels January 2019.

10 Art 29 Working Party, Opinion 13/2011 on Geolocation services on smart mobile devices, adopted on 16 May 2011.

— location data can be considered personal data where it is relatable to an identifiable individual. Furthermore, even if the location data is concerning an object, it can indirectly become personal data where it is highly likely the object is where the data subject is. For example, the location of a person's smart phone reveals the location of the owner of the phone via the phone's unique ID.[1] This could then reveal special categories of personal data if it can be seen that the data subject is visiting a particular political rally, or a hospital.[2]

While the name of the person who owns the device may not be apparent, every smart device has at least one unique identifier. Thus, the combination of the location data with a unique identifier must be treated as personal data.[3]

WP29 identified three types of entities that provide location services and may hold personal data:[4]

1. Controller of a geolocation infrastructure; if they collect location data and WiFi data, there is a collection of personal data;
2. Provider of a specific geolocation application service / browser service; the provider of an application that is capable of processing geolocation data (like the Facebook App) is the controller for the processing of personal data resulting from the installation and use of the application. Furthermore, often such services can be provided via browsers as well;
3. The developer of the operating system of a smart device; if the developer interacts directly with the user for the provision of the services, they would act as a controller.

In all cases, due to privacy by default and design, location tracking must by default be off unless turned on by the data subject. Providers usually initiate a "pop-up" to remind data subject's to turn on location tracking for a certain functionality.[5]

---

1 Art 29 Working Party, Opinion 13/2011 on Geolocation services on smart mobile devices, adopted on 16 May 2011, at 7.

2 Art 29 Working Party, Opinion 13/2011 on Geolocation services on smart mobile devices, adopted on 16 May 2011, at 7.

3 Art 29 Working Party, Opinion 13/2011 on Geolocation services on smart mobile devices, Adopted on 16 May 2011, at 11.

4 Art 29 Working Party, Opinion 13/2011 on Geolocation services on smart mobile devices, Adopted on 16 May 2011, at 11-13.

5 Art 29 Working Party, Opinion 13/2011 on Geolocation services on smart mobile devices, Adopted on 16 May 2011, at 13.

Cloud Computing and High Performance Computing

There is large support in the EU to utilise the capabilities of cloud computing and high-performance computing, including quantum technologies, for the Digital Single Market.[6] There is movement toward a governance structure for the management and development of data infrastructure and services, as well as to encourage interoperability.[7] The European Cloud initiative emphasises that high levels of "quality, reliability and confidentiality" are necessary to ensure protection of personal data and compliance with the GDPR.[8]

Blockchain

Blockchain raises GDPR concerns.[9] The nature of blockchain technology necessitates that it would retain data on the history of events relating to the blockchain. For example, if blockchain is used to support the IoT infrastructure, it would create a history of IoT activity. The nature of blockchain technology means that information can only be added to and may not be removed, which goes against several principles of the GDPR i.e. data minimisation. Furthermore, the fact that blockchain is a distributed ledger raises concerns regarding data transfers, within and outside the EU. On the other hand, blockchain would act as a security measure in that any attempt at altering data would need to be carried out on multiple copies of the data set because blockchain technology functions in a decentralised manner. On 03 October 2018 the EU Parliament passed a resolution on blockchain technology, showing support for the use of blockchain technology within the EU.[10] Parts of the EU are already planning to utilise blockchain.[11] The resolution

---

6 See Communication from the Commission to the European Parliament, The Council, The European Economic and Social Committee and the Committee of the Regions European Cloud Initiative – Building a competitive data and knowledge economy in Europe, COM/2016/0178 final [SWD(2016) 106 final].

7 s 2, [SWD(2016) 106 final].

8 s 3, [SWD(2016) 106 final].

9 The French data protection authority was the first data protection authority to detail concerns and potential solutions, see Commission Nationale Informatique & Libertes, Solutions for a responsible use of the blockchain in the context of personal data, 6 November 2018, available at https://www.cnil.fr/en/blockchain-and-gdpr-solutions-responsible-use-blockchain-context-personal-data.

10 European Parliament resolution of 3 October 2018 on distributed ledger technologies and blockchains: building trust with disintermediation (2017/2772(RSP)).

11 The European Union Intellectual Property Office launched a new platform based on blockchain technology to aid in minimising counterfeiting, see European Union Intellectual Property Office, Using blockchain in the fight

emphasised that blockchain technology must be compliant with the GDPR and called on the EDPS to provide further guidance on this.[12]

Further Discussion

Article 29 Working Party, Opinion 13/2011 on Geolocation services on smart mobile devices, adopted on 16 May 2011.

Article 29 Working Party, Opinion 8/2014 on the on Recent Developments on the Internet of Things, adopted on 16 September 2014.

Communication from the Commission to the European Parliament, The Council, The European Economic and Social Committee and the Committee of the Regions European Cloud Initiative – Building a competitive data and knowledge economy in Europe, COM/2016/0178 final [SWD(2016) 106 final].

European Economic and Social Committee, INT/846 Opinion on Trust, privacy and security for consumers and businesses in the Internet of things (IoT)

---

against counterfeiting–EUIPO launches a Forum to support concrete solutions in that field, 07 February 2019, at https://euipo.europa.eu/ohimportal/en/web/guest/news/-/action/view/4963920

12 Part 33, European Parliament resolution of 3 October 2018 on distributed ledger technologies and blockchains: building trust with disintermediation (2017/2772(RSP)).

The Different Risk Assessments under the GDPR

Risk* assessment needed for	Assess risk in relation to	Risk assessment criteria	Meaning of results
Activities of controller (Article 24 GDPR)	Risks presented by the personal data processing	Must be an objective assessment that takes into consideration the likelihood and severity of the risk	Technical and organisational measures, for the purposes of security, are required, which are proportionate to the risk
Data protection by design and data protection by default (Article 25 GDPR)	Risks presented by the planned personal data processing and during the personal data processing itself	Must be an objective assessment that takes into consideration the likelihood and severity of the risk	Data protection by design and default measures are required, which are proportionate to the risk
Records of processing activities (data inventory) (Article 30 GDPR)	Risks presented by the personal data processing	Assessment that takes into consideration the likelihood of the risk	If the risk is likely then a record of processing activities/ data inventory is required
Security of processing (Article 32 GDPR)	Risks presented by the planned personal data processing	Must be an objective assessment that takes into consideration the likelihood and severity of the risk	Technical and organisational measures, for the purposes of security, are required, which are proportionate to the risk

Risk* assessment needed for	Assess risk in relation to	Risk assessment criteria	Meaning of results
Data Protection Impact Assessment (Article 35 GDPR)	Risks arising from the processing of personal data and from a hypothetical personal data breach		If the risk is high, then a DPIA is required
Personal Data Breach (Article 33 – 34 GDPR)	Risks arising from the personal data breach that occurred	Must be an objective assessment that takes into consideration the likelihood and severity of the risk	If the risk is unlikely, there is no notification requirement to the supervisory authority; If the risk is high, there is an additional notification requirement to the data subjects impacted
Representatives of controllers or processors not established in the EU (Article 27 GDPR)	Risks presented by the personal data processing		If the risk is unlikely, this is a factor towards determining whether a representative is needed

* Note that the risk assessment is in relation to the rights and freedoms of natural persons; this not only includes the right to data protection and privacy, but also all other rights such as free speech and freedom of movement.[1]

1 Art 29 Working Party, Statement on the role of a risk-based approach in data protection legal frameworks, at 4; Art 29 Working Party, Guidelines on Data Protection Impact Assessment (DPIA) and determining whether processing is "likely to result in a high risk" for the purposes of Regulation 2016/679, at 6.

GDPR Check List

Every entity involved in the processing of personal data should establish answers to all the following questions; ideally the entity would have a complete excel or other documentation of the following information, answered in as much detail as possible. If anything does not appear to be compliant, or the information is not obtainable yet – ensure to flag it as a risk and keep a log of all risks.

Information to be documented	Examples/ further questions, where applicable
Is personal data collected?	
What personal data is collected?	Names, addresses, IP address, etc
Is sensitive personal data or the personal data of a child collected?	
Who are the data subjects?	Employees, clients, students, refugees, etc
Number of data subjects?	
Purpose of processing personal data?	Marketing, human resources, provision of a service
In what capacity is personal data being processed?	Controller, processor, sub-processor
Legal basis for personal data processing?	Consent: Is consent documented? Contractual: Is the contract documented? Legitimate interest: Is there documentation assessing whether the legitimate interest is valid? etc
How was the personal data acquired?	Via an online form, via a survey, via a third party
Does automatic decision making, including profiling, occur?	
Where is the personal data held?	Where can the personal data be accessed from?
Is there a system for personal data deletion?	Is there a clear retention policy?

Information to be documented	Examples/ further questions, where applicable
Is the personal data transferred abroad?	Are the correct legal mechanisms in place for the transfer? What is the purpose for the transfer? Is the data subject informed of the transfer, either via privacy policy or other?
Is the personal data transferred to another entity?	Are the correct legal mechanisms in place for the transfer? What is the name and address of the entity to whom the personal data is transferred? What is the purpose for the transfer? Is the data subject informed of the transfer, either via privacy policy or other?
Who has access to the personal data?	CEOs, certain employees, etc; are they under a duty of confidentiality? Under what circumstances can they access the personal data? What can the individual see? Is access to personal data tracked?
What security, organisational measures and risk management processes are in place?	Pseudonymisation, encryption, regular testing of the security in place, data minimisation, data protection by design, data protection by default
Is a DPIA required?	
Is a data record (data inventory) required?	
Are data subjects appropriately informed of the data processing and associated information required under the GDPR (right to be informed)?	
What policies are in place?	Privacy policy, retention policy, cookie policy, acceptable use policy, security policy, data breach policy, data access request policy
Who is in control of maintaining a log for data incidents, data risks, data breaches and data subject requests?	
Is a Data Protection Officer or Data Protection Representative required?	
Is there insurance in place for any data protection liability incidents?	

Index